CHANGING NUMBERS, CHANGING NEEDS

American Indian Demography and Public Health

Gary D. Sandefur, Ronald R. Rindfuss,
and Barney Cohen, Editors

Committee on Population

Commission on Behavioral and Social Sciences and Education

National Research Council

NATIONAL ACADEMY PRESS
Washington, D.C.   1996

NATIONAL ACADEMY PRESS • 2101 Constitution Ave., N.W. • Washington, D.C. 20418

Support for this project was provided principally by the Public Health Service of the U.S. Department of Health and Human Services. The National Institute of Aging also provided funding to the Committee on Population for this project.

Library of Congress Catalog Card No. 96-70052
International Standard Book Number 0-309-05548-2

Changing Numbers, Changing Needs: American Indian Demography and Public Health is available for sale from the National Academy Press, 2101 Constitution Avenue, N.W., Box 285, Washington, D.C. 20055. Call 800-624-6242 or 202-334-3313 (in the Washington Metropolitan Area). Order electronically via Internet at http://www.nap.edu.

CONTRIBUTORS

ANNIE C. ABELLO, Economics Program, Research School of Social Sciences, Australian National University

BARNEY COHEN, Committee on Population, National Research Council

PETER J. CUNNINGHAM, Center for Studying Health System Change, Washington, D.C.

EUGENE P. ERICKSEN, Departments of Sociology and Statistics, Temple University

ROBERT G. GREGORY, Economics Program, Division of Economics and Politics, Research School of Social Sciences, Australian National University

ROBERT JOHN, Minority Aging Research Institute, University of North Texas

JAMIE JOHNSON, Department of Economics, University of Chicago

CAROLYN A. LIEBLER, Center for Demography and Ecology, University of Wisconsin, Madison

PHILIP A. MAY, Center on Alcoholism, Substance Abuse, and Addictions, University of New Mexico

K.M. VENKAT NARAYAN, National Institute of Diabetes and Digestive and Kidney Diseases, National Institutes of Health, U.S. Department of Health and Human Services

JEFFREY S. PASSEL, The Urban Institute, Washington, D.C.

RONALD R. RINDFUSS, Carolina Population Center, University of North Carolina, Chapel Hill

GARY D. SANDEFUR, Department of Sociology, University of Wisconsin, Madison

C. MATTHEW SNIPP, Department of Rural Sociology, University of Wisconsin, Madison

RUSSELL THORNTON, Department of Anthropology, University of California, Los Angeles

RONALD L. TROSPER, Native American Forestry Program, Northern Arizona University

T. KUE YOUNG, Department of Community Health Sciences, Faculty of Medicine, University of Manitoba

COMMITTEE ON POPULATION

RONALD D. LEE (*Chair*), Departments of Demography and Economics, University of California, Berkeley
CAROLINE H. BLEDSOE, Department of Anthropology, Northwestern University
JOSE-LUIS BOBADILLA, The World Bank, Washington, D.C.
JOHN BONGAARTS, The Population Council, New York
JOHN B. CASTERLINE, The Population Council, New York
LINDA G. MARTIN, RAND, Santa Monica, California
ROBERT A. MOFFITT, Department of Economics, Brown University
MARK R. MONTGOMERY, The Population Council, New York
W. HENRY MOSLEY, Department of Population Dynamics, Johns Hopkins University
ALBERTO PALLONI, Department of Sociology, University of Wisconsin, Madison
ANNE R. PEBLEY,* RAND, Santa Monica, California
RONALD R. RINDFUSS,* Carolina Population Center, University of North Carolina, Chapel Hill
JAMES P. SMITH, RAND, Santa Monica, California
BETH J. SOLDO, Department of Demography, Georgetown University
MARTA TIENDA, Population Research Center, University of Chicago
AMY O. TSUI, Carolina Population Center, University of North Carolina, Chapel Hill

JOHN G. HAAGA, *Director*
BARNEY COHEN, *Program Officer*
TRISH DeFRISCO, *Senior Project Assistant*
KAREN A. FOOTE, *Program Officer*
JOEL A. ROSENQUIST, *Project Assistant*
JOYCE E. WALZ,** *Administrative Associate*

*through October 1995
**through May 1996

v

The National Academy of Sciences is a private, nonprofit, self-perpetuating society of distinguished scholars engaged in scientific and engineering research, dedicated to the furtherance of science and technology and to their use for the general welfare. Upon the authority of the charter granted to it by the Congress in 1863, the Academy has a mandate that requires it to advise the federal government on scientific and technical matters. Dr. Bruce M. Alberts is president of the National Academy of Sciences.

The National Academy of Engineering was established in 1964, under the charter of the National Academy of Sciences, as a parallel organization of outstanding engineers. It is autonomous in its administration and in the selection of its members, sharing with the National Academy of Sciences the responsibility for advising the federal government. The National Academy of Engineering also sponsors engineering programs aimed at meeting national needs, encourages education and research, and recognizes the superior achievements of engineers. Dr. William A. Wulf is interim president of the National Academy of Engineering.

The Institute of Medicine was established in 1970 by the National Academy of Sciences to secure the services of eminent members of appropriate professions in the examination of policy matters pertaining to the health of the public. The Institute acts under the responsibility given to the National Academy of Sciences by its congressional charter to be an adviser to the federal government and, upon its own initiative, to identify issues of medical care, research, and education. Dr. Kenneth I. Shine is president of the Institute of Medicine.

The National Research Council was organized by the National Academy of Sciences in 1916 to associate the broad community of science and technology with the Academy's purposes of furthering knowledge and advising the federal government. Functioning in accordance with general policies determined by the Academy, the Council has become the principal operating agency of both the National Academy of Sciences and the National Academy of Engineering in providing services to the government, the public, and the scientific and engineering communities. The Council is administered jointly by both Academies and the Institute of Medicine. Dr. Bruce M. Alberts and Dr. William A. Wulf are chairman and interim vice chairman, respectively, of the National Research Council.

Preface

The Committee on Population was established by the National Research Council in 1983 to bring the knowledge and methods of the population sciences to bear on major issues of science and public policy. The committee's mandate is to conduct scientific assessments of major population issues and to provide a forum for discussion and analysis of important public policy issues related to population.

The papers in this volume were first presented at a Committee on Population workshop on the demography of American Indians and Alaska Natives. The workshop, which was held in May 1995 at the request of the Public Health Service, brought together researchers from different disciplines to discuss recent issues in American Indian demography and their implications for health service delivery. At that time, a number of alternative plans for reforming healthcare were being considered, each of which offered explicitly and implicitly different options for providing healthcare to beneficiaries of the IHS. The papers prepared for the workshop were not designed to present the needed information directly, but to provide background data that could be used by the Public Health Service and the IHS in preparing such estimates for their deliberations.

A major challenge for demographers concerned with American Indian and Alaska Native populations is to differentiate between changes in the size, characteristics, and distribution of these populations caused by fertility, mortality, and migration trends and changes caused by the increased tendency of people to identify themselves as Indians in response to census or survey questions on race, ethnicity, and ancestry. Over the last 20 years, changes in self-identification have been substantial and have affected estimates of birth and death rates, as well as estimates of the geographic and income distributions of American Indians.

Changes in self-identification and eligibility affect the estimates and projections, particularly the long-range projections, of the population relevant to Indian Health Service (IHS) and other agencies that provide services for American Indians. Many of the people newly identifying themselves as American Indian are unlikely to have been served in the past by the IHS. Hence, designing plans for coverage of eligible IHS beneficiaries, projecting enrollments, and estimating utilization and premiums, requires up-to-date estimates of the size, composition, distribution, economic characteristics, and health care needs of the potentially eligible populations.

This volume pulls together information on the demography and health status of American Indians. The work would not have been possible without the efforts of several people, but two deserve special recognition. First, the committee was extremely fortunate in being able to enlist the services of Gary D. Sandefur, a distinguished scholar of American Indian demography, to collaborate on the project and ensure that it was a success. Second, committee member Ronald R. Rindfuss worked diligently to organize the workshop and share the editorial duties for this volume. The committee expresses its heartfelt appreciation to both of them for contributing so much of their valuable time and expertise.

The committee is grateful to the Public Health Service for its financial support and to staff members Susanne Stoiber and Maruta Zitans for their interest and efforts during the development of the workshop. The Committee would also like to thank the National Institute on Aging for providing funding for this project.

Finally, we thank the staff at the National Research Council, who made it all possible. The work took place under the general direction of John Haaga, director of the Committee on Population. Barney Cohen, program officer, provided a constant intellectual and managerial presence for the project, from the organization of the workshop to the publication of this volume. Trish DeFrisco, senior project assistant, efficiently and diligently took care of all the logistical arrangements and prepared the papers for publication. We also thank Rona Briere for her skillful editing of the manuscript. We are grateful to them all.

Ronald D. Lee, *Chair*
Committee on Population

Contents

CHANGING NUMBERS, CHANGING NEEDS

American Indian Demography and Public Health

1

Introduction

Gary D. Sandefur, Ronald R. Rindfuss, and Barney Cohen

American Indians[1] trace their roots in the geographic area that now comprises the United States to an earlier point in time than any other racial or ethnic group, yet ironically, we know less about their current demographic and health situation than that of African Americans, Hispanics, Asian Americans, or European Americans.

This volume includes a selection of papers prepared for a workshop on the demography and health of American Indians, conducted by the National Research Council's Committee on Population in May 1995. The papers were intended to summarize the state of knowledge about the demography of the American Indian and Alaska Native populations, about the major health problems they face today, and about their utilization of healthcare.

The organizers of the workshop and the authors of the papers also attempted to fill a gap in knowledge about American Indians resulting from the absence of a monograph on the American Indian population based on the 1990 census. After the 1980 census, the Russell Sage Foundation commissioned a series of monographs, including one devoted specifically to American Indians, *American Indians: The First of This Land*

---

[1]The chapters in this volume use the terms American Indian and Native American interchangeably. Moreover, unless otherwise indicated, both terms include the Alaska Native population, which comprises Aleuts (Aleutian Islanders), Eskimo, and other Native American people residing in Alaska.

(Snipp, 1989). After the 1990 census, the Russell Sage Foundation commissioned only two volumes to report all recent social and economic trends in the United States (Farley, 1995). Several of the chapters in Volume Two, including one on racial and ethnic groups, contain some analysis of data on American Indians from the 1990 census. These two volumes could not, however, cover in any depth the changing demography of American Indians. In addition, no volume has ever pulled together information on American Indian demography along with data on American Indian health issues.

The present volume has four major sections. The first contains two chapters that examine major demographic and epidemiological trends among American Indians during the past few decades. These two chapters discuss trends in fertility, mortality, morbidity, and migration.

The second section explores issues involved in identifying and studying the American Indian population. These issues are critical in the case of American Indians for a number of reasons, two of which are well known: the above-noted changes in self-identification from non-Indian to Indian over recent censuses, and the more general issues involved in enumerating and/or sampling a relatively rare population. The latter set of issues is of concern because less than 1 percent of the U.S. population identified itself as American Indian by race in the 1990 census; this makes it particularly difficult to use national surveys to study American Indians.

The third section examines the social and economic characteristics of the general, reservation, and urban Indian populations. The authors examine the economic situation of urban and reservation Indians, the characteristics of American Indian children and families, and the characteristics of the elderly Indian population.

The final section addresses healthcare issues and healthcare access and utilization. This section contains three papers. Two papers summarize and assess our understanding of two major public health issues for Native Americans: alcohol abuse and related diseases and diabetes, especially the adult-onset type. A final paper examines healthcare utilization and expenditures for insurance coverage for American Indians eligible for IHS services.

QUESTIONS AND ISSUES

This volume has two goals: first, to achieve a better understanding of some of the reasons for this relative paucity of knowledge and second, to review and extend our knowledge of the contemporary demographic and health situation of American Indians. The paths to these goals are closely intertwined, and it is difficult to discuss one without considering the other. We know relatively little about the demographic and health situation of contemporary American Indians in part because they are difficult to study with conventional social science techniques. Conversely, the lack of current and detailed knowledge exacerbates the difficulty involved in studying American Indians. The result is that many of the papers in this volume that treat the demographic or health status of American Indians also address the methodological difficulties involved, while those papers that are concerned with methodological issues bring trends and differentials into their discussion. Indeed, these two sets of issues are so intertwined that the editors vacillated regarding which should be covered first in the volume, and we recommend that the reader keep both in mind when reading the papers that follow.

Several factors make it difficult to apply conventional social demographic techniques to the American Indian population: (1) American Indians are a relatively small proportion of the total U.S. population; (2) their residences tend to be either highly clustered in a small number of geographic areas or spread lightly over a large number of geographic areas; (3) they have experienced relatively high rates of marital exogamy, resulting in ambiguity about the extent to which their offspring are "American Indians"; and (4) over time and across types of data collection systems, there have been shifts in whether self-identifying or being identified as an American Indian is perceived as an advantage or a disadvantage.

Alone or in combination, these factors make it more problematic to compare results over time or across studies for American Indians than for other groups. Upon seeing a change, the substantively oriented want to speculate about the causes of that change, whereas the methodologically oriented want to suggest there was no change, invoking one or several explanations involving data "error." These two groups can frequently talk past one another, and the policymaker can be left wondering which orientation to accept. In fact, one of the main challenges faced by policymakers is sorting through the changing numbers to identify needs and shifts in those needs over time.

A historical example, involving data technologies quite different from those used today, serves to illustrate one of many methodological problems involved in studying American Indians— the problem of using a national survey or census to draw inferences about a small fraction of the total population. In the published tabulations of the 1950 U.S. census, there was a surprising increase in the number of teenage American Indian widowers as compared with either the 1940 census or the patterns one might expect from common sense. In a display of statistical and demographic sleuthing, Coale and Stephan (1962) found that with the punch card data entry technology being used for the 20 percent sample in the 1950 census, a shift of one column to the right would transform a middle-

aged white male into a teenage American Indian widower. They estimated that there was an error rate of approximately 14 to 20 per 10,000
middle-aged white males. This is a very low error rate, one that was
invisible for the numbers published for middle-aged white males, but
quite visible for the teenage American Indian widower category.

The lesson is not that the Census Bureau did a poor job with the 1950
census, but rather that studying the American Indian population with
conventional social, demographic, and epidemiological approaches is difficult. Nevertheless, for a number of reasons, it is extremely important
that we continue to advance our knowledge of the demographic and
health situation of the American Indian population and that our policies
affecting American Indians be informed by the highest-quality demographic and health research.

The American Indian population is growing rapidly. Between the
1890 and 1960 censuses, it doubled from 248,000 to 552,000, with an average annual growth rate of only 1.1 percent. Between 1960 and 1990, the
population increased almost four-fold to just under 2 million, representing an average annual growth rate of 4.2 percent. In the absence of large-
scale immigration, this very high rate of population growth is incompat-
ible with what we know about the prevailing fertility and mortality
regimes. Indeed, much of this increase is attributable to an increase in
self-identification, i.e., people identifying themselves as non-Indian in
one census and as Indian in the next. It has been estimated that three-
fifths of the growth in the American Indian population between 1970 and
1980 is attributable to an increase in self-identification and two-fifths to
natural increase. The increase in self-identification has also affected estimates of the geographic and income distributions of American Indians:
many of those newly identifying themselves as Indian live in areas with
low concentrations of American Indian populations, and on average they
have higher incomes than those living on or near reservations.

Issues of race and ethnicity and their interaction with public policy
are never higher on the agenda than when policymakers and planners are
designing programs to serve better the needs of American Indian populations. Designing and evaluating alternative plans for the coverage of the
Indian Health Service (IHS) population requires projections of tribal enrollment, estimates of current and future utilization of IHS services, and
estimates of the availability and utilization of private healthcare coverage
among individuals within the IHS service population. Furthermore, planners need to understand how the changing characteristics of American
Indians could affect healthcare and insurance needs, as well as future
expenditures. For example, the IHS relies on a combination of membership in federally recognized tribes and residence in geographically defined areas to identify the size and scope of its service population. The

effect of changing self-identification on the geographic and income distributions of American Indians noted above has resulted in a population profile that is less concentrated in the West and less poor. Much of the population increase has been among those not eligible for IHS services. Analysts need to estimate the extent to which the observed trends are due to changes relevant to the health service needs of a defined population versus changing ethnic identification.

MAJOR FINDINGS

What Are the Major Population and Health Trends?

In the first of two overview papers in this volume, C. Matthew Snipp summarizes what we know about the classic demographic issues of fertility, mortality, and migration. His analysis, like Passel's research in the next section, shows that the rapid growth of the American Indian population since the turn of the century is due in part to changes in self-identification, but also to the relatively high fertility of American Indians, currently higher than that of either blacks or whites. This represents a major change from the beginning of the century, when the deprivations of reservation life limited American Indian fertility. Moreover, the population would have grown even more rapidly if it had not experienced such high mortality, although there is considerable uncertainty about the relative mortality levels of whites, blacks, and American Indians.[2]

Careful examination of National Center for Health Statistics (NCHS) data has confirmed systematic inconsistencies in the coding of race and ethnicity between birth and death in U.S. infants (Hahn et al., 1992; Sorlie et al., 1992). Nevertheless, Indian infant mortality rates have improved substantially over the last 15 years, both in absolute terms and relative to the trend among whites and blacks. However, the death rates for American Indian youths and young adults remain high, exceeding those for comparable groups of blacks and whites.

With regard to migration and population redistribution, the removal

---

[2]Based on special tabulations of data from the National Center for Health Statistics, the U.S. Census Bureau calculates that life expectancy for American Indians is similar to whites and approximately 6 years longer than for blacks; 76.2 years for American Indians, 76.8 years for whites, and 69.7 years for blacks (U.S. Bureau of the Census, 1996:Table A, p. 2). However, because of the problems surrounding the misclassification of American Indian deaths, we believe that these estimates are seriously in error. For further discussion on this point, see Indian Health Service (1995) as well as the chapters by Snipp and Young in this volume.

policies of the 1800s resulted in a concentration of the American Indian population west of the Mississippi River, a pattern that continues today. The American Indian population has also become increasingly urbanized, a trend promoted by World War II and the relocation programs of the 1950s. Currently, over one-half of American Indians reside in urban areas. Ongoing migration is likely to increase the proportion residing in urban areas, though it is unlikely to alter substantially the regional distribution of the American Indian population.

The second overview paper, by T. Kue Young, examines in more depth the trends in diseases associated with mortality trends among American Indians. The major trends include a decline in infectious diseases, though stabilized at a level still higher than that for the non-Native population; an increase in chronic diseases, especially diabetes; and the overwhelming importance of social causes of injury and death—violence, accidents, and alcohol and drug abuse. The latter are important in accounting for the relatively high mortality among American Indian youth documented by Snipp.

How Do We Identify, Enumerate, and Sample the Population?

As noted above, previous research by Jeffrey S. Passel and others has shown that much of the recent growth in the American Indian population is attributable to changes in self-identification. In his paper in this volume, Passel demonstrates that the shifts in self-identification between 1980 and 1990 were smaller than those in the previous decades since 1960, and that these shifts do not preclude the *careful* use of census data to examine the demographic characteristics of American Indians, especially in those geographic areas where their populations are most concentrated.

A large proportion of those changing their reported identity from one census to the next are of mixed race. However, as Russell Thornton points out, intermarriage not only has affected how people identify themselves, but in some cases has also made tribes reconsider how they define themselves. American Indian tribes are governmental entities with the right to establish their own criteria for membership. As tribes have been faced with increasing rates of intermarriage involving other tribes and non-Indians, some have responded by relaxing their "blood quantum" requirements for membership (that is, the proportion of one's ancestors required to be American Indians). Some tribes use documented descent from earlier membership rolls rather than blood quantum as the principal criterion for tribal membership.

Finally in this section, Eugene P. Ericksen reckons with the implications for sampling of both the unstable self-identification and the small size of the American Indian population. He also assesses some of the other challenges facing those who want to sample the American Indian population: (1) American Indians are not as segregated or as concentrated as some other populations; (2) they are very culturally diverse; (3) the over 300 tribal groups recognized by the federal government and the as many as 200 other non-federally recognized entities have very diverse histories; and (4) visual inspection is often not a good way to identify American Indians because of the long history of intermarriage. Ericksen concludes that there is no easy solution to these identification and sampling problems, but that sampling is possible in most cases where the objective of the study and the purposes of sampling are clear, and where researchers pay close attention to the difficulties involved. His paper is a guide to the issues that must be addressed in studying the American Indian population and segments within it.

How Are American Indians Faring Economically and Socially?

The first two papers in the third section deal with the economic situation of American Indians in general, on reservations, and in urban areas. The final two papers deal with two components of the American Indian population that are of special concern for health policy: families and the elderly.

Analyzing micro-level data from the 1980 and 1990 censuses, Robert Gregory and colleagues characterize the decade of the 1980s as one of "moving backwards" economically for Native American men and women. The average income of American Indian men, for example, was 63 percent that of white men at the beginning of the 1980s, but 54 percent that of white men at the end of the decade. The pattern was similar for American Indian women. The reasons for this decline include both the poor performance of the general economy and factors specific to Native Americans. Two facts in particular emerge: (1) American Indians receive lower returns to education in terms of earnings than do whites, and (2) earnings of American Indians lost ground at each educational level during the 1980s.

Ronald L. Trosper looks at the economic situation of American Indians at the macro level by focusing on 23 major reservations and changes in their situation over the period 1969 to 1989. During 1969-1979, the percentage of families who were poor declined on all but 2 of the reservations. In contrast, during 1979-1989, the percentage of all families who were poor increased on all but 3 of the reservations. Consequently, the setbacks documented by Gregory et al. for the overall Indian population in the 1980s are reflected on most of these reservations. Multivariate analysis of macro-level data suggests that changes in federal expenditures on reservations may have an important role to play in explaining changes in American Indian poverty.

Children and the elderly are two of the most vulnerable groups in society. Furthermore, both have unique needs with respect to healthcare access and utilization, and both use disproportionately large shares of total healthcare services. By analyzing trends in family patterns, Gary D. Sandefur and Carolyn A. Liebler show that in addition to economic and housing problems, American Indians have a higher percentage of children residing in single-parent families than does the general population. They also find that trends in marriage and divorce over time among American Indians parallel those in the general population, and that American Indian women are less likely to marry and more likely to divorce than women in general. They find further that the extent of single parenthood, never marrying, and divorce is considerably higher on some of the major reservations than among the general Indian population.

As Robert John points out, the American Indian elderly population has grown substantially over the last decade. The proportion of the American Indian population aged 60 and older grew from 8 percent in 1980 to 9 percent in 1990, though it still remained well below the 17 percent of the general U.S. population who were 60 or older. This differential reflects the much lower median age of the American Indian population, resulting from the relatively high fertility and high mortality discussed in other papers in the volume. Significantly, approximately 29 percent of elderly American Indians were poor as compared with approximately 10 percent of non-Hispanic whites in the same age group.

In sum, the papers in this section show that American Indian families, adults, children, and elders remain economically disadvantaged relative to the general U.S. population. Moreover, they show that these disadvantages are present among the overall Indian population, as well as among those residing both on reservations and in urban areas.

What Are Some Major Health Problems Facing American Indians?

The overviews by C. Matthew Snipp and T. Kue Young discussed above show accidents, suicide, and homicide, all three of which are often alcohol-related, to be the three leading causes of death among American Indians aged 15-24 in IHS service areas. Among American Indians aged 65 and older in IHS service areas, heart disease, cancer, cerebrovascular disease, diabetes, and pneumonia and influenza are the five leading causes of death.

Alcohol abuse, along with associated diseases and accidents, is a health issue that has been important historically for American Indians and continues to be of concern. Philip A. May's review of previous and ongoing research shows that drinking prevalence varies greatly across tribal communities. Heavy drinking is quite common among some subgroups in many Indian communities. Because the American Indian population is so young, and heavy drinking is concentrated among teens and young adults, alcohol-involved mortality continues to be a substantial problem for Indians. The bulk of this mortality results from alcohol-related causes such as motor vehicle crashes, other accidents, suicide, and homicide, rather than alcohol-produced diseases such as cirrhosis of the liver. More recent intervention efforts have begun to consider the importance of behavioral patterns in accounting for high alcohol-related mortality. On the other hand, a number of tribes are characterized by a lower prevalence of drinking than is found among the general U.S. population. Moreover, Indian women have a substantially lower overall prevalence of drinking than U.S. women, and many Indian men "mature out" of heavy problem drinking in middle age to become abstainers.

A second problem of particular concern among American Indians is diabetes mellitus. K. M. Venkat Narayan reviews what we know about the prevalence, causes, consequences, and prevention of diabetes among American Indians. His assessment shows clearly that the rates of diabetes and its complications, including premature death, renal failure, and limb amputation, are substantially higher among Native Americans than among the general population and that the frequency of diabetes among Native Americans is increasing. Diabetes was relatively rare among American Indians until the middle of the twentieth century. Since that time, it has become one of their most common diseases. One group of Indians, the Pima, has the highest recorded prevalence of diabetes in the world.

Several of the causes of diabetes among Native Americans, including obesity, dietary composition, and physical inactivity, are preventable, and recent intervention efforts have shown some progress in addressing these causes.

Are American Indians Receiving Adequate Healthcare?

Given the clear social and economic disadvantages of American Indians and their well-documented health problems, one may ask to what extent the current healthcare delivery system is meeting their needs. As Snipp points out, the IHS service population numbered about 1.21 million in 1990, or 62 percent of the total population of 1.96 million American Indians enumerated by the 1990 census. Because of the information collected by the IHS for its service population, as well as a federally commissioned study of this population that produced a data set known as the Study of American Indians and Alaska Natives (SAIAN), we know more about how we are meeting the needs of the IHS service population than we do with regard to the remaining 38 percent of the American Indian population.

Peter J. Cunningham uses the SAIAN data to examine healthcare coverage and utilization for those eligible for IHS services. He points out that those who are eligible for IHS services have some advantages over those who are not. IHS beneficiaries do not pay premiums, nor do they pay deductibles or copayments, regardless of personal or family income level. Also, while many in the general U.S. population live in medically underserved rural areas or inner-city areas, IHS facilities and resources are targeted specifically to many rural and sparsely populated areas where eligible Indians are concentrated.

On the other hand, because of geographic isolation, many Indians have difficulty reaching IHS service centers, and the amount of money spent each year on services is limited. In addition, expensive diagnostic and treatment services may be delayed or denied if funds are not available to purchase such services through contractual arrangements. Partly for this reason, many members of the IHS service population have other sources of healthcare coverage, either purchased or available through Medicare or Medicaid. Cunningham points out that, given the growing size of its service population and its resource constraints, the IHS will increasingly have to rely on utilizing and coordinating with other sources of healthcare services.

IMPLICATIONS FOR HEALTHCARE AND OTHER POLICIES

One theme that emerges clearly from the chapters in this volume is that the socioeconomic disadvantages of American Indians make them a vulnerable population. American Indians are a relatively young population with higher levels of poverty, unemployment, single-parent families, fertility, and mortality than the general U.S. population. These conditions are present among both urban and reservation Indians, but they are especially pronounced on some reservations.

Such conditions call for both short- and long-term approaches. In the short term, safety-net programs, such as accessible healthcare provided through the IHS, are important to ensure that vulnerable individuals—particularly those who live on reservations with poverty rates that sometimes approach or exceed 50 percent—are able to receive preventive and other healthcare services.

In the long term, improving the situation of American Indians will require substantial efforts to improve their education and health, along with efforts to provide employment opportunities both on and off the reservations. The IHS may be an important part of such a long-term strategy, working to improve the health of American Indians so they will be able to take advantage of any enhanced employment opportunities.

Existing research on health issues indicates several problems that are more prevalent among American Indians than among other Americans, including alcohol-related problems, diabetes, suicide, and homicide. Addressing some of these problems may require intervention programs targeted at behavior. Both alcohol-related problems and diabetes, for example, are strongly affected by behavior. In recent years, researchers have begun to develop and demonstrate the effectiveness of efforts designed to lead to healthier drinking, eating, and exercise behaviors. The successful programs deserve wider dissemination and utilization.

Another set of implications for healthcare and related policies flows from the very reasons why it is methodologically difficult to study the American Indian population. Consider the identification issue. Thornton shows how various American Indian tribes have changed their own criteria for membership. These changes are related to the high rates of marital exogamy among American Indians as compared with whites or blacks (Sandefur and McKinnell, 1986). Further, at the individual level, Passel and others have shown that each of the last three decennial censuses provides overwhelming evidence that individuals and households shifted to identifying themselves as American Indian from one census to the next.

From the perspective of the IHS or any other organization whose mandate is to serve the American Indian population, the potential for shifts in either tribal criteria for membership or individual self-identification means that predicting the size of the population to be served is problematic. Further, the size of the population to be served may be influenced by the nature of the federal programs involved, thus introducing feedback into the system. For example, Nagel (1995) has argued that prior federal American Indian policies, by affecting patterns of migration and intermarriage, have influenced the ambiguity of identification of those whose heritage is not completely American Indian and subsequently influenced their increased self-identification as American Indian. Both federal and state policies also influence the advantages or disadvantages accruing to tribes by increasing their size through a change in their criteria for membership or to individuals by identifying as American Indian. Growth of this type could strain the facilities and programs of the IHS, as well as other agencies. Predicting the effect of a change in any given American Indian program on the actual size of the eligible and self-designated American Indian population is difficult, yet deserves consideration.

QUESTIONS FOR FUTURE RESEARCH

It is customary to end papers on American Indian demography or health with a lament about the lack of good data on American Indians. This lack of data is indeed a real problem. The large national datasets that are used to examine blacks, whites, and Latinos, such as the National Longitudinal Surveys and the Panel Study of Income Dynamics, do not sample consciously among the American Indian population. Consequently, we know less about American Indians than about many other groups in our society.

The papers in this volume show, however, that there are data of good quality available for those who wish to study American Indians. These include data from the censuses; the Survey of American Indians and Alaska Natives (SAIAN); and some of the medical studies of specific groups of Indians, such as the study of diabetes among the Pima. The papers in this volume hardly exhaust what can be done with these data. There is room for a good deal more in-depth research on American Indian economic well-being; fertility and mortality; families, elders, and children; incidence, prevalence, and treatment of specific diseases; and health-care utilization. Nevertheless, given the uncertainties surrounding the size and characteristics of the American Indian population, policymakers and planners dealing with these populations might best be served by using ranges rather than point estimates for their projections of the potential growth of their service populations. When dealing with an ambiguously defined population, it is particularly important to test the sensitivity of forecasts and cost estimates based on alternate assumptions.

REFERENCES

Coale, A.J., and F.F. Stephan
    1962   The case of the Indians and the teen-age widows. *Journal of the American Statistical Association* 57:338-347.
Farley, R., ed.
    1995   *State of the Union: America in the 1990s*. Volume One: Economic Trends. Volume Two: Social Trends. New York: Russell Sage Foundation.
Hahn, R.A., J. Mulinare, and S.M. Teutsch
    1992   Inconsistencies in coding of race and ethnicity between birth and death in US infants. *JAMA* 267(2):259-263.
Indian Health Service
    1995   *Regional Differences in Indian Health, 1995*. Rockville, MD: U.S. Department of Health and Human Services.
Nagel, J.
    1995   American Indian ethnic renewal: Politics and the resurgence of identity. *American Sociological Review* 60:947-965.
Sandefur, G.D., and T. McKinnell
    1986   American Indian intermarriage. *Social Science Research* 15:347-371.
Snipp, C.M.
    1989   *American Indians: The First of This Land*. New York: Russell Sage Foundation.

Sorlie, P.D., E. Rogot, and N.J. Johnson
  1992   Validity of demographic characteristics on the death certificate. *Epidemiology*
         3(2):181-184.
U.S. Bureau of the Census
  1996   *Population Projections of the United States by Age, Sex, Race, and Hispanic Origin: 1995
         to 2050.* Current Population Reports, P25-1130. Washington D.C.: U.S. Govern-
         ment Printing Office.

I

Overview of Demographic and Health Conditions

2

The Size and Distribution of the American Indian Population: Fertility, Mortality, Migration, and Residence

C. Matthew Snipp

Knowledge about the size and distribution of the American Indian[1] population is fundamental for understanding its demography. In particular, such knowledge represents a logical point of departure for any effort to assess other salient characteristics of the population. This paper examines the natural events determining the size of the American Indian population—fertility and mortality—as well as data showing how the American Indian population is distributed and the migration processes responsible for these patterns.

The American Indian population is an especially interesting and challenging subject for demographic research. Data are often sparse and difficult to locate. An even more vexing problem is the fluid boundaries of the population. Over the past 20 years, the American Indian population has grown remarkably as a result of the increased numbers of persons choosing to claim American Indian as their racial identity, as opposed to some other category, such as black or white (Passel, 1976; Passel and Berman, 1986; Snipp, 1989; Harris, 1994). Harris (1994) reports the percentages of population growth exceeding natural increase among the American Indian population as 8.5 for 1970, 25.2 for 1980, and 9.2 for 1990. This growth in the population numbers makes temporal comparisons

---

[1]Although the term "American Indian" is used throughout this paper, this is done purely for editorial convenience. Readers should be mindful that the data presented are for American Indians and Alaska Natives, unless otherwise specified.

difficult, but it also makes such comparisons imperative for purposes of understanding how compositional changes may be reflected in statistics for the American Indian population (Eschbach et al., 1995).

The next section reviews briefly the most important literature on patterns of fertility, mortality, and migration among American Indians. This is followed by some observations about the limitations of available data on these patterns. With these limitations in mind, we turn to examine what the data can tell us about the patterns in these three areas. The final section presents concluding remarks.

REVIEW OF THE LITERATURE

Fertility

Modern American Indian fertility patterns are the subject of several publications from the 1930s and 1940s. These studies were carried out by anthropologists working within a single tribe or region (Aberle, 1931; Aberle et al., 1940; Wissler, 1936). Of course, the findings from this research have limited applicability to other groups of American Indians. After a long hiatus of several decades in the study of American Indian fertility, anthropologists were joined in their study of the subject by demographers and other social scientists (e.g., Kunitz, 1976; Rindfuss and Sweet, 1977).

A brief report published by Thornton et al. (1991) presents data from the 1910 U.S. census showing that early in this century, fertility rates for American Indians were relatively low. The mean number of children ever born to so-called "full-blood" couples was 4.5, notably lower than the number born to interracial couples involving mixed-race and full-blood Indian spouses, with 5.4 and 5.1 children ever born, respectively. Likewise, nearly 11 percent of endogamous full-blood couples were childless in 1910, compared with about 8 percent of full-blood/white couples and 4 percent of mixed-blood/white couples. These decidedly lower rates of fertility among full-blood American Indians led the Census Bureau to predict their eventual disappearance (U.S. Bureau of the Census, 1915).

In the absence of data, it is impossible to determine conclusively why endogamous American Indians had lower fertility than those married to whites in the early part of this century. Since that time, however, fertility rates among American Indians have risen apace. In 1940, there was a marked shift in the fertility of endogamous American Indian couples vis-à-vis that of American Indian women with non-Indian spouses—the former now had higher fertility than the latter. This pattern persisted through the baby boom years; indeed, the gap between endogamous and exogamous couples became larger (Thornton et al., 1991).

As in the rest of the nation, American Indian fertility declined noticeably in the 1970s. By the late 1970s, however, it was rising again, and now outstrips by a substantial margin the fertility of either the white or the black populations. In addition, the fertility of endogamous American Indian couples or American Indians residing on reservations was noticeably higher than that of exogamous couples or couples living in urban areas. Predictably, endogamous American Indian couples are more common on reservations (Snipp, 1989).

Mortality

In the nineteenth century (and earlier), epidemic disease, warfare, and occasionally genocide were recurring events that took a spectacular toll on American Indians (Thornton, 1987). Once American Indians had settled on reservations, most were plagued by the loss of traditional subsistence, economic impoverishment, and unsanitary living conditions. Episodes of epidemic disease continued to be a problem on many reservations (Campbell, 1991), and the influenza epidemic of 1918 caused an observable decline in the American Indian population between 1910 and 1920.

The Meriam Report (Institute for Government Research, 1928) documented the dire conditions and noted the ill health of American Indians. In addition to outbreaks of influenza and dysentery, tuberculosis and alcoholism were widespread. High levels of infant mortality were also noted, no doubt due to poor prenatal and neonatal care, as well as poor sanitation. Indoor plumbing was uncommon in many Indian communities until the 1950s, and it is still uncommon in many Alaska Native villages (Snipp, 1989).

Nonetheless, the conditions that contributed to the rise in fertility among American Indians during the middle of this century very likely also contributed to the observed declines in mortality among American Indian populations in the United States, as well as in Canada (Snipp, 1989; Young, 1994). In 1940, the life expectancy of American Indians was about 52 years, lower than that of either blacks or whites at that time. However, the life expectancy of American Indians improved remarkably in subsequent decades, reaching 71.5 years in 1987-1989—higher than the 70-year expectancy for blacks and lower than the 75.6-year expectancy for whites (Snipp, 1989).

These gains in life expectancy were no doubt the function of a remarkable decline in rates of infant mortality among American Indians (Young, 1994). Indeed, of all the changes in patterns of American Indian mortality, the decline in infant mortality has been perhaps most dramatic. In the period 1956-1960, the infant mortality rate for American Indians was 53 per 1,000 live births, while that for the rest of the United States was 26 per 1000 live births. However, by 1981-1985, infant mortality among American Indians had declined to 11 per 1,000 live births, the same rate as that for the rest of the United States.[2] This decline coincides with the transfer of the Indian Health Service to the Public Health Service in 1955. Sorkin (1988) argues that this transfer led to an expansion of American Indian healthcare services, and indeed appropriations for such services tripled between 1955 and 1965. The result was a number of improvements in public health measures such as sanitary waste disposal and water supplies, vaccinations, and prenatal and neonatal care. As a consequence, deaths from most infectious diseases declined during this period. Taffel (1987) also documents higher-than-average birth weights for American Indian babies during this same period, no doubt improving their chances for survival.

In a frequently cited article, Omran (1971) describes a shift in mortality patterns that he labels an "epidemiologic transition." This transition takes place in a population when degenerative diseases, such as cancer, supplant infectious diseases as the major causes of death. As Sorkin (1988) points out, the public health measures introduced by the Indian Health Service in the 1950s and 1960s succeeded in significantly reducing infectious disease. At the same time, however, the American Indian population has continued to be plagued by violence and substance abuse, health problems rooted deep in conditions stemming from economic disadvantage, family disorganization, and personal malaise (Bachman, 1992). Rogers and Hackenberg (1987) extend Omran's model by presenting their concept of the "hybristic stage" of the transition, in which deaths from causes associated with risky behavior, such as AIDS, drug abuse, and accidents, supplant other causes of death as a major source of mortality. This concept appears to be an apt characterization of the American Indian population, especially among its younger members.

Accidents and violence continue to be major causes of death among the American Indian population. For example, in the years 1989-1991, the suicide rate for American Indians was 16.5 per 100,000 population—85 percent higher than the suicide rate of 11.5 per 100,000 for the rest of the United States (Indian Health Service, 1994). Likewise, in 1989-1991, the alcoholism mortality rate for American Indians was 51.8 per 100,000 population—630 percent higher than the total U.S. rate of 7.1 per 100,000.

---

[2]Young (1994:40) reports infant mortality rates of 10 and 16 per 1,000 live births, respectively, for American Indians and Alaska Natives.

Social pathologies are not the only distinctive characteristic of American Indian mortality. Historically, tuberculosis has been a persistent problem among American Indians, though in recent years infection rates have been low in absolute terms (Young, 1994). Nonetheless, according to the Indian Health Service, deaths from tuberculosis are about seven times higher for American Indians than for the general population. Moreover, diabetes mellitus, primarily type II maturity-onset, is a serious problem among American Indians. Young (1994:145) points out that diabetes increases among populations undergoing urbanization and life-style changes, factors that characterize the American Indian population. Diabetes rates vary substantially across the American Indian population, but deaths due to this disease are more than 230 percent greater for American Indians than for the U.S. population as a whole (Indian Health Service, 1994).

Migration

American Indians began their occupation of the western hemisphere by migration approximately 20,000 years ago. In the intervening centuries, they established permanent settlements across the North American continent. The American Indian population also included a substantial number of nomadic societies, especially on the Great Plains, until they were forcibly settled in the late nineteenth century.

The distribution of the American Indian population across the continent was profoundly altered by the arrival of Europeans and most directly by the actions of the U.S. federal government. About three-fourths of the American Indian population is concentrated in the western United States, and a relatively small proportion is found in New England or the southeast. This pattern is not a coincidence. The tribes in New England were decimated by disease and warfare with colonial settlers (Thornton, 1987; Merrell, 1989). American Indians in the south and the Ohio River Valley were subjected to forced migrations that began early in the nineteenth century and accelerated when Andrew Jackson signed the Indian Removal Act in 1830. Eventually, the entire American Indian population was resettled on reservations or in the Indian territory of what is now Oklahoma.

American Indians continue to be concentrated not only in the west, but also in rural areas. The purpose of the removal legislation and the creation of reservations was to place American Indians in remote sites distant from the mainstream of American society. These policies were remarkably successful. In 1930, barely 10 percent of the American Indian population lived in urban areas, as compared with slightly over half of all Americans (Snipp, 1989). In 1990, after more than half a century of rural-urban migration, nearly half of the American Indian population remained outside of metropolitan areas, while more than three-quarters of all Americans were living in cities.

Two events, one unplanned and the other planned, were responsible for the rapid urbanization of American Indians. The first and obviously unplanned event was the outbreak of World War II. Small numbers of American Indians had participated in World War I, but over 25,000 American Indians were active in military service in World War II, while another 50,000 joined the war effort by working in munitions plants, shipyards, and other war-related industries (Hagan, 1979; Bernstein, 1991). The impact of World War II on American Indians, especially those in the service, is difficult to underestimate. For many if not most, it was an opportunity to become immersed in non-Indian culture and to learn to adapt to the expectations of the dominant society. For some, it provided job skills that helped them become employed once they left the military. For many others, the GI Bill was an opportunity to acquire an education and job skills that helped them find employment. The upshot was that many of these American Indians chose to remain in urban labor markets instead of returning to the poverty and joblessness of reservation life (Fixico, 1986; Bernstein, 1991).

Besides World War II, American Indians were affected by federal plans intended to cause the greatest resettlement of American Indians since the Indian Removal Act. Following World War II, the federal government enacted a series of policies that have become known as "Termination and Relocation." The objectives of these policies were to settle outstanding claims made by American Indian tribes against the federal government, dissolve the reservation system, and move American Indians to preselected urban locations. It was expected that once American Indians had been relocated from reservations to urban locations, they would become employed and assimilated into the mainstream of American society (Fixico, 1986).

It has been estimated that from 1952 to 1972, approximately 100,000 American Indians were relocated to cities such as Los Angeles, San Francisco, and Chicago (Sorkin, 1978). Of course, not all of these urban immigrants remained in cities; a substantial number returned to their reservation homes, and this became grounds for criticizing the relocation program (O'Brien, 1989). These programs also were criticized for being ineffective, and although some studies showed that some of those who relocated benefited from the program (Clinton et al., 1975), other studies were more equivocal about the prospects for these rural-urban migrants (Gundlach and Roberts, 1978; Snipp and Sandefur, 1988). The policies of termination and relocation were widely attacked, especially by American Indian advocacy groups. Eventually, these policies were repudiated symbolically by the restoration of the once-terminated Menominee reservation and officially by the passage of the Indian Self-Determination and Educational Assistance Act, both of which took place in 1975.

The impacts of participation in World War II and the relocation program cannot be judged separately. In combination, these two events had a major impact on the settlement patterns of American Indians. By one estimate, fewer than 10,000 American Indians lived in cities in 1926. By 1960, this number had risen to about 160,000, and by 1970, it had risen to 340,000. Between 1960 and 1970, the percentage of American Indians in urban areas climbed from 30 to 45. However, the decreased emphasis on the relocation program in the late 1960s and early 1970s may have slowed this trend. In 1980, 51 percent of the American Indian population lived outside of metropolitan areas, and in 1990, this number had decreased modestly to 49 percent. Such temporal comparisons are fraught with methodological problems, changing census definitions for urban areas, compositional changes in the Indian population due to changes in self-identification noted earlier, and procedural changes in the census. Nonetheless, it should be beyond question that the American Indian population can be characterized as having experienced recent and rapid urbanization and as still having large numbers concentrated in rural areas.

SOME OBSERVATIONS ABOUT THE DATA

Fertility and Mortality Data

Data for studying fertility and mortality are extremely sparse for American Indians as compared with other groups, but there are several sources from which these data can be obtained. The decennial census is the largest and most comprehensive source of demographic information about American Indians. It provides information about social and economic characteristics, as well as details about family and household structure. As noted earlier, in terms of fertility, the census is limited to identifying the number of children ever born to Indian women. However, it is possible to use this information to examine the relationships between total fertility and other characteristics, such as education or labor force participation.

Because the census is conducted only once a decade, it is not useful for calculating annual birth rates, and it contains no data about mortality. Vital statistics produced by the National Center for Health Statistics include birth and death data about American Indians, yet these data provide little additional information about newborns or deceased persons. As a result, it is nearly impossible to use these data for anything except the computation of simple rates. A third source, also produced by the National Center for Health Statistics, is a special data file in which birth and death records are linked (National Center for Health Statistics, 1995:261). Hahn et al. (1992) have used these data very effectively to uncover racial classification errors in birth and death records.

Migration Data

It might be accurate to say that migration data for American Indians are plagued by relatively fewer problems than the data for fertility and mortality—but only because there are fewer migration data and because those data have just one source: the decennial census. Although there are a number of case studies dealing with American Indian migration (Price, 1968; Hackenburg and Wilson, 1972; Weibel-Orlando, 1991), the decennial census is the only large-scale source of data about American Indian migration patterns nationwide. In particular, the Census Bureau provides data about two types of migration, as well as about patterns of residence.

One type of migration data relates to mobility between respondents' current residence and their birthplace. The second and more commonly used type relates to respondents' current place of residence and their residence 5 years earlier, e.g., place of 1985 residence in the 1990 census. For both of these measures, current residence is defined according to the respondent's "usual place of residence" and does not refer to temporary quarters, such as labor camps or vacation places.

Place of residence 5 years earlier is an arbitrary reference point for determining residential mobility, though not unreasonable because it does represent the intercensal midpoint. However, this choice does limit the kinds of migration that can be studied, especially relocations of less than 5 years' duration. For American Indians, this is a potential problem because anecdotal evidence suggests that there is a great deal of short-term mobility between reservations and urban labor markets. For example, Mohawk Indian men travel to New York City to work in construction, but keep close ties with their reservation and return during slack work periods (Blumenfield, 1965). This kind of short-term circular mobility between reservations and cities is impossible to study using census data.

FERTILITY

Age at First Birth

A key to explaining the high rates of American Indian fertility is that American Indian women begin their childbearing at a relatively early age.

TABLE 2-1 Percentage Distribution of Ages of
Mothers at First Birth by Race of Mother, 1990

Age at First Birth	American Indians	Whites
Under 20	45.2	20.6
20-24	35.1	30.7
25-29	13.2	29.4
30-34	4.9	14.6
35 and Over	1.6	4.8

SOURCE: Indian Health Service (1994).

Women who begin childbearing at an early age typically have more children than those who defer motherhood until they are older. The percentages in Table 2-1 show the age distribution of mothers at the time of their
first birth. They also leave no doubt about the differences in fertility
behavior between American Indian and white women.

A very high number of American Indian women, about 45 percent,
have their first child as teenagers, as compared with about 21 percent of
white women. About equal percentages of American Indian and white
women become mothers during their 20s. At the other end of the spec-
trum, it is clear that more white women than American Indian women
defer childbearing: only 6.5 percent of American Indian mothers wait
until their 30s to have their first child, as compared with about 20 percent
of white women.

Children Ever Born

Children ever born, or parity, is a widely used measure of fertility. It
gauges cumulative fertility and allows comparisons of changes in fertility
behavior across cohorts of women. Table 2-2 shows the mean number of
children ever born to black, white, and American Indian women aged 15-
44. A glance at these numbers makes two conclusions quickly evident.

One is that American Indian fertility equals or exceeds the fertility of
either black or white women. In particular, these numbers suggest that
young American Indian and black women have about the same fertility
levels. In 1970, for example, American Indian women aged 15-24 had 0.65
children ever born, and black women had 0.67, a negligible difference. In
1990, the number of children ever born to black and American Indian
women was smaller than in 1970—0.54—but identical for both groups. A
second, related conclusion is that American Indians continue to have children and eventually to exceed the number of children ever born to black
women. Black women appear to curtail their childbearing in their late 20s

TABLE 2-2 Mean Number of Children Ever Born to
Women Aged 15 to 44, by Race in 1970, 1980, and 1990

Year and Age	American Indian	Black	White
1970			
15-24	0.65	0.67	0.35
25-34	2.93	2.77	2.12
35-44	4.41	3.54	2.83
1980			
15-24	0.53	0.57	0.27
25-34	2.04	1.86	1.40
35-44	3.46	3.21	2.54
1990			
15-24	0.54	0.54	0.27
25-34	1.95	1.62	1.31
35-44	2.55	2.22	1.92

SOURCE: U.S. Bureau of the Census public-use microdata samples.

and early 30s, while American Indian women continue to have children. In 1990, the mean number of children ever born to American Indian women aged 25-34 (1.95) was 20 percent higher than the mean number for black women (1.62).

This gap persists in the older cohort as well. At the same time, while the mean number of children ever born declined for all three groups of women from 1970 to 1990, the decrease was greatest for American Indian women. Among American Indian women aged 35-44, the mean number of children ever born fell from 4.41 in 1970 to 2.55 in 1990, a 42 percent decrease. In the same period, the decrease was 37 and 32 percent for black and white women, respectively. Needless to say, this decrease among American Indian women may reflect changes in population composition due to changing racial identities as much as "real" changes in fertility behavior.

Tribal Differences in Children Ever Born

Racial differences in fertility are the result of a complex array of social, cultural, and even physiological factors that govern conception, the desirability of children, and normative beliefs about ideal family size. A plausible argument can be made that black and American Indian women have somewhat similar fertility patterns in part because they often share similar economic circumstances, whereas the remaining differences between them may be due in part to differences in cultural backgrounds. By the same token, American Indians do not have a monolithic culture. Indeed, there is a great deal of heterogeneity among tribal cultures that in most cases cannot be considered because the necessary data are not available. However, there is a small amount of data by tribe in the 1990 census. These data allow comparison of children ever born to determine whether there are significant cultural differences across tribes with respect to childbearing and family size.

The tribes shown in Table 2-3 are the ten largest, listed in descending order. Perhaps the single most important conclusion that can be drawn from this table is that there are clear tribal differences in this measure of fertility behavior. With respect to childbearing, these data suggest that Sioux women are the most likely to begin their families at a young age, while Lumbee women are least likely to do so: young Sioux women aged 15-24 have an average of 0.65 children ever born, while Lumbee women of the same age have 0.3. One way to visualize this difference is to realize that among 10 young Sioux women, 6 or 7 would have 1 child each, and the others would be childless, whereas among 10 young Lumbee women 3 would have 1 child each, and the others would be childless. Considering that many Sioux women begin their families at an early age, it should not be surprising that older Sioux women have relatively large numbers of children (3.05). However, Navajo women have even higher levels of lifetime fertility, with 3.13 children ever born. Iroquois women have the lowest levels of lifetime fertility, nearly one-third lower than those of Navajo women, with 2.05 children ever born. The reasons for these differ-

TABLE 2-3 Mean Number of Children Ever Born to American Indian Women Aged 15 to 44, by Tribe,[a] 1990

Tribe	15-24	25-34	35-44
Cherokee	0.48	1.77	2.26
Chippewa	0.61	2.09	2.64
Navajo	0.56	2.23	3.13
Sioux	0.65	2.18	3.05
Apache	0.59	2.10	2.97
Choctaw	0.43	1.72	2.23
Iroquois	0.46	1.68	2.05
Pueblo	0.52	1.82	2.57
Lumbee	0.30	1.81	2.52
Creek	0.50	1.78	2.27

[a]Ten largest tribes based on self-reports in the census.

SOURCE: U.S. Bureau of the Census, public-use microdata sample.

ences are not readily apparent, but may involve cultural and/or socioeconomic factors; regrettably, a detailed analysis of these issues is beyond the scope of this discussion.

Residential Differences in Children Ever Born

Residential differences in children ever born are important because they underscore the differences between reservation and nonreservation American Indians. Most reservations are located in nonmetropolitan areas, and though not all Indians living in such areas are reservation residents, this distinction still serves as a convenient proxy for reservation residence (see Snipp, 1989). The data in Table 2-4 show the mean number of children ever born to women living in metropolitan and nonmetropolitan areas, over the decades from 1970 to 1990.

Table 2-4 shows the same declines in fertility over time that are visible in other tables, the result of both compositional changes and real declines. Furthermore, this downward trend is evident in metropolitan and nonmetropolitan areas alike. It is somewhat more pronounced in metropolitan areas, but this may reflect more the influence of compositional changes over time than a real change in fertility, given that changes in racial self-identification have been greatest in urban areas. And as with other groups, the fertility of American Indian women is higher in nonmetropolitan than in metropolitan areas. There are various explanations for why fertility levels are typically higher in rural areas, and they are just as plausible for American Indian as for other women. For example, traditional values that reinforce the desirability of large families are often more prevalent in rural areas. Perhaps more important, correlates of fertility such as education and labor force participation also tend to be lower in rural areas.

TABLE 2-4 Mean Number of Children Ever Born to American Indian Women Aged 15-44, by Place of Residence in 1970, 1980, and 1990

	1970		1980		1990	
Age	Metro	Nonmetro	Metro	Nonmetro	Metro	Nonmetro
15-24	0.37	0.44	0.30	0.40	0.30	0.37
25-34	2.11	2.31	1.39	1.74	1.24	1.70
35-44	2.78	3.12	2.55	2.84	1.90	2.25

SOURCE: U.S. Bureau of the Census public-use microdata samples.

MORTALITY

The largest and most comprehensive source of data about American Indian mortality is that available from the Indian Health Service, which obtains data for its reports from special tabulations produced by the National Center for Health Statistics. The most significant limitation of these data is that they are tabulated only for those areas served by the Indian Health Service. The coverage of these tabulations for 1990 included an estimated 1.21 million persons, or about 62 percent of the total American Indian population of 1.96 million. It is important to note that the population served by the Indian Health Service is heavily concentrated on reservations in rural areas. Some urban areas are included; nonetheless, the American Indian population represented by these data is more rural, has a lower standard of living, and has more health problems than the complete population enumerated by the census. Still, these data illustrate the mortality and health problems experienced by the majority of American Indians and accurately represent the mortality experience of the most economically disadvantaged segment of the American Indian population.

Summary Measures of Mortality

Table 2-5 shows data for American Indians and whites for several measures that reflect mortality patterns.

Life expectancy at birth is one such measure. Table 2-5 shows that here the gap between American Indians and whites was greatest about 20 years ago; in earlier decades, it was even larger (see Snipp, 1989). In the

TABLE 2-5 Summary Measures of Mortality, American Indians and Whites

Race/Year	Life Expectancy	YPLL[a]	Age-Adjusted Mortality
American Indians			
1987-89	71.5	93.1	60.0
1980-82	68.5	119.1	71.0
1972-74	61.0	188.3	100.7
Whites			
1988	75.6	49.2	51.3
1981	74.8	57.4	54.5
1973	72.2	70.8	65.9

[a]Years of productive life lost.

SOURCE: Indian Health Service (1993).

period of 1972-1974, the life expectancy of American Indians was 61.0 years as compared with 72.2 years for whites, a difference of over 11 years or 18 percent. Fifteen years later, this gap had narrowed considerably. In 1988, American Indians had a life expectancy at birth of 71.5, while for whites the figure was 75.6, a gap of just 5 years or 6 percent. Some of this relative improvement in life expectancy is probably due to compositional changes resulting from the changes in racial self-identification discussed earlier. However, based on data yet to be discussed, this increase can also be attributed to significant declines in infant mortality.

Another useful measure of mortality is years of productive life lost (YPLL)—the difference between age 65 and age at death, summed over all deaths in a given year. This measure especially captures the impact of mortality among younger adults. For American Indians in 1972-74, years of productive life lost (YPLL) was over 188, about 166 percent higher than for the white population. However, 15 years later, this number had decreased significantly to 93.1, or less than half its previous value; YPLL had also declined for whites, from 70.8 to 49.2, about a 31 percent reduction. Despite these improvements in both populations, YPLL was still about 89 percent higher for American Indians than for whites.

Age-adjusted mortality is a third way of describing mortality. This measure allows comparisons between populations with substantially different age distributions. In particular, it takes into account the differences in mortality that may arise because of differences in age structure. Specifically, because of high rates of fertility and mortality, the American Indian population is relatively young, with a median age of 26.2 years. In contrast, the non-Hispanic white population has lower fertility and mortality and a correspondingly older population, with a median age of 34.9. Table 2-5 shows that, age differences aside, the American Indian population still experiences substantially higher mortality than other Americans, notably the white population. In 1973, the age-adjusted mortality rate for American Indians was 53 percent higher (100.7) than the rate for whites (65.9). Fifteen years later, the gap between whites (51.3) and American Indians (60.0) had diminished significantly, but American Indians continued to have persistently high rates of mortality.

Infant Mortality

High levels of socioeconomic distress are frequently accompanied by high levels of infant mortality. This is because poverty-stricken areas have limited access to medical care, prenatal and neonatal care is limited, and the nutrition of mothers is poor, among other problems. In this regard, American Indians are an anomaly. There is no question that American Indians are one of the poorest groups in American society.

Infant mortality rate (per 1000 births)

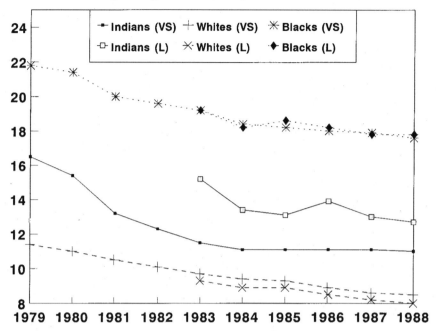

FIGURE 2-1 Infant mortality rates per 1,000 births.

About 32 percent of American Indians in Indian Health Service areas have incomes below the official poverty threshold, compared with 13 percent for the total U.S. population. Yet remarkably, American Indians have relatively low infant mortality rates.

Figure 2-1 shows trends from two sources of data. The longer lines, labeled "(VS)", are based on vital statistics reports. These reports are widely used and have the virtue of being available for lengthy periods in the past. However, there is some evidence that American Indian infant deaths are underreported (Hahn, 1992; Hahn et al., 1992). In contrast, the special National Center for Health Statistics data file in which birth and death records are linked (National Center for Health Statistics, 1995) significantly reduces reporting errors, but has the disadvantage of being available only for the period since 1983. Infant mortality rates from this special data file are shown in Figure 2-1 as lines labeled "(L)".

The infant mortality rates from vital statistics show a downward trend from 1979 to 1990. As suggested earlier, this trend can be traced back to 1955, when the Indian Health Service was transferred to the Public Health Service (Sorkin, 1988). Around 1979, American Indian infant mortality was about 16.5 per 1,000 live births, approximately 45 percent higher than the rate of 11.4 among the white population. Within 5 years, American Indian infant mortality had continued its decline and leveled off at about 11 deaths per 1,000 live births—very near the rate of 8.5 among whites, though still about 29 percent higher.

Overall, American Indian infant mortality has declined steeply over the last four decades, and the Indian Health Service undoubtedly deserves a great deal of credit for the care it provides to expectant mothers and newborns. Without this care, it is very likely that American Indians would have much higher numbers of infant deaths and infant mortality rates more closely resembling those found among other impoverished groups. As shown in Figure 2-1, blacks in particular have substantially higher rates of infant mortality. At the same time, as discussed below, there are good reasons to believe that these declines are not as great as they appear. Furthermore, it is important to underscore the regional variation in these rates, lest it be assumed that infant mortality is universally low for all groups of American Indians.

Evidence indicating that American Indian infant deaths are underreported is clearest when one compares infant mortality rates from vital statistics with those from the linked special file. While the estimates for blacks and whites are fairly consistent across data sources, estimates of American Indian infant mortality from vital statistics are substantially lower than those from the linked file. For example, for 1986, vital statistics show an infant mortality rate of 11.1 per 1,000 births, while for the same year, the rate derived from the linked file is 13.9, or 25 percent higher.

In its own estimates, the Indian Health Service cautions that American Indian infant deaths are underreported for its Portland, Oregon, service area, covering the states of Oregon, Washington, and Idaho; for its Oklahoma service area, covering the states of Oklahoma, Kansas, and Texas; and for its California service area. Notably, the Oklahoma and California service areas have the two lowest reported rates of infant mortality—5.1 and 4.8 per 1,000 live births, respectively. When these three service areas are excluded, the 1990 American Indian infant mortality rate rises to about 12 per 1,000 live births. Furthermore, it is important to point out that infant mortality continues to be a serious problem in the northern plains. Some of the poorest reservations in the nation are located in this region, including Shannon County, South Dakota, the poorest county in the nation and the site of the Pine Ridge reservation. In this region, infant mortality rates are in the range of 16 to 18 per 1,000 live births, well above the 8.5 rate for whites.

Leading Causes of Death

The numbers in Table 2-6 chronicle the main causes of death among American Indians in 1988 and show the corresponding rates for the white population. Note that these are not necessarily the leading causes of death among whites. In addition, it should be no surprise that the major causes of death change as the population becomes older. For this reason, the figures in Table 2-6 show the leading causes of death for young adults (ages 15 to 24), early adulthood (ages 25 to 44), and older adulthood (ages 65 and older).

Examination of the death rates in Table 2-6 makes it clear that the overwhelming majority of these deaths were preventable, at least in principle. In 1988, younger American Indians aged 15-24 had a death rate from all causes of 221 per 100,000 persons—133 percent higher than the death rate among whites of the same age. The tragedy of this figure is that so many of these deaths need not have happened: 85 percent were the result of accidents, suicide, and homicide. Although suicides are 172 percent higher for young American Indian adults than for young whites, and homicides kill nearly three times more American Indians than whites per capita, accidents, especially car accidents, are the true scourge of American Indians at this age. Tribal leaders could reduce deaths among their young people by a third or more if they simply could successfully encourage safe driving and seat belt use and discourage drunk driving— the major causes of auto fatalities. This would certainly not be easy, but would have enormous benefit in many Indian communities; for this age group, it would save more lives than finding a cure for cancer.

Although accidents and violent deaths are the most lethal agents of American Indian mortality, liver disease is also a deadly but possibly avoidable problem for American Indians aged 25-44. In this age group, liver disease claims nearly six times more American Indian than white lives. The reason so many of these deaths are unnecessary is because they no doubt reflect the aftermath of chronic alcoholism and alcohol abuse. Of course, liver disease is not always the result of alcohol consumption. But the problem of alcohol abuse is well known among American Indians, and to find so many deaths due to this disease in a relatively young population is both extraordinary and alarming. Ironically, for American Indians who reach middle age, the chances of survival improve significantly, especially as compared with the white population. While younger American Indians die at a much higher rate than whites of the same age, the death rate from all causes for American Indians aged 45-64 is only about 21 percent higher than the death rate for whites of the same age— 968 and 798, respectively. In this age group, heart disease and cancer are the major killers, but the number of deaths due to heart disease is about

TABLE 2-6 Five Leading Causes of Adult Deaths, 1988

Cause	American Indians	Whites
Ages 15-24		
All causes	221.0	95.1
All accidents	125.4	52.0
Vehicular accidents	90.0	41.3
Suicide	38.3	14.1
Homicide	23.3	7.8
Cancer	4.8	5.1
Heart disease	2.5	2.4
Ages 25-44		
All causes	304.7	150.6
All accidents	112.2	34.7
Vehicular accidents	69.2	21.0
Liver disease	27.8	4.9
Suicide	26.2	16.1
Homicide	25.8	8.0
Heart disease	21.9	17.1
Ages 45-64		
All causes	968.0	797.8
Heart disease	248.2	246.5
Cancer	180.4	291.4
All accidents	97.4	31.2
Vehicular accidents	45.3	15.5
Liver disease	84.1	24.2
Diabetes	64.9	16.0
Ages 65 and Older		
All causes	4067.5	5127.6
Heart disease	1368.8	2088.1
Cancer	738.6	1066.5
Cerebrovascular disease	299.7	427.1
Diabetes	234.0	90.9
Pneumonia and influenza	232.5	231.7

NOTE: Rates are per 100,000 population.

SOURCE: Indian Health Service (1993).

the same for American Indians and whites, and cancer is noticeably less common among American Indians, by about 38 percent. Indeed, the total death rate for American Indians in this age group is higher than for whites, mainly because of excessive deaths due to accidents and liver disease. As noted earlier, American Indians are also susceptible to mature-onset (Type II) diabetes, another reason for the excess of American Indian deaths. Indeed, there are more than four times as many deaths due to diabetes among American Indians aged 45-64 as among whites of the same age.

Finally, it may be surprising, but American Indians who reach old age actually enjoy a small advantage over whites of the same age. This may reflect some selectivity in the factors that contribute to survival and the fact that so many American Indians die at younger ages. Yet American Indians who reach age 65 are less likely than whites to die from cancer, stroke, or heart disease. In fact, only diabetes stands out as a unique cause of excessive deaths for these American Indians, causing about 2.6 times more deaths than for whites. However, another plausible explanation is that mortality for older American Indians, like infant mortality, is underestimated as a result of racial misclassification on death certificates. Similarly, there is evidence that for nonwhites, there is a tendency to underestimate the age of decedents on death certificates, and this would artificially lower mortality rates for older American Indians (Hambright, 1968).

POPULATION DISTRIBUTION AND MIGRATION

Regional Distribution

The Census Bureau uses a standard set of geographic regions that are subdivided into multistate divisions. The percentages in Table 2-7 show the geographic distribution of the American Indian population across these areas between censuses since 1970. The distributional changes shown in Table 2-7 should be interpreted with caution, however. Some of these differences may be due to the movement of persons around the country or to differential rates of natural increase among areas. Yet there is also another, less obvious source of change: the changing patterns of self-identification noted earlier. Regional variations in racial self-identification have been described as "implied migration." Harris (1994) found that rates of implied migration ranged from as little as 0.4 percent in the Mountain Division to 37.5 percent in the East South Central Division. Hence, what may appear to be a significant demographic shift may reflect changing ideas about racial identity more than the actual mobility of the population.

Despite the substantial increase in the number of American Indians since 1970, especially that due to changes in racial self-identification, the basic distribution of the American Indian population has remained surprisingly stable for the past two decades. In 1990, as in 1970 and 1980, the West Region had the largest number of American Indians. Similarly, the Northeast Region had the fewest numbers of American Indians over the 20-year period. This pattern clearly reflects the impact of the Indian Removal Act, which targeted American Indians east of the Mississippi River. The latter area includes the entire Northeast Region and the East North Central, South Atlantic, and East South Central divisions. As his-

TABLE 2-7 Regional Distribution of the American Indian and Alaska Native Population, 1970-1990 (percentage of totals in parentheses)

Region and Division	1970		1980		1990		Percent Change	
							1970-1980	1980-1990
Northeast Region	45,720	(5.8)	79,038	(5.6)	125,148	(6.4)	72.9	58.3
New England	10,362	(1.3)	21,597	(1.5)	32,794	(1.7)	108.4	51.9
Mid-Atlantic	35,358	(4.5)	57,441	(4.0)	92,354	(4.7)	62.5	60.8
Midwest Region	144,254	(18.2)	248,413	(17.5)	337,899	(17.3)	72.2	36.0
East North Central	54,578	(6.9)	105,927	(7.4)	149,939	(7.7)	94.1	41.6
West North Central	89,676	(11.3)	142,486	(10.0)	187,960	(9.6)	58.9	31.9
South Region	194,406	(24.5)	372,825	(26.2)	562,731	(28.7)	91.8	50.9
South Atlantic	65,367	(8.2)	118,938	(8.4)	172,281	(8.8)	82.0	44.9
East South Central	8,708	(1.1)	22,472	(1.6)	40,839	(2.1)	158.1	81.7
West South Central	120,331	(15.2)	231,410	(16.3)	349,611	(17.8)	92.3	51.1
West Region	408,350	(51.5)	722,769	(50.8)	933,456	(47.6)	77.0	29.2
Mountain	229,669	(29.0)	366,291	(25.7)	480,516	(24.5)	59.5	31.2
Pacific	179,681	(22.5)	356,478	(25.1)	452,940	(23.1)	99.5	27.1
U.S. Total	792,730		1,423,045		1,959,234		79.5	37.7

SOURCES: U.S. Bureau of the Census (1992); Snipp (1989).

tory suggests, there are relatively few American Indians living in this area: approximately 488,000 or about one-quarter of the total U.S. American Indian population.

One additional observation that can be made about the population changes shown in Table 2-7, is that the rate of growth in all areas was smaller in the 1980s than in 1970s, reflecting in part changes in racial self-identification. In the 1980s, the total growth of the American Indian population was about 38 percent, with natural increase accounting for about 22 percent. Natural increase was higher in the 1970s, about 28 percent, but shifting patterns of racial self-identification raised the total growth to nearly 80 percent. These intercensal differences are reflected across regions and divisions with percentage changes ranging from 59 to 158 percent in the 1970s and 27 to 82 percent in the 1980s. Predictably, those places with the smallest numbers of Indians (e.g., the East South Central Division) also had the largest increases, and vice versa for areas with large numbers of American Indians, such as the divisions of the West.

Place of Residence: Urban and Rural Population

The percentages in Table 2-8 show the distribution of the U.S. population, including American Indians and Alaska Natives, by metropolitan

TABLE 2-8 Residential Distribution of the American Population by Race and Hispanic Origin, 1990 (percent)

| Race/Origin | Inside MSAs* | | | Outside MSAs | Inside and Outside MSAs |
	Inside Central Cities	Outside Central Cities	Total		
American Indian and Alaska Native					
1990	23.3	28.0	51.3	48.7	100.0
1980	20.9	28.1	49.0	51.0	100.0
Asian and Pacific Islander	46.5	47.4	93.9	6.1	100.0
Black	57.3	26.4	83.7	16.3	100.0
Hispanic[a]	51.5	38.9	90.4	9.6	100.0
White	24.5	50.3	74.8	25.2	100.0
Total U.S. Population	31.3	46.2	77.5	22.5	100.0

[a]Hispanics may be of any race.
*MSA = Metropolitan Service Area.

SOURCES: U.S. Bureau of the Census (1993); Snipp (1989).

residence (metropolitan statistical areas or MSAs). Comparing American Indians with other groups makes it abundantly clear that American Indians continue to be heavily concentrated outside of urban areas. In 1990, about 78 percent of all Americans resided in MSAs, as compared with slightly over half (51.3 percent) of all American Indians. Other minority groups, such as Asians or Hispanics, were concentrated in cities at rates of 90 percent or higher. Furthermore, most minority populations living in metropolitan areas were concentrated in "downtown" central city locations. This was not the case for American Indian city dwellers, about 55 percent of whom lived outside of central city areas.

Table 2-8 also shows a change in the urbanization of American Indians between 1980 and 1990: the numbers suggest a slight increase in metropolitan residence, from 49.0 to 51.3 percent. However, it would be a mistake to read too much into this shift. One reason is that these numbers are influenced not only by changes in racial self-identification, but also by changes in the Census Bureau's metropolitan definitions, with some places being designated as metropolitan in 1990 but not in 1980. Given the small difference involved, it is probably reasonable to conclude that the rapid urbanization of American Indians that took place in the 1940s, 1950s, and 1960s reached a point of stasis, and there is little reason to believe that the American Indian population of 1990 was significantly more urbanized than that of 20 years before.

Although American Indians are one of the least urbanized groups in American society, they are nonetheless concentrated in a relatively small number of cities. In fact, roughly half of all urban American Indians can be found in as few as 16 cities. These cities and their numbers of American Indian inhabitants are shown in Table 2-9. These figures reflect the aftermath of the urban relocation programs that were winding down by 1970: 8 of the cities shown in Table 2-9—Tulsa, Oklahoma City, the Los Angeles area, the San Francisco Bay area, Dallas, Seattle, and Chicago— were officially designated relocation sites for American Indians desiring to leave the reservations with Bureau of Indian Affairs sponsorship.

The three sets of population estimates for 1970, 1980, and 1990 shown in Table 2-9 make it tempting to reach conclusions about changes in urban settlement. Though these data are interesting, it would be a mistake to place much emphasis on the changes over time. These changes reflect not only changes in the physical boundaries of these places, but also the changing definitions of what constitutes a metropolitan area noted above. Thus, it appears that Los Angeles and Albuquerque lost American Indian population between 1980 and 1990, but there is no way of determining whether this loss reflects a real decline in the number of people in these places or these other changes.

TABLE 2-9 Metropolitan Statistical Areas with 15,000 or More American Indians and Alaska Natives in 1990

MSA	1970	1980	1990
Tulsa, OK	15,183	38,463	48,348
Oklahoma City, OK	12,951	24,695	46,111
Los Angeles-Long Beach, CA	23,908	47,234	43,689
Phoenix, AZ	19,996	27,788	38,309
Seattle-Tacoma, WA	8,814	15,162	32,980
Riverside-San Bernadino, CA	5,941	17,107	25,938
New York City, NY	9,984	13,440	24,822
Minneapolis, MN	9,911	15,831	23,338
San Diego, CA	6,007	14,355	21,509
San Francisco-Oakland, CA	12,041	17,546	21,191
Tucson, AZ	8,704	14,880	20,034
Dallas-Fort Worth, TX	5,500	11,076	19,933
Detroit-Ann Arbor, MI	5,203	12,372	19,331
Sacramento, CA	3,548	10,944	18,164
Chicago, IL	8,203	10,415	16,513
Albuquerque, NM	5,822	20,721	16,008
Total in MSAs	161,716	312,029	436,218
Percent of Total U.S. Indian Population	20.4	21.9	22.3

SOURCES: U.S. Bureau of the Census (1993); Snipp (1989).

Place of Residence: Reservation Populations

Reservations, along with the former Indian nations of Oklahoma, make up the majority of territory known as "Indian Country." Reservations were once places where American Indians were quarantined from the mainstream of the dominant society, but have since become places whose importance cannot be overestimated. Reservations represent the last remaining lands belonging to people who once claimed all of North America. For most American Indians, including many urban residents, they are also the touchstones of cultural identity—places with sacred sites, the locus of ceremonial activity, and an essential symbol of tribal life.

There are 279 federal and state reservations located around the nation, and for reasons already mentioned, most are in the west (see Figure 2-2). A quick glance at Figure 2-2 also makes clear that reservations vary enormously in size, ranging from a few acres, such as the small rancherias scattered around California, to the Navajo reservation in the Four Corners area, which is about the same size as the state of West Virginia or the nation of Ireland.

As important as reservations are to American Indian tribal life, it is

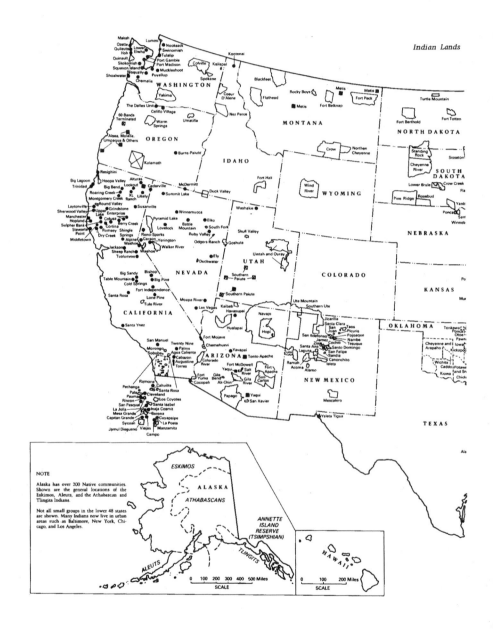

FIGURE 2-2 Indian lands and communities. SOURCE: Snipp (1989). Used with permission of the Russell Sage Foundation.

and Communities

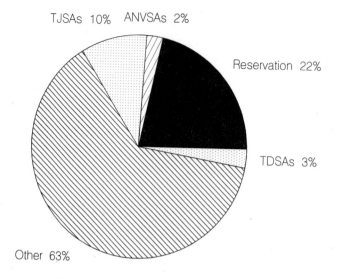

FIGURE 2-3 American Indian places of residence. NOTE: ANVSAs, Alaska Native Village Statistical Area; TJSAs, Tribal Jurisdiction Statistical Areas; TDSAs, Tribal Designated Statistical Areas.

not true that most American Indians live in these places. In fact, as Figure 2-3 shows, many more American Indians live off reservation than on. For the 1990 census, the Census Bureau introduced a new set of geographic designations to delineate "Indian Country"; these are shown in Figure 2-3.

In 1990, about 438,000 American Indians lived on state and federally recognized reservations and trust lands. In absolute numbers, there were more American Indians living on reservations then than at any time in the past; roughly 370,000 American Indians occupied reservations and trust lands in 1980. In relative terms, however, the percentage of Indians living on reservation land declined, from about 27 percent in 1980 to slightly less than 22 percent in 1990.

Tribal Jurisdiction Statistical Areas (TJSAs) and Tribal Designated Statistical Areas (TDSAs) were newly defined in the 1990 census. TJSAs correspond to areas designated as the Oklahoma Historic Areas in the 1980 census, and they follow approximately the boundaries of the Indian nations that existed in Oklahoma before statehood in 1907. Collectively, these areas contain a significant number of American Indians—over 200,000—and they are areas in which tribal governments have a major responsibility for providing services and benefits to tribal members. TDSAs constitute a much smaller group of about 54,000 persons in 17 locations, mostly on state-recognized reservations. Alaska Native Village

Statistical Areas (NVSAs) were a third innovation in the 1990 census, designating villages that were recognized in the Alaska Native Claims Settlement Act of 1972. About 47,000 persons lived in these places in 1990. Overall, about 37 percent of the total U.S. Indian population lived within the boundaries of areas served by tribal governments in 1990.

TDSAs, TJSAs, and Alaska NVSAs are in many respects a significant improvement over past efforts by the Census Bureau to demarcate the boundaries of Indian Country, and especially the areas for which tribal governments have some form of jurisdiction or obligation. Yet these designations have one serious shortcoming: they exclude the numbers of persons who live within close proximity of these areas, participate regularly in tribal affairs, have extensive social ties to the tribe, and possibly even receive services. Tulsa, Oklahoma, has nearly 20,000 American Indians living within a 2- or 3-hour drive to several TJSAs, but this population is considered outside of Indian Country. In 1980, the Census Bureau reported that nearly 15 percent of the total American Indian population lived near but outside reservation land. The point to be made is that while 63 percent of American Indians live outside of lands served by tribal governments, it would be a mistake to assume that this statistic represents the number of persons outside of tribal life.

As Figure 2-3 shows, about one-third of all American Indians live on reservations, and it is worth noting that in most instances, these reservations are very small communities or collections of small communities by modern standards. Of the 279 recognized reservations, only 18 had populations of 5,000 or more in 1990. Table 2-10 shows these reservations and their populations in 1970, 1980, and 1990.

Several interesting observations can be made about Table 2-10. Very clearly, the Navajo reservation stands out as the most populous (as well as the physically largest) reservation. With 143,000 persons, it is nearly 13 times larger than the next-largest reservation, the Pine Ridge Sioux reservation in South Dakota. Another observation is that these reservations grew substantially in the 1970s and 1980s, more than doubling in population size. Yet in relative terms, they represent a slowly declining share of the total U.S. Indian population. Evidence of enumeration problems are also noticeable in this table. In 1980, the Cheyenne River experienced a very steep (and improbable) population loss, followed by an even steeper population recovery in 1990. Similarly, the Turtle Mountain population was virtually unchanged between 1970 and 1980, but experienced a very sharp increase in 1990. The population decline at the Pine Ridge reservation between 1980 and 1990 may also reflect an undercount in 1990, but in the absence of corroborating evidence, this is impossible to determine with certainty.

TABLE 2-10 Population Sizes of Reservations with 5,000 or More American Indians and Alaska Natives in 1990

Reservation	1970	1980	1990	Percent Change		Percent in Different House in 1985
				1970-1980	1980-1990	
Navajo	56,949	104,968	143,405	84.3	36.6	25.9
Pine Ridge	8,280	11,882	11,182	43.5	-6.0	36.5
Fort Apache	5,903	6,880	9,825	16.6	42.8	41.0
Gila River	4,573	7,067	9,116	54.5	29.0	38.1
Papago	4,879	6,959	8,480	42.6	21.9	17.5
Rosebud	5,656	5,688	8,043	0.6	41.4	49.1
San Carlos	4,525	5,872	7,110	29.8	21.1	38.4
Zuni Pueblo	4,736	5,988	7,073	26.4	18.1	18.0
Hopi	7,726	6,601	7,061	b	7.0	35.9
Blackfeet	4,757	5,080	7,025	6.8	38.3	36.8
Turtle Mountain	3,386	3,955	6,772	16.9	71.2	46.1
Yakima	2,509	4,983	6,307	98.6	26.6	43.1
Osage	a	4,749	6,088	a	28.2	42.7
Fort Peck	3,182	4,273	5,782	34.3	35.3	54.2
Wind River	3,319	4,150	5,676	25.0	36.8	48.1
Eastern Cherokee	3,455	4,844	5,388	40.2	11.2	24.9
Flathead	2,537	3,504	5,130	38.1	46.4	53.3
Cheyenne River	3,440	1,557	5,100	-54.7	227.6	53.9
Reservation Total	128,812	199,000	264,563	54.5	33.0	—
Percent of Total U.S. Indian Population	16.3	14.0	13.5			

aNot reported for 1970 and not included in reservation total.
bFigures for 1970 and 1980 are not strictly comparable because of administrative changes in reservation boundaries.

SOURCES: U.S. Bureau of the Census (1993); Snipp (1989).

Migration

Data from the 1980 census provide evidence that the contemporary American Indian population was highly mobile (Snipp, 1989). The data for migration in the 1990 census are more limited, but they do not contradict the 1980 findings. One indication of this mobility appears in the last column of Table 2-11. The percentages in this column are for persons aged 5 and older who were living in a different house in 1990 than the one they inhabited in 1985. These numbers range from a low of 18 percent for the Papago reservation and the Zuni Pueblo in the southwest to a high of 54 percent for the Fort Peck and Cheyenne River reservations in the northern plains.

These remarkably high rates of mobility are even more noteworthy because to a large extent they probably represent mobility to and from the reservation and not intra-reservation migration. This is impossible to determine beyond doubt, but is likely for two reasons. One is that housing stocks on these reservations are extremely limited, and overcrowding is a persistent housing problem on most reservations (Snipp, 1989). There is simply not enough housing available to allow persons to move freely within the reservation, and indeed the lack of housing often limits migration to reservations. A second, related point is that new housing might foster neighborhood mobility or an influx of migrants, but during the 1980s, housing construction and especially federally subsidized housing came to a virtual halt. In sum, whatever neighborhood mobility occurred during the 1980s was not in response to housing availability and thus was probably much less common than mobility between the reservation and nearby towns and cities, where housing was more plentiful.

The residential mobility of persons living on reservations may seem high, but the residential mobility of urban American Indians is even higher. Figure 2-4 shows the percentage of American Indians who lived in a different house in 1990 than in 1985, by place of residence—metropolitan or nonmetropolitan area and central city or not. About 45 percent of American Indians living in nonmetropolitan areas changed residences between 1985 and 1990. This is consistent with the percentages in Table 2-11 for reservations and not surprising because most reservations are located in nonmetropolitan areas. Residential mobility was highest for American Indians living in central cities, where about 65 percent of this population changed residences between 1985 and 1990.

Figure 2-4 also shows the residential mobility of whites and blacks, and there is no question that American Indians are considerably more mobile than either of these groups. In central cities, the gap between American Indians and whites or blacks is about 15 to 18 percent. In nonmetropolitan areas, the gap is smaller, but American Indians are still

Percentage

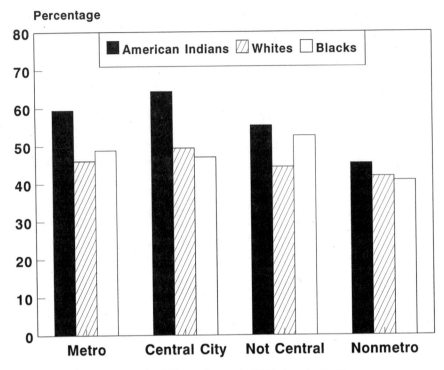

FIGURE 2-4 Percentage in different house in 1990 than in 1985.

more mobile than either blacks or whites. The high level of mobility among urban Indians is difficult to explain, but there are two possibilities. One is that because American Indians are relative newcomers to cities, they do not have established communities or ethnic enclaves in which to settle and become attached to existing social networks. This lack of social ties to an area or neighborhood may contribute to higher levels of residential mobility. Another possible explanation is the substantial anecdotal evidence that American Indians routinely and frequently move between reservations and urban areas. Nonmetro mobility rates remain low because persons return to the same house on the reservation, but live in different places when residing in cities. Hence, residential mobility on the reservation appears low, while urban residential mobility stays at a high level.

In view of the earlier finding that the distribution of the American Indian population across regions, states, and cities has remained fairly stable for the past two decades, the above high rates of residential mobility may be surprising, presuming that residential mobility frequently leads to population redistribution. On the other hand, if residential mo-

TABLE 2-11 Migration Rates Between 1985 and 1990 Place of Residence for America Indians and Alaska Natives

Region/Division	In Migration	Out Migration	Net Migration
Northeast	14.2	12.0	2.1
New England	16.5	14.6	1.9
Mid-Atlantic	13.3	11.0	2.2
Midwest	11.9	11.0	0.9
East North Central	10.3	9.5	0.8
West North Central	13.3	12.3	0.9
South	12.3	11.7	0.5
South Atlantic	16.9	13.1	3.7
East South Central	16.2	15.1	1.1
West South Central	9.3	10.6	−1.3
Mountain	10.6	10.0	0.6
Pacific	10.7	9.2	1.6

NOTE: The data in this table are for persons age 5 and older.

SOURCE: U.S. Bureau of the Census public-use microdata sample (1990).

bility follows established, long-term patterns of exchange, such as those that might exist between certain reservations and certain cities, there is no reason to expect that residential flows would have any effect on population distribution.

Table 2-11 shows rates of in, out, and net migration per 100 population for census regions and divisions between 1985 and 1990. The South and Northeast regions had relatively small American Indian populations, but relatively high rates of in and out migration. In contrast, the Mountain and Pacific regions had much larger populations, but somewhat lower rates of in and out migration. Despite these relatively high rates of in and out migration, net migration in virtually all of these areas was negligible, between 1 and 2 percent, lending credence to the idea that high rates of residential mobility do not signal a large-scale distributional shift in the American Indian population. Significantly, the West South Central Division, including Oklahoma with its large Indian population, was the only area to experience a net loss, which was dispersed across the other regions.

In closing, it is worth noting that in the 1970s, American Indian migration patterns mirrored those of other Americans, especially in flows toward the so-called "sunbelt" (Snipp, 1989). Because American Indians were already concentrated in the west, these migration patterns did not substantially alter the distribution of the Indian population, and these flows were also offset by return mobility to reservation communities.

However, in the 1980s, as sunbelt opportunities diminished, the American Indian population, though highly mobile, appeared to be in stasis insofar as no place, state, or region appeared to hold a strong attraction. Needless to say, this buttressed the stability of the American Indian population distribution, which apparently remained fundamentally unchanged from 1970 to 1990.

CONCLUDING REMARKS

From the arrival of Europeans until the dawn of the twentieth century, the indigenous societies of North America appeared destined for extinction. Most observers fully expected American Indians to disappear, and their beliefs were well founded; the American Indian population dwindled from perhaps as many as 5-7 million to as few as a quarter million in 1890. However, as the twentieth century progressed, a remarkable event took place: instead of disappearing, the American Indian population staged a surprising comeback.

Throughout the first half of this century, growth in the American Indian population gathered momentum, starting slowly at first, then gradually increasing over the decades. Despite signs of renewed vigor in the form of rising fertility and declining mortality, no one could have predicted the spectacular growth in the American Indian population since 1950. In the second half of the twentieth century, the American Indian population has increased five-fold, and at least in the short term, there are few reasons to expect this trend to reverse itself.

The staggering growth in the American Indian population, coupled with the unique legal and political status accorded to American Indian tribes, is no less than a mandate for acquiring better knowledge about the demography of this population. Insofar as demography is the study of how human populations reproduce themselves, as well as the conditions in which they live, there are obvious and compelling reasons why a better understanding of American Indian demography is essential for social scientists and policymakers alike—and perhaps even more so for American Indians themselves.

This chapter has been devoted to two fundamental dimensions of American Indian demography: the size and the distribution of the American Indian population. In particular, because population size is primarily an outcome of natural events related to births and deaths, fertility and mortality are central to understanding American Indian population dynamics. Likewise, the distribution of the American Indian population is tied to settlement patterns, and especially to patterns of migration or residential mobility.

With regard to fertility, American Indian birth rates were relatively low at the beginning of this century. The reasons for these low rates are not well understood, but the rates are consistent with the slow population growth among American Indians prior to 1930. Since that time, the fertility rate of American Indians has climbed to a level that now exceeds most other groups in American society. There can be little doubt that high fertility rates have made a significant contribution to the growth of the American Indian population. Indeed, from 1970 to 1980, the excess of births over deaths helped increase the population by 28 percent, and it added another 22 percent in the decade of the 1980s.

Natural increase would have an even greater impact on the size of the American Indian population if somehow mortality could be reduced. Death rates for American Indians are especially high for younger persons. Ironically, the Indian Health Service probably deserves much of the credit for severing the link between poverty and infant mortality among American Indians—infant mortality rates are relatively low in most areas of Indian Country. Yet American Indian youth and young adults die at rates far out of proportion to their numbers. Moreover, an overwhelming number of these deaths are unnecessary in that they do not result from chronic disease; instead, they are the result of violence, auto accidents, and alcohol abuse. Many tribal leaders are acutely aware of these problems, but as a matter of public health, they should be accorded foremost priority.

Finally, perhaps more than fertility or mortality, the distribution of the American Indian population clearly bears the marks of historical events and especially the influence of federal policies. The removal policies of the nineteenth century, for example, pushed American Indians out of the east and into the west, where the majority still reside. About one-third still live on the reservations first designed to quarantine them and now serving as a final homeland. World War II and the relocation programs of the 1950s and 1960s had a profound impact on American Indians by bringing them to urban areas, where slightly over one-half now live, with the largest numbers being concentrated in cities once designated as relocation centers. American Indians continue to be a highly mobile population, but their moves follow patterns that do not appreciably alter the existing residential distribution. Since 1970, there have been no major developments to cause a significant redistribution of the American Indian population, and the current distribution of American Indians appears to be a relatively stable one for the foreseeable future.

There can be no doubt that the American Indian population, once on the brink of extinction, has rebounded in a dramatic way. Equally certain is the fact that, at least numerically, the existence of the American Indian population is assured for the foreseeable future. Yet the future vitality of the American Indian population will depend on more than growth alone.

Growing numbers bring hope, but they also bring challenges. Tribal leaders and others concerned with the future well-being of American Indians must find innovative ways to provide for the material needs and ensure the cultural survival of Indian people. As American Indians move into the next century, meeting the many challenges of preserving cultural traditions and improving economic well-being will, more than numbers alone, be the foundation for sustaining the place of American Indians within the mosaic of American society.

REFERENCES

Aberle, S.B.D.
    1931   Frequency of Pregnancies and Birth Interval Among Pueblo Indians. *American Journal of Physical Anthropology* 16:63-80.
Aberle, S.D., J.H. Watkins, and E.H. Pitney
    1940   The vital history of the San Juan Pueblo. *Human Biology* 12:141-87.
Bachman, R.
    1992   *Death and Violence on the Reservation*. Westport, CT: Auburn House.
Bernstein, A.R.
    1991   *American Indians and World War II: Toward a New Era in Indian Affairs*. Norman, OK: University of Oklahoma Press.
Blumenfield, R.
    1965   Mohawks: Round trip to the high steel. *Transaction* 3:19-22.
Campbell, G.R.
    1991   Changing patterns of health and effective fertility among the Northern Cheyenne of Montana, 1886-1903. *American Indian Quarterly* 15:339-58.
Clinton, L., B.A. Chadwick, and H.M. Bahr
    1975   Urban relocation reconsidered: Antecedents of employment among Indian males. *Rural Sociology* 40:112-33.
Eschbach, K., K. Supple, and C.M. Snipp
    1995   Changes in racial self-identification and changes in the educational attainments of American Indians, 1970-1990. Paper presented at the annual meetings of the Population Association of America, San Francisco, CA.
Fixico, D.L.
    1986   *Termination and Relocation: Federal Indian Policy, 1945-1960*. Norman, OK: University of Oklahoma Press.
Gundlach, J.H., and A.E. Roberts
    1978   Native American Indian migration and relocation: Success or failure. *Pacific Sociological Review* 12:117-128.
Hackenberg, R.A., and C.R. Wilson
    1972   Reluctant emigrants: The role of migration in Papago Indian adaptation. *Human Organization* 31:171-186.
Hagan, W.T.
    1979   *American Indians*. Chicago, IL: University of Chicago Press.
Hahn, R.A.
    1992   The state of federal statistics on racial and ethnic groups. *Journal of the American Medical Association* 267:268-71.

Hahn, R.A., J. Mulinara, and S.M. Teutsch
   1992   Inconsistencies in coding of race and ethnicity between birth and death in U.S.
           infants. *Journal of the American Medical Association* 267:259-63.
Hambright, T.Z.
   1968   *Comparability of Age on the Death Certificate and Matching Census Record.* National
           Center for Health Statistics. Series 2, No. 29. Washington, D.C.: U.S. Government
           Printing Office.
Harris, D.
   1994   The 1990 census count of American Indians: What do the numbers really mean?
           Social Science Quarterly 75:580-93.
Indian Health Service
   1993   *Trends in Indian Health.* Washington, D.C.: U.S. Department of Health and Human
           Services.
   1994   *Trends in Indian Health.* Washington, D.C.: U.S. Department of Health and Human
           Services.
Institute for Government Research
   1928   *The Problem of Indian Administration* [The Meriam Report]. Baltimore, MD: Johns
           Hopkins University Press.
Kunitz, S.J.
   1976   Fertility, mortality, and social organization. *Human Biology* 48:361-77.
Merrell, J.
   1989   *The Indian's New World: The Catawba and Their Neighbors from European Contact
           Through the Period of Removal.* Chapel Hill, NC: University of North Carolina Press.
National Center for Health Statistics
   1995   *Health, United States, 1994.* Hyattsville, MD: Public Health Service.
O'Brien, S.
   1989   *American Indian Tribal Governments.* Norman, OK: University of Oklahoma Press.
Omran, A.R.
   1971   The epidemiological transition: A theory of the epidemiology of population
           change. *Milbank Memorial Fund Quarterly* 49:509-38.
Passel, J.S.
   1976   Provisional evaluation of the 1970 census count of American Indians. *Demography*
           13:397-409.
Passel, J.S., and P.A. Berman
   1986   Quality of 1980 census data for American Indians. *Social Biology* 33:163-82.
Price, J.A.
   1968   The migration and adaptation of American Indians to Los Angeles. *Human Organi-
           zation* 27:168-75.
Rindfuss, R.R., and J.A. Sweet
   1977   *Postwar Fertility Trends and Differentials in the United States.* New York: Academic
           Press.
Rogers, R.G., and R. Hackenberg
   1987   Extending epidemiologic transition theory: A new stage. *Social Biology* 34:234-43.
Snipp, C.M.
   1989   *American Indians: The First of This Land.* New York: Russell Sage Foundation.
Snipp, C.M., and G.D. Sandefur
   1988   Earnings of American Indians and Alaska Natives: The effects of residence and
           migration. *Social Forces* 66:994-1008.
Sorkin, A.L.
   1971   *American Indians and Federal Aid.* Washington, D.C.: Brookings Institution.

Sorkin, A.L.
   1978   *The Urban American Indian.* Lexington, MA: D.C. Heath.
Sorkin, A.L.
   1988   Health and economic development on American Indian reservations. Pp. 145-165
          in C.M. Snipp, ed., *Public Policy Impacts on American Indian Economic Development.*
          Albuquerque, NM: Institute for Native American Development, University of New
          Mexico.
Taffel, S.M.
   1987   Characteristics of American Indian and Alaska Native births: United States. *NCHS*
          Monthly Vital Statistics Report. Vol. 36, No. 3. Hyattsville, MD: National Center for
          Health Statistics.
Thornton, R.
   1987   *American Indian Holocaust and Survival.* Norman, OK: University of Oklahoma
          Press.
Thornton, R., G.D. Sandefur, and C.M. Snipp
   1991   American Indian fertility patterns: 1910 and 1940 to 1980. A research note. *Ameri-*
          can Indian Quarterly 15:359-67.
U.S. Bureau of the Census
   1915   *Indian Population in the United States and Alaska, 1910.* Washington, D.C.: U.S.
          Government Printing Office.
   1992   *General Population Characteristics, United States, 1990.* Washington, D.C.: U.S. Gov-
          ernment Printing Office.
   1993   *Social and Economic Characteristics, United States, 1990.* Washington, D.C.: U.S. Gov-
          ernment Printing Office.
Weibel-Orlando, J.
   1991   *Indian Country, L.A.* Urbana, IL: University of Illinois Press.
Wissler, C.
   1936   Changes in population profiles among the Northern Plains Indians. *Anthropologi-*
          cal Papers of the American Museum of Natural History 36:1:1-7.
Young, T.K.
   1994   *The Health of Native Americans.* New York: Oxford University Press.

3

Recent Health Trends in the Native American Population

T. Kue Young

INTRODUCTION

The health of Native Americans has undergone substantial changes in the second half of the twentieth century. In broad terms, the recent epidemiologic history of Native American populations can be characterized by several key features: the decline but persistence of infectious diseases, stabilizing at a level still higher than that of the non-Native population; the rise in chronic diseases, especially diabetes; and the overwhelming importance of the so-called social pathologies—violence, unintentional injuries, and the ill effects of alcohol and drug abuse. The rise of chronic diseases also characterizes various indigenous populations around the world that are undergoing rapid sociocultural changes. Such diseases collectively have also been called "Western" diseases (Trowell and Burkitt, 1981).

The long-term temporal changes in the pattern of health and disease of a population have been termed epidemiologic or health transition. One particular conception of that transition, originally proposed by Omran (1971, 1977, 1983), consists of three stages: the age of pestilence and famines, the age of receding pandemics, and the age of degenerative and man-made diseases. The pace of the transition differs among populations. Omran distinguishes among the classical or western model, exemplified by western Europe and North America; the accelerated model, characterized by Japan and eastern Europe; and the delayed model, which encompasses most developing countries. Other researchers (Olshansky and Ault, 1986) have added a fourth stage —the age of delayed degenerative diseases—to account for the phenomena observed in the industrialized countries of a decline in mortality from such causes as heart disease and later age at death among the elderly.

The concept of epidemiologic transition has gained some currency in the population and health literature, and a variety of case studies from around the world have attempted to fit available health statistics to the theory. Furthermore, the theory has found applications in the area of health policy and planning, particularly in the context of developing countries (Gribble and Preston, 1993; Jamison et al., 1993; Mackenbach, 1994; Phillips, 1994). Several authors have specifically investigated the applicability of the theory to some Native American populations, for example, the Navajo (Broudy and May, 1983; Kunitz, 1983) and Canadian Indians (Young, 1988). Such attempts are difficult and infrequent, however, because they require the reconstruction of historical time series of mortality/morbidity rates. It is interesting to speculate whether the Native American population has diverged sufficiently from the broader North American experience to merit a separate model, or merely is experiencing a time lag of several decades, or fits better the model for developing countries. However, this issue is of less public health importance than discerning the major health trends to inform the planning and targeting of intervention programs.

This paper does not review the extensive literature on Native American health; a comprehensive review is available elsewhere (Young, 1994). Rather, the focus here is on broad trends based on U.S. data, especially those published by the U.S. Indian Health Service (IHS) (1990a, 1990b, 1994a, 1994b) on the population it serves. The following questions are addressed:

- What are the changes in Native American mortality/morbidity since the mid-1950s?
- Do Native Americans differ from non-Natives in their disease patterns?
- Are there regional and tribal differences within the Native American population?
- What are the determinants of the current patterns?

Before discussing these questions, we examine some methodological issues involved in the use and interpretation of Native American health data. This is followed by sections addressing overall health trends among Native Americans, relative risks of dying from various diseases, regional variations, and health determinants. A final section presents conclusions.

METHODOLOGICAL ISSUES

In the calculation of rates of occurrence of various events of interest among the Native American population (e.g., mortality, incidence, prevalence, health service use), there are problems associated with both the numerator and denominator. In the United States, the IHS began publishing data on Indians it served starting in 1955, the year it was formed. The IHS provides an important source of time-series data on some health indicators for a substantial proportion of the Native American population nationally. The IHS population, however, should not be equated with the total population of Native Americans in the United States. Data that are truly national in scope are sparse.

The issue of the number of Native Americans in the United States is a topic of major concern that is discussed elsewhere. Generally, there are two main sources of these data: the U.S. census (data based on self-identification) and the IHS (data based on eligibility for and use of service). The IHS in fact uses two populations: a *service* population, which is ultimately derived from the census, and a *user* population, based on the agency's own patient registration system.

The IHS estimates the service population by counting those Native Americans identified by the census who reside in geographical areas—on or near reservations—in which the IHS has responsibilities. The service population, which may or may not use IHS services, is used primarily for vital statistics. Service population data for intercensal years are estimated by a smoothing technique; with each new revision to decennial census counts, previously estimated intercensal populations are adjusted accordingly. Rates for 1981-89 differ among the 1991, 1992, 1993, and 1994 *Trends in Indian Health* reports as a result of revisions of the intercensal estimates using two versions of the 1990 census counts of Native Americans and a revision of the 1980 census itself (Indian Health Service, 1994a).

The IHS user population comprises Indian patients who have obtained direct or contract health services from the IHS or tribally operated facilities at least once during the past 3 years and thus are registered in the Patient Registration System. This population serves as the denominator for rates of morbidity and healthcare utilization.

In this paper, national estimates of mortality rates from various causes are derived primarily from the IHS *Trends* series, unless otherwise noted. For vital rates, the IHS receives Native American data from the National Center for Health Statistics (NCHS), extracted from records submitted electronically by state health agencies. There is a further complication in that vital rates prior to the 1992 *Trends* report were not based strictly on the IHS service population, but on the total Native American population in the "reservation states," i.e., states that contain Indian reservations (or legally equivalent entities) and in which the IHS has responsibility. Thus Native Americans living in counties or cities not on or near a reservation but in the same state are included. The reservation state-based vital rates tend to be lower than the "true" IHS service population-based rates. For this paper, vital rates for 1955 to 1972 were obtained from the 1990 *Trends* report, which still used the reservation state method, whereas data for 1973 to 1990 were obtained from the 1994 *Trends* report, which used the IHS service population. However, while the subtle difference between the two data series should be recognized, it does not affect the overall conclusions to be drawn about long-term trends.

Another methodological issue arises from the considerable under-reporting of Native American status that has been shown to occur with birth and death certificates. This is a phenomenon that varies widely among states/IHS areas; the problem is most serious for the California, Oklahoma, and Portland, Oregon areas (Centers for Disease Control and Prevention, 1993). (Note that California data are not included in any of the figures/tables in this paper.)

To illustrate the problem, a study that linked infant death records nationally with their birth records showed that more than a third of the deaths classified as Native American at the time of birth were coded as belonging to other races on the death certificates. The infant mortality rate would have increased from 9.8 to 14.4 per 1,000 if the improved race data drawn from this linkage had been used (Hahn et al., 1992). In a national study that linked deaths at all ages to the census, only 74 percent of deaths among individuals who had self-identified themselves as Native American in the census were found to be coded as such on their death certificates; this discrepancy could result in an underestimation of the death rate by 22 percent (Sorlie et al., 1992). Similar discordances were found in linkage studies conducted in specific regions. Examples are a study of infant deaths in Washington State that linked birth and death certificates (Frost and Shy, 1980) and a later study that linked deaths at all ages with the IHS patient registry (Frost et al., 1994). As noted above, the IHS patient registry includes Native Americans who actually use some IHS services and hence are *bona fide* Native Americans according to legal/bureaucratic criteria. This study also found that Native American status was more likely to be coded correctly for alcohol-related deaths than for diseases such as cancer. Concordance was highest for "full-blooded" Native Americans, and lowest for those with less than one-quarter Native American "blood quantum" (Frost et al., 1994).

Many regional/tribal studies of disease incidence rely on special disease registries. Identification of Native American status in such local registries has also been shown to be incomplete and inaccurate, particularly when it is validated through linkage with the IHS patient registry.

Examples include the Oregon Injury Registry (Sugarman et al., 1993); the Puget Sound Surveillance, Epidemiology and End Results cancer registry (Frost et al., 1992); and the Pacific Northwest Renal Network registry of end-stage renal disease (Sugarman and Lawson, 1993). In the Los Angeles County AIDS registry, only 6 cases had been identified as Native Americans by January 1, 1989; however, when community organizations providing support services to AIDS victims were surveyed, at least 60 Native American cases were identified (Lieb et al., 1992).

The population with which Native Americans are most often compared is the national "all-races" population of the United States, although sometimes specific subgroups such as blacks, whites, Asians, and Hispanics may be compared. It should be noted that the Native American population is younger than the U.S. national population. In the 1990 census, the median age of Native Americans was 26 years, compared with 33 years nationally, and 39 percent of the Native American population was under the age of 20, compared with 29 percent nationally. In most IHS publications, age-standardized rates (by the direct method) are usually provided, with the 1940 U.S. population as the standard. Because of the smaller size of the Native American population, 3-year moving averages are used, whereas single-year data for the U.S. all races population are reported.

Despite the above deficiencies and limitations of existing data sources, it is still possible to discern broad trends in the health and disease status of the Native American population. Indeed, one has the choice of basing planning and policy decisions on imperfect existing data or on no data at all.

OVERALL TRENDS

There is little doubt that the overall health status of Native Americans has substantially improved. Between 1940 and 1990, life expectancy at birth among Native Americans increased by 17.8 years to 69.1 years among men and by 25.6 years to 77.5 years among women. The gap between Native Americans and whites (both sexes combined) narrowed from 13.2 to 2.9 years (Indian Health Service 1990a, 1994a, 1994b). Figure 3-1 compares the infant mortality rate of Native Americans and the U.S. national population since 1955. The substantial decline and convergence is evident, although the low rate shown for Native Americans may have to be adjusted upward to account for underenumeration of Native American infant deaths.

Figure 3-2 shows, in semi-logarithmic scale, trends in age-standardized mortality rates from six causes: tuberculosis, gastroenteritis, cancer, motor vehicle accidents, homicide, and suicide. These six causes were

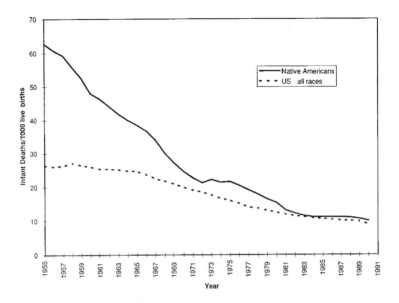

FIGURE 3-1 Trends in infant mortality rates: Native Americans and U.S. all-races national population. SOURCES: 1955-1972 data from Indian Health Service (1990a); 1973-1990 data from Indian Health Service (1994a).

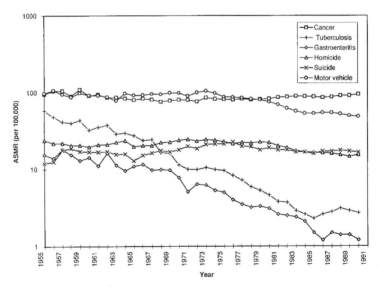

FIGURE 3-2 Trends in age-standardized mortality rates for selected causes among Native Americans. SOURCES: 1955-1972 data from Indian Health Service (1990a); 1973-1990 data from Indian Health Service (1994a).

selected because of the availability of data, as well as general trends they illustrate.

The most dramatic decline in mortality is for the two infectious diseases—tuberculosis and gastroenteritis—which are now insignificant causes of death among Native Americans. Of the six causes shown, cancer and motor vehicle accidents are the most important contributors to mortality, while suicide and homicide occupy an intermediate position. It should be noted that all three causes of injury, especially motor vehicle accidents, have shown some decline since the early 1970s, whereas the rate for cancer has remained relatively unchanged.

It should be cautioned that trend data are subject to variation in coding rules and practices over the years. Between 1955 and 1990, three different revisions of the International Classification of Diseases (ICD)—the seventh, eighth, and ninth—were in use. Moreover, ascription of a death to a specific diagnosis is often based solely on clinical impression and unsubstantiated by medical record or autopsy confirmation. The deficiencies of death certificates as a source of mortality information are well recognized in epidemiologic research (e.g., Kirchner et al., 1985; Israel et al., 1986).

RELATIVE RISKS

The risk of dying from various diseases among Native Americans relative to the total U.S. population can be determined from the age-standardized mortality rates of selected causes for the two populations. Native Americans experience excessive risk for most conditions listed in Table 3-1, with the exception of cardiovascular diseases and cancer.

As the rates of mortality from infectious diseases have declined substantially among both populations, the enormous gap between the two populations has also narrowed (Figure 3-3). However, this should not be interpreted to mean that infectious diseases are no longer a threat to the health of Native Americans. Unfortunately, with the exception of notifiable diseases such as tuberculosis, on which reasonably accurate statistics on the incidence of new active cases are kept, there is a general lack of national data on disease incidence. Figure 3-4 shows incidence data for tuberculosis, indicating that although a substantial decline in incidence has occurred, the gap between Native Americans and the national population is still wide. Moreover, many regional and local studies have demonstrated that Native Americans are still at high risk for such infections as meningitis, acute respiratory infections, viral hepatitis, sexually transmitted diseases, and intestinal infections (reviewed in Young, 1994).

Figure 3-5 shows the trends in age-standardized mortality rates for two chronic diseases, diabetes and cancer. In terms of mortality risk

TABLE 3-1 Age-Standardized Mortality Rates for Selected Causes:
Native Americans (1989-91) and Total U.S. Population (1990)

Cause	ICD-9 Code	Native Americans	U.S. Population	Ratio
Heart diseases	390-8,402,404-29	132.1	152.0	0.9
Cancer	140-208	94.5	135.0	0.7
Unintentional injuries	E800-949	86.0	32.5	2.6
Motor vehicle	*E810-825*	*48.4*	*18.5*	*2.6*
All other	*E800-7,826-949*	*37.6*	*14.0*	*2.7*
Chronic liver disease/ cirrhosis	571	30.3	8.6	3.5
Diabetes mellitus	250	29.7	11.7	2.5
Cerebrovascular disease	430-438	25.2	27.7	0.9
Pneumonia/influenza	480-487	20.5	14.0	1.5
Suicide	E950-959	16.5	11.5	1.4
Homicide	E960-978	15.3	10.2	1.5
Tuberculosis	010-018	2.7	0.5	5.4
All causes		571.7	535.5	1.1

NOTE: All rates are per 100,000.

SOURCE: Indian Health Service, 1994a.

among Native Americans relative to the total U.S. population, the two
diseases are very different: elevated for diabetes and reduced for cancer.
It has been recognized since the pioneering work of West (1974) that
diabetes is a "new" disease among Native Americans, having developed
from a rarity before World War II to an "epidemic" in recent years. Mortality from diabetes does not convey the excessive burden of this disease
among most Native American tribes. Many glucose tolerance surveys
have been conducted among Native Americans over the years (Gohdes,
1995), and estimates of prevalence of the disease can be derived from IHS
patient care data (Valway et al., 1993). A national estimate of self-reported diabetes is also available from the Survey of American Indians and
Alaska Natives, a special component of the 1987 National Medical Expenditures Survey, which covered Native Americans residing in IHS service
areas who self-identified as being eligible for IHS services. The estimated
age-adjusted prevalence of diabetes among Native Americans was 11 percent in men and 13 percent in women, more than twice the rates of the
total U.S. population (Johnson and Taylor, 1991). A detailed review of
diabetes among Native Americans is provided by Narayan in this volume.

A chronic disease of increasing concern among Native Americans is
end-stage renal disease (ESRD). While the etiology of ESRD is varied,

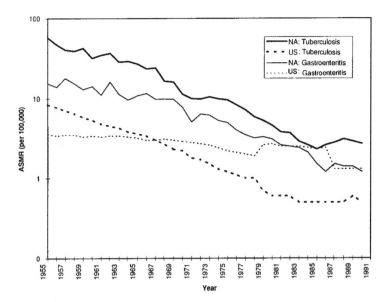

FIGURE 3-3 Trends in age-standardized mortality rates for tuberculosis and gastroenteritis: Native Americans and total U.S. population (semi-logarithmic scale). SOURCES: 1955-1972 data from Indian Health Service (1990a); 1973-1990 data from Indian Health Service (1994a).

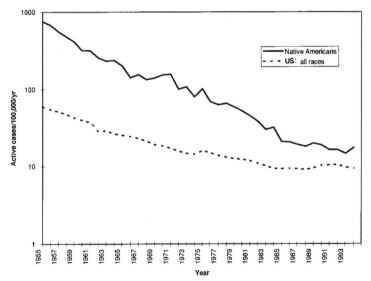

FIGURE 3-4 Trends in incidence of active tuberculosis: Native Americans and total U.S. population. SOURCES: 1955-1978 data from Indian Health Service (1979); other years from unpublished data from National Center for Health Statistics.

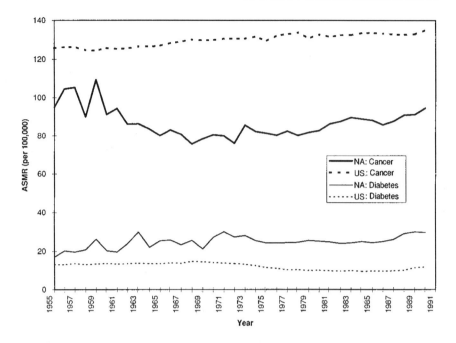

FIGURE 3-5 Trends in age-standardized mortality rates of diabetes and cancer; Native Americans and total U.S. population. SOURCES: 1955-1972 data from Indian Health Service (1990a); 1973-1990 data from Indian Health Service (1994a).

diabetes is an important cause. A national survey using Medicare data indicated that the incidence of ESRD was three times higher among Native Americans than among whites, and the incidence of ESRD due specifically to diabetes was six times higher (Newman et al., 1990).

Incidence data support the lower mortality risk for cancer among Native Americans relative to the total U.S. population. In a meta-analysis of seven published epidemiological studies on Native Americans in four U.S. states and two Canadian provinces from the mid-1950s to early 1980s, a low incidence was found when all cancer sites were combined. There are a few sites, however, for which Native Americans are at increased risk: kidney in men and gallbladder and cervix in women. On the other hand, Native Americans have a reduced risk of the most common cancers in the total U.S. population, such as lung, breast, and colon (Mahoney and Michalek, 1991). Similar findings were obtained from a national study using IHS hospital discharge data (Nutting et al., 1993).

Table 3-1 indicates that the risk of death from heart disease and stroke is slightly lower among Native Americans than among the total U.S. population, after adjustment for age. Incidence data are not readily available, as there are no registries of myocardial infarction, stroke, or other cardio-vascular disorders on a national scale. The hospital discharge rates for IHS facilities do offer one measure of morbidity for cardiovascular dis-eases, and indicate a lower rate than that shown by U.S. national data (Welty and Coulehan 1993). Self-reported prevalence data are available from the Survey of American Indians and Alaska Natives (Table 3-2); however, these data do not truly represent the risk of disease as cross-sectional data can capture only survivors of rapidly progressing and sometimes fatal diseases. A review of NCHS data on stroke shows that Native Americans had lower mortality rates than both blacks and whites between 1980 and 1990. Moreover, the trend has also been declining (Gillum, 1995).

Injuries, both intentional (homicide and suicide) and unintentional (accidents), constitute the second largest group of causes of mortality (after cardiovascular diseases) among Native Americans. While a decline in the past two decades can be observed, there is still a substantial gap as compared with the national population (Figures 3-6 and 3-7). Young adults are at highest risk for death from motor vehicle accidents, drown-ing, and firearm accidents, while falls and house fires disproportionately affect the elderly. One national survey of mortality from childhood inju-ries during 1980-85 showed that overall, the risk among Native Ameri-cans was 1.8 times that of the total U.S. population. For individual causes, the relative risks were 2.2 for motor vehicle occupant accidents, 3.9 for

TABLE 3-2 Prevalence (%) of Selected Self-Reported Chronic Diseases from the Survey of American Indians and Alaska Natives, 1987

Chronic Condition	Male		Female		Total	
	Native	U.S.	Native	U.S.	Native	U.S.
Cardiovascular disease	12.1	10.5	7.8	9.6	9.8	10.0
Cancer	2.6	4.0	3.4	5.3	3.0	4.7
Emphysema	2.4	2.7	1.4	2.3	1.8	2.5
Gallbladder disease	3.8	3.2	10.7	7.4	7.4	5.4
Hypertension	23.2	22.2	22.2	23.4	22.7	22.8
Rheumatism	5.3	4.2	4.0	5.4	4.5	4.8
Arthritis	18.0	16.8	21.3	23.6	19.7	20.4
Diabetes	11.0	4.8	13.2	5.6	12.2	5.2

NOTE: Prevalence among Native Americans is age- and sex-adjusted to the total U.S. population.

SOURCE: Johnson and Taylor (1991).

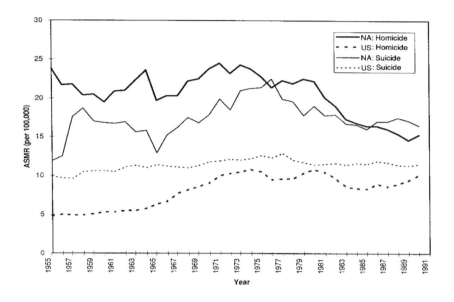

FIGURE 3-6 Trends in age-standardized mortality rates of homicide and suicide; Native Americans and total U.S. population. SOURCE: 1955-72 data from Indian Health Service (1990a); 1973-1990 data from Indian Health Service (1994a).

pedestrian accidents, 1.7 for drowning, 3.5 for poisoning, and 2.6 for aspiration (Waller et al., 1989).

REGIONAL VARIATIONS

The preceding sections address disease and injury rates among Native Americans nationally. While Native Americans do share common experiences as a group, particularly as compared with the dominant North American society, they live in different ecological zones; have different genetic lineages; have different historical experiences; lead different lifestyles; and maintain different values, customs, and traditions. All of these factors have some impact on the distribution of disease and injury, and indeed, substantial regional variations can be observed for almost all indicators.

Administratively, the IHS divides the United States into various areas, each of which serves a tribally mixed population, with the exception of the Navajo Area. Certain groups, however, are found mainly in one area, such as Eskimo and Aleuts in Alaska, various tribes belonging to the

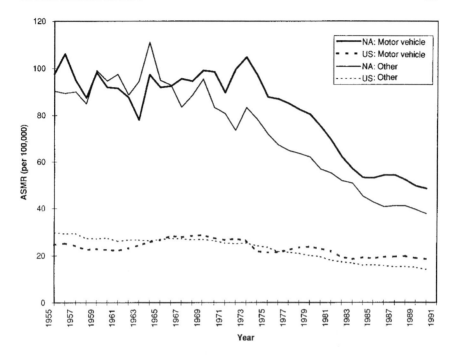

FIGURE 3-7 Trends in age-standardized mortality rates of unintentional injuries, Native Americans and total U.S. population. SOURCES: 1955-1972 data from Indian Health Service (1990a); 1973-1990 data from Indian Health Service (1994a).

Northwest Coast culture in the Portland Area, and Siouan-speaking tribes in the Aberdeen Area. On the other hand, the Nashville Area, for example, covers the entire eastern United States from Maine to Louisiana. Nevertheless, in the absence of data disaggregated into tribes, language families, or culture areas, the IHS administrative divisions provide a readily available perspective on geographic variation.

Figures 3-8, 3-9, and 3-10 show the variation in mortality rates by IHS region for selected infections, chronic diseases, and injuries, respectively. Where prevalence or incidence data exist, they tend to correspond to the regional variation in mortality, for example, in diabetes (Valway et al., 1993) and cancer (Nutting et al., 1993). For diabetes, the Alaska Area has the lowest rates, a reflection of its large Eskimo (Inuit) population. While the rates have increased in recent years, the circumpolar Eskimo in Russia, Alaska, Canada, and Greenland continue to be at substantially lower risk for diabetes than other American Indians (Young et al., 1992). At the other extreme are the Pima, who have the world's highest known prevalence of the disease and have been monitored extensively over the past

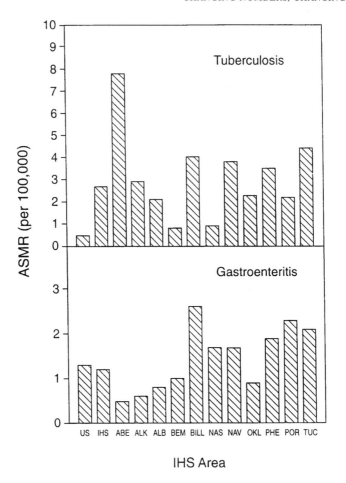

FIGURE 3-8 Regional variation in age-standardized mortality rates for selected infectious diseases, 1989-1991. SOURCE: Indian Health Service (1994b).

three decades (Knowler et al., 1990). With regard to cancer, the Eskimo are at high risk for certain sites, especially nasopharynx and liver (Lanier et al., 1989), contributing to the overall high cancer mortality and incidence rates of the Alaska Area.

The Navajo Area tends to have low mortality rates for cardiovascular disease. A relatively low risk of ischemic heart disease has been observed for some years among the Navajo and Apache, members of the Athapaskan language family who migrated to the Southwest from the northern reaches of the continent around the tenth century (and whose kin today largely inhabit the subarctic boreal forests of Alaska and north-

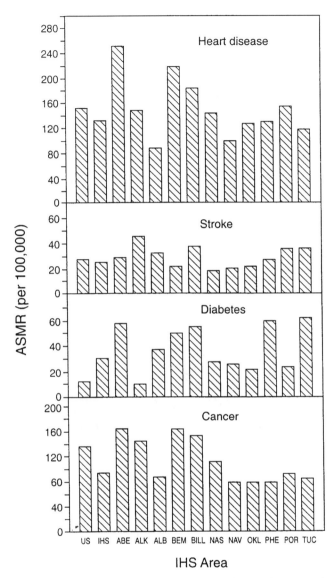

FIGURE 3-9 Regional variation in age-standardized mortality rates for selected chronic diseases, 1989-1991. SOURCE: Indian Health Service (1994b).

ern Canada). A study among the Navajo based on clinical records confirmed the low incidence of the disease in the mid-1980s, although even this group seems to be "catching up" (Klain et al., 1988).

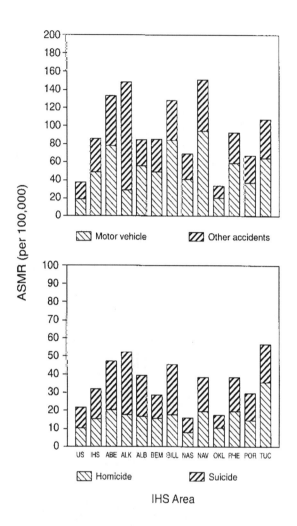

FIGURE 3-10 Regional variation in age-standardized mortality rates for injuries, 1989-1991. SOURCE: Indian Health Service (1994b).

HEALTH DETERMINANTS

While individual diseases and health conditions have their unique causes or risk factors, there are some common factors which are responsible, by and large, for the observable *pattern* of health and disease. Some of these determinants relate to individual physiology and genetics, some to individual life-styles and health practices; and still others to socioeconomic status, community infrastructure, and environmental quality.

Native Americans provide an excellent case study of how genetics and environment interact to affect health status and the distribution of disease. For the chronic diseases, especially diabetes, there is strong evidence that genetic susceptibility is an important factor, and theories such as the "thrifty gene" (Neel, 1982) have been proposed to explain the explosive emergence of these diseases among Native Americans. The metabolic mechanisms are complex and not completely elucidated. From an evolutionary perspective, the diabetic genotype probably conferred a survival advantage under harsh, "feast-or-famine" conditions, but became a liability with an increasingly sedentary life-style and the assurance of a continuous and ample food supply, resulting in obesity and diabetes. There are also alternative theories (e.g., Ritenbaugh and Goodby, 1989; Szathmary, 1990) that can be applied more appropriately to Native American groups in the arctic and subarctic with a hunting tradition and a low-carbohydrate diet. The co-occurrence of gallbladder disease, obesity, and diabetes observed among diverse Native American populations led to the proposal of a "New World Syndrome" of disorders that are likely to be genetically based and mediated through the metabolism of lipids (Weiss et al., 1984).

Historically, the high incidence of and mortality from infectious diseases among Native Americans have contributed to the view that such diseases as tuberculosis are "racial." It has since been recognized that conditions in the social environment probably play the leading etiologic role (Kushigemachi et al., 1984). However, the pendulum has again swung the other way, and recent research on ethnic differences in disease susceptibility and the molecular basis of host resistance suggests that there is a role for genetics in infectious diseases after all (Skamene, 1994).

While genetics are likely to contribute least to injuries among causes of mortality and morbidity, genetically determined enzyme differences affecting alcohol metabolism between Native Americans and other populations have been recognized (Reed, 1985), although the evidence is not consistent. It is also important to note that even if metabolic differences do exist, they are not sufficient to explain the high risk of alcohol abuse and its health effects in terms of accidents and violence among Native Americans populations.

An important factor among the determinants of health is individual health risk behaviors, which have increasingly become the focus of health promotion. Such behaviors as smoking, diet and nutrition, alcohol and drug use, safety knowledge and practices, sexual behavior, and physical activity are implicated in diverse health problems. For Native Americans, national data on health determinants are far more limited than data on health outcomes such as mortality. Surveys such as the Survey of American Indians and Alaska Natives provide useful data on smoking habits;

obesity; and the use of preventive health services, such as screening for hypertension and for cervical and breast cancer (Lefkowitz and Underwood, 1991). Such data are not encouraging: Native Americans smoke more, are more overweight, and use preventive services less often.

Another source of national survey data on health determinants is the Behavioral Risk Factor Surveillance System, a telephone survey conducted since 1984 by the Centers for Disease Control in collaboration with state health departments. Data have been reported on 1,055 Native Americans between 1985 and 1988, covering such areas as seatbelt nonuse, drinking, drinking and driving, high blood pressure, sedentary life-style, cigarette smoking, use of smokeless tobacco, and obesity. In general, the sex-specific prevalences for Native Americans compared with whites do not differ by more than 4 percent, except for current smoking (substantially higher among Native Americans in all regions except the Southwest, where it is lower), and obesity (substantially higher among Native American women). Interestingly, regional differences among Native Americans are similar in magnitude to the regional differences among whites (Sugarman et al., 1992). A recent update on the prevalence of smoking showed that 33 percent of Native American men and 27 percent of women are smokers (Centers for Disease Control and Prevention, 1992). Regionally based data on cardiovascular risk factors, including serum lipids, hypertension, obesity, physical activity, and smoking, can be found in a recent review (Ellis and Campos-Outcalt, 1994).

Broader socioeconomic and environmental factors, such as income, education, housing, and employment, affect health through a variety of pathways. Thus overcrowding and inadequate sanitation promote the acquisition and transmission of respiratory, intestinal, and skin infections; low education and low income affect food choices and nutritional status and contribute to the development of chronic diseases; and unemployment engenders family breakdown and increases the likelihood of violence and injuries. According to the 1990 census, Native Americans nationally continue to be at a disadvantage in terms of a variety of indicators, as summarized in Table 3-3.

It should be emphasized that Native American health must be examined and understood in its historical and political context, beyond the mere cataloging of isolated, individual determinants and outcomes. The evolution of health and disease among Native Americans has been termed an "unnatural history" (Campbell, 1989), and resolution of the major health problems of Native Americans requires redressing the underlying social, cultural, and political causes of those problems.

TABLE 3-3 Selected Socioeconomic Indicators from the 1990 Census: Native Americans and Total U.S. Population

Indicator	Native Americans	U.S. Population
% families maintained by female householder without husband	27	17
% adults 25 years+ with high school graduation	66	75
% adults 16 years+ in the labor force	62	65
% employed persons 16 years + in managerial and professional occupations	18	26
Median family income	$21,750	$35,225
% individuals below poverty level	3	13

SOURCE: Bureau of the Census, 1993.

CONCLUSIONS

The health of Native Americans is undergoing both quantitative and qualitative changes. While the absolute burden of mortality and morbidity has decreased substantially in the decades since World War II, the relative contributions of various diseases and health conditions have also changed. Whether one calls this an "epidemiologic transition" in the sense intended by the theory's original proponents—as well as the associated issues of what stage of the transition currently characterizes Native Americans and whether they should constitute a model distinct from that which characterizes developing countries—is not as important as the utility of the theory in advancing our ability to monitor and predict trends. Clearly, planning for future health interventions must be based on how the current burden of illness will evolve (Rhoades et al., 1987). On a theoretical level, the data are insufficient, particularly at a national level, to characterize more clearly "health" beyond mortality. Among Native Americans, one must also proceed beyond the descriptive to the analytic to help understand and explain why the Native American pattern of health has changed and is continuing to do so. This will be a challenge to demographers and epidemiologists interested in Native Americans.

REFERENCES

Broudy, D.W., and P.A. May
  1983   Demographic and epidemiologic transition among the Navajo Indians. *Social Biology* 30:1-16.

Bureau of the Census
1993 *We the First Americans*. Washington, DC: Racial Statistics Branch, Population Division.
Campbell, G.R.
1989 The changing dimension of Native American health: A critical understanding of contemporary Native American health issues. *American Indian Culture and Research Journal* 13(3 & 4):1-20.
Centers for Disease Control and Prevention
1992 Cigarette smoking among American Indians, Alaska Natives—Behavioral Risk Factor Surveillance System, 1987-1991. *Journal of the American Medical Association* 268:3052, 3055.
1993 Classification of American Indian race on birth and infant death certificates— California and Montana. *Morbidity and Mortality Weekly Reports* 42:220-223.
Ellis, J.L., and D. Campos-Outcalt
1994 Cardiovascular disease risk factors in Native Americans: A literature review. *American Journal of Preventive Medicine* 10:295-307.
Frost, F., and K.K. Shy
1980 Racial differences between linked birth and infant death records in Washington State. *American Journal of Public Health* 70:974-976.
Frost, F., V. Taylor, and E. Fries
1992 Racial misclassification of Native Americans in a Surveillance, Epidemiology and End Results registry. *Journal of the National Cancer Institute* 84:957-962.
Frost, F., K. Tollestrup, A. Ross, E. Sabotta, and E. Kimball
1994 Correctness of racial coding of American Indians and Alaska Natives on the Washington State death certificate. *American Journal of Preventive Medicine* 10:290-294.
Gohdes, D.
1995 Diabetes in North American Indians and Alaska Natives. Pp. 683-701 in *Diabetes in America*, 2nd ed. National Diabetes Data Group. NIH Pub. No. 95-1468. Bethesda, MD: National Institutes of Health, National Institute of Diabetes and Digestive and Kidney Diseases.
Gillum, R.F.
1995 The epidemiology of stroke in Native Americans. *Stroke* 26:514-521.
Gribble, J.N., and S. Preston, eds.
1993 *The Epidemiological Transition: Policy and Planning Implications for Developing Countries*. Committee on Population, National Research Council. Washington, DC: National Academy Press.
Hahn, R.A., J. Mulinare, and S.M. Teutsch
1992 Inconsistencies in coding of race and ethnicity between birth and death in U.S. infants: A new look at infant mortality, 1983-1985. *Journal of the American Medical Association* 267:259-263.
Indian Health Service
1979 *Illness Among Indians and Alaska Natives, 1970 to 1978*. Rockville, MD.
1990a *Trends in Indian Health 1990*. Rockville, MD.
1990b *Regional Differences in Indian Health 1990*. Rockville, MD.
1994a *Trends in Indian Health 1994*. Rockville, MD.
1994b *Regional Differences in Indian Health 1994*. Rockville, MD.
Israel, R.A., H.M. Rosenberg, and L.R. Curtin
1986 Analytical potential for multiple cause-of-death data. *American Journal of Epidemiology* 124:161-179.
Jamison, D.T., W.H. Mosley, A.R. Measham, and J.L. Bobadilla, eds.
1993 *Disease Control Priorities in Developing Countries*. New York: Oxford University Press.

Johnson, A., and A. Taylor
1991 *Prevalence of Chronic Diseases: A Summary of Data from the Survey of American Indians and Alaska Natives.* Pub. No. 91-0031. Rockville, MD: Agency for Health Care Policy and Research.

Kirchner, T., J. Nelson, and H. Burdo
1985 The autopsy as a measure of accuracy of the death certificate. *New England Journal of Medicine* 313:1263-1269.

Klain, M., J.L. Coulehan, V.C. Arena, and R. Janett
1988 More frequent diagnosis of acute myocardial infarction among Navajo Indians. *American Journal of Public Health* 78:1351-1352.

Knowler, W.C., D.J. Pettit, M.F. Saad, and P.H. Bennett
1990 Diabetes mellitus in the Pima Indians: Incidence, risk factors and pathogenesis. *Diabetes Metabolism Reviews* 6:1-27.

Kunitz, S.J.
1983 *Disease Change and the Role of Medicine: The Navajo Experience.* Berkeley, CA: University of California Press.

Kushigemachi, M., L.J. Schneiderman, and E. Barrett-Connor
1984 Racial differences in susceptibility to tuberculosis: Risks of disease after infection. *Journal of Chronic Diseases* 37: 853-62.

Lanier, A.P., L.R. Bulkow, and B. Ireland
1989 Cancer in Alaska Indians, Eskimos and Aleuts, 1969-83: Implications for etiology and control. *Public Health Reports* 104:658-664.

Lefkowitz, D., and C. Underwood
1991 *Personal Health Practices: Findings from the Survey of American Indians and Alaska Natives.* Pub. No. 91-0034. Rockville, MD: Agency for Health Care Policy and Research.

Lieb, L.E., G.A. Conway, M. Hedderman, J. Yao, and P.R. Kerndt
1992 Racial misclassification of American Indians with AIDS in Los Angeles County. *Journal of AIDS* 5:1137-1141.

Mackenbach, J.P.
1994 The epidemiologic transition theory [editorial]. *Journal of Epidemiology and Community Health* 48:329-331.

Mahoney, M.C., and A.M. Michalek
1991 A meta-analysis of cancer incidence in United States and Canadian Native population. *International Journal of Epidemiology* 20:323-327.

Neel, J.V.
1982 The thrifty gene revisited. Pp. 283-293 in J. Kobberling and R. Tattersall, eds., *The Genetics of Diabetes Mellitus.* New York: Academic Press.

Newman, J.M., A.A. Marfin, P.W. Eggers, and S.D. Helgerson
1990 End stage renal disease among Native Americans, 1983-86. *American Journal of Public Health* 80:318-319.

Nutting, P.A., W.L. Freeman, D.R. Risser, S.D. Helgerson, R. Paisano, J. Hisnanick, S.K. Beaver, I. Peters, J.P. Carney, and M.A. Speers
1993 Cancer incidence among American Indians and Alaska Natives, 1980 through 1987. *American Journal of Public Health* 83:1589-1598.

Olshansky, S.J., and A.B. Ault
1986 The fourth stage of the epidemiologic transition: The age of delayed degenerative diseases. *Milbank Quarterly* 64:355-391.

Omran, A.R.
1971 The epidemiological transition: A theory of the epidemiology of population change. *Milbank Memorial Fund Quarterly* 49:509-538.

1977   A century of epidemiologic transition in the United States. *Preventive Medicine* 6:30-51.
1983   The epidemiologic transition theory: A preliminary update. *Journal of Tropical Pediatrics* 29:305-316.

Phillips, D.R.
1994   Does epidemiological transition have utility for health planners? [editorial]. *Social Science and Medicine* 38:vii-x.

Reed, T.E.
1985   Ethnic differences in alcohol use, abuse and sensitivity: A review with genetic interpretation. *Social Biology* 32:195-209.

Rhoades, E.R., J. Hammond, T.K. Welty, A.O. Handler, and R.W. Amler
1987   The Indian burden of illness and future health interventions. *Public Health Reports* 102:361-8.

Ritenbaugh, C., and C. Goodby
1989   Beyond the Thrifty Gene: Metabolic implications of prehistoric migration into the New World. *Medical Anthropology* 11: 227-36.

Skamene, E.
1994   The Bcg gene story. *Immunobiology* 191: 451-60.

Sorlie, P.D., E. Rogot, and N.J. Johnson
1992   Validity of demographic characteristics on the death certificate. *Epidemiology* 3:181-184.

Sugarman, J.R., C.W. Warren, L. Oge, and S.D. Helgerson
1992   Using the Behavioral Risk Factor Surveillance System to monitor Year 2000 Objectives among American Indians. *Public Health Reports* 107:449-456.

Sugarman, J.R., and L. Lawson
1993   The effect of racial misclassification on estimates of end-stage renal disease among American Indians and Alaska Natives in the Pacific Northwest, 1988 through 1990. *American Journal of Kidney Diseases* 21:383-386.

Sugarman, J.R., R. Soderberg, J.E. Gordon, and F.P. Rivara
1993   Racial misclassification of American Indians: Its effect on injury rates in Oregon, 1989 through 1990. *American Journal of Public Health* 83:681-684.

Szathmary, E.J.E.
1990   Diabetes in Amerindian populations: The Dogrib studies. Pp. 75-103 in A. Swedlund and G. Armelagos, eds., *Health and Disease of Populations in Transition*. New York: Bergin and Garvey.

Trowell, H.C., and D.P. Burkitt, eds.
1981   *Western Diseases: Their Emergence and Prevention*. Cambridge, MA: Harvard University Press.

Valway, S., W. Freeman, S. Kaufman, T. Welty, S. Helgerson, and D. Ghodes
1993   Prevalence of diagnosed diabetes among American Indians and Alaska Natives, 1987. *Diabetes Care* 16 (Suppl 1):271-276.

Waller, A.E., S.P. Bakes, and A. Szocka
1989   Childhood injury deaths: national analysis and geographic variations. *American Journal of Public Health* 79:310-315.

Weiss, K.M., R.E. Ferrell, and C.L. Hanis
1984   A New World Syndrome of metabolic diseases with a genetic and evolutionary basis. *Yearbook of Physical Anthropology* 27:153-178.

Welty, T.K., and J.L. Coulehan
1993   Cardiovascular disease among American Indians and Alaska Natives. *Diabetes Care* 16 (Suppl 1):277-83.

West, K.M.
   1974   Diabetes in American Indians and other native populations of the New World. *Diabetes* 23:841-855.
Young, T.K.
   1988   *Health Care and Cultural Change: The Indian Experience in the Central Subarctic.* Toronto: University of Toronto Press.
   1994   *The Health of Native Americans: Toward a Biocultural Epidemiology.* New York: Oxford University Press.
Young, T.K., C.D. Schraer, E.V. Shubnikoff, E.J. Szathmary, and Y.P. Nikitin
   1992   Prevalence of diagnosed diabetes in circumpolar indigenous populations. *International Journal of Epidemiology* 21:730-736.

II

Identification:
Indications and Consequences

4

The Growing American Indian Population, 1960–1990: Beyond Demography

Jeffrey S. Passel

INTRODUCTION

For decades through 1960, the American Indian[1] population, as enumerated in U.S. censuses, grew little if at all. From a population of 248,000 in 1890, American Indians[2] increased to 524,000 in 1960. While this does represent a doubling of the population, the average annual growth rate over the entire 70-year period was only 1.1 percent—a very low figure resulting from high fertility and very high mortality. Since 1960, the Native American[3] population has exhibited explosive growth, increasing from 552,000 to 1,959,000, or 255 percent. The average annual growth rate of 4.3 percent, extending over a 30-year period, is demographically impossible without immigration. Previous research (Passel, 1976; Passel and Berman, 1986) has shown that this extraordinary growth was achieved through changing patterns of racial self-identification on the part of people with only partial or distant American Indian ancestry, coupled with relatively high fertility and improving mortality.

---

[1]In general, the terms "American Indian" and "Native American" are used interchangeably here to refer to the combined census categories of American Indian, Eskimo, and Aleut. Any use of other definitions is noted in the text.

[2]The census figures cited in this sentence for 1890 and 1960 refer only to American Indians; Alaska Natives are not included.

[3]Including American Indians, Eskimo, and Aleuts.

Data Collection Methods

Data on the American Indian population collected in the 1970, 1980, and 1990 censuses are based on self-identification. That is, persons answering the census choose their response to the race question. A person choosing the American Indian racial response did not have to provide any substantiation or documentation of this identification. There was no requirement that an "American Indian" be enrolled as a member of a recognized tribe or that any tribal group recognize the respondent as a member, and there was no "blood quantum" requirement. This method of identification differs from that of previous censuses, in which a person's racial identification tended to be assigned by an enumerator, usually based on observation, local knowledge, or custom. Thus before 1970, a person would be classified as American Indian if he or she "looked" Indian, was recognized by the local community as American Indian, or lived in an American Indian area.

Collection of racial data based on self-identification aids overall census taking by permitting respondents to fill out their own census forms, thus reducing the need for expensive in-person interviews. At the same time, self-identification adds a temporal component to the data. The responses elicited from the same individual (or group of individuals) may change over time in response to social, political, or economic conditions or variations in question wording. New identities may emerge, or old ones may disappear. Even though the names of groups or categories often remain the same from census to census, each census actually represents a "snapshot" in time, capturing the content of the moment, especially when data are based on self-identification. Analysts and other data users must be aware of underlying response patterns to interpret changes correctly.

For the American Indian population, the changes in method of identification between the pre-1960 and post-1960 periods[4] have been associated with substantial changes in the nature of the data. In addition, the American Indian population has undergone rapid demographic change, including sizeable population growth coupled with substantial geographic redistribution. Many of these decadal changes have already been documented—Passel (1976) for the 1960–1970 decade; Passel and Berman

---

[4]The 1960 census represented a transition from the enumerator-conducted censuses through 1950 and the almost entirely mail censuses since 1970. The 1960 census was actually a hybrid of data collection methodologies, with most census forms being mailed to respondents, but all forms being collected in person by enumerators. The 1960 data themselves also appear to be transitional between enumerator identification and self-identification.

(1986) and Snipp (1989) for 1970–1980; and Passel (1992), Eschbach (1993), and Harris (1994) for 1980–1990.

Overview of the Chapter

This chapter expands on previous work by using various demographic measures to illustrate the magnitude of changing self-identification among the American Indian population and draws some implications for data analysis. It provides some basic demographic background on the size, growth, and geographic structure of the American Indian population, while explaining some of the factors contributing to the extraordinary increase in this population. Specifically, the next section focuses on differentiating the growth nationally according to demographic versus nondemographic factors. For example, the 1990 census count of 1,959,000 American Indians exceeds by 10 percent or 189,000 the figure expected on the basis of the 1980 census and demographic components of change (i.e., births and deaths) during the 1980s. This relatively large "excess" count comes on top of a 26 percent "excess" in the 1980 census count (Passel and Berman, 1986). Put another way, of the 1.4 million growth in the American Indian population between 1960 and 1990, about 762,000 is attributable to natural increase (i.e., births minus deaths) and 645,000 to nondemographic factors.

The section that follows explores some of the sources of both the demographic and nondemographic dimensions of the increase in the 1980s and earlier. Specifically, we use data on self-reported ancestry to demonstrate how such large increases could have occurred and what potential there might be for further increases in the future. We then use various demographic measures to pinpoint changes in the age structure of the American Indian population. Census survival ratios for this population over the last three decades show clearly that large increases are occurring for all age groups above age 10, with very notable concentrations at ages 10-19 and above age 30. In spite of the basic demographic constraint that age cohorts should decrease in size over time as people die, the American Indian cohorts aged 10 to 59 in 1990 were all larger in 1990 than in 1980.

The next section uses additional demographic methods to demonstrate how the dramatic growth in the American Indian population is distributed unevenly across states. The analysis shows clearly that, with the exception of Oklahoma, most of the population increase attributable to changing self-identification has occurred in states that have *not* historically been major centers of the American Indian population. With minor exceptions, this pattern has persisted over the last three decades.

The paper closes with a discussion of the implications of response patterns for data analysis pertaining to American Indians.

NATIONAL DEMOGRAPHIC FACTORS

Population Size and Growth Rate

For three decades, from 1890 through 1920, the American Indian population hovered around 250,000, changing little from census to census (see Table 4-1). In 1930, the population jumped to roughly 330,000, where it remained for another two decades. Since 1950, the American Indian population has shown a steady upward trend, with huge numerical increases since 1970, culminating in a 1990 census count of 1,959,000.

Average annual growth rates track these trends. From the 1890–1900 decade through 1940–1950, only the decade of the 1920s (3.1 percent) showed average annual growth exceeding 1.1 percent. In fact, for the 1890s and 1910s, the growth rates were negative as the enumerated American Indian population decreased. In 1950, growth rates began to jump

TABLE 4-1 American Indian Population: 1890-1990 Censuses

Census Year	Population	Decadal Change	
		Amount	Average Annual Rate
American Indian, Eskimo, Aleut (50 states and D.C.)			
1990	1,959,200	538,800	3.27
1980	1,420,400	593,100	5.55
1970	827,300	275,600	4.13
1960	551,700	208,300	4.01[a]
American Indian Only (48 states and D.C.)			
1960	508,700	165,300	4.01
1950	343,400	9,400	0.28
1940	334,000	1,600	0.05
1930	332,400	88,000	3.12
1920	244,400	−21,200	−0.83
1910	265,700	28,500	1.14
1900	237,200	−11,100	−0.45
1890	248,300	n.a.	n.a.

NOTE: Populations rounded to hundreds.

[a]Rate set equal to 48 state rate.
n.a., not applicable.

substantially—to 4 percent for the 1950s and 1960s and reaching a measured annual rate of 5.6 percent in the 1970s, before dropping to 3.3 percent in the 1980s. Such rates are extremely high, and the 5.6 percent rate for the 1970s is demographically impossible without international migration—a situation that characterizes the American Indian population, as shown below.

Error of Closure

We can gain some insight into the nature of these recent increases in the American Indian population with some simple analytic tools of demography. For a population not experiencing immigration, demographic increases come only from births and decreases only from deaths. We can express this relationship with the demographic "balancing equation," which relates the size of the population at one point in time to its size in the past:

$$P_1 = P_0 + B - D + e$$

where P_1 = the population at time 1 (e.g., 1990)

P_0 = the population at time 0 (e.g., 1960)
B = births during the time interval (e.g., 1960–1990)
D = deaths during the time interval
e = error of closure.

The final term in the equation, e or error of closure, is the amount needed to make the equation balance. Error of closure is normally small and usually represents changes in census coverage, unmeasured demographic change (such as immigration), or shifts in the makeup of the population. As we will see, errors of closure since 1960 have been large for the American Indian population. They appear to have resulted from increases in the population caused by changes in self-identification, that is, individuals who previously did not choose to call themselves American Indian, but did so in more recent censuses.

Table 4-2 shows the growth of the American Indian population and errors of closure for the last four decades (1950–1960 through 1980–1990). For the 1950–1960 decade, the error of closure amounts to only 1,900, or 0.4 percent of the 1960 American Indian population. This error is negligible and can easily be attributed to inaccuracies in measuring any of the four components in the balancing equation. For the 1960–1970 decade, however, the error of closure is very large, amounting to 91,000, or 11 percent of the 1970 population. In earlier work, Passel (1976) proved that the

TABLE 4-2 Components of Change and Error of Closure for American Indians: 1950–1990 Censuses

Component or Population	30-Year Period 1960-1990	Intercensal Period			
		1980-1990	1970-1980	1960-1970	1950-1960 [a]
Final census	1,959,200	1,959,200	1,420,400	827,300	508,700
Error of closure					
Amount	645,400	188,700	365,500	91,200	1,900
Percent[b]	32.9	9.6	25.7	11.0	0.4
Estimated population at final census	1,313,900	1,770,600	1,054,900	736,100	506,900
Component for period					
Natural increase	762,200	350,200	227,600	184,400	163,500
Births	948,700	422,200	290,700	235,800	207,000
Deaths	186,500	72,100	63,100	51,300	43,500
Initial census	551,700	1,420,400	827,300	551,700	343,400
Average annual rate of natural increase[c]	27.2	21.9	24.2	28.6	38.5
Births	33.9	26.5	30.9	36.6	48.7
Deaths	6.7	4.5	6.7	8.0	10.2

[a]American Indian only.
[b]Base of percent is final census.
[c]Per 1,000 mid-period population, as estimated.

error of closure could not be attributed to errors in measuring the population (i.e., changes in census coverage), immigration, births, or deaths, but
could be explained only by the creation of "new Indians," that is, individuals who had not previously identified as American Indian but chose
to do so in the 1970 census.

For the 1980 census, the error of closure was unprecedented, amounting to 366,000, or 26 percent of the 1980 census count. This increase, too,
can be attributed only to changing self-identification (Passel and Berman,
1986). The 1970–1980 increase is particularly noteworthy in that it occurred after the large 1960–1970 increase. Thus, not only did new individuals choose to identify as American Indian, but the previous shifts
were maintained.

With the 1990 census, not only were these historical shifts further
consolidated, but the trend toward shifting identity continued. The
1990 census count of 1,959,000 resulted in an error of closure for the decade of the 1980s of 189,000, or almost 10 percent. Given that the 1980s
were marked by unprecedented levels of immigration (Fix and Passel,
1994), some of the error of coverage in 1990 has been attributed to the
immigration of American Indians from Canada, Latin America, or the
Caribbean (e.g., Harris, 1994). However, the foreign-born American Indian population increased only slightly between the 1980 and 1990 censuses—from 41,700 to 48,700,—while the percentage foreign-born decreased—from 2.7 to 2.4 percent. Although the error of closure is not as
large, numerically or in percentage terms, as those of the previous decades, the continued, considerable shift in identity in 1990 again shows
the enduring nature of the change.

Combining the data for the 1960–1990 period shows the magnitude of
the shifts that have occurred. Between 1960 and 1990, the American Indian population increased by 1,407,000, from 552,000 to 1,959,000. During
these three decades, the measured natural increase of the American Indian population (i.e., the excess of births over deaths) amounted to 762,000
(see Table 4-2). This leaves almost 645,000 persons, or 33 percent of the
1990 census count of American Indians, that cannot be accounted for by
demographic factors, but must be explained by the changing nature of
American Indian self-identification during the 30 years.

SOURCES OF NONDEMOGRAPHIC INCREASE

The 1980 and 1990 censuses provide some data that point to the source
of the shifts in American Indian self-identification. In addition, some
simple demographic measures can be used to demonstrate which age
groups have been driving these changes.

Ancestry and Race

The data discussed above are from decennial census questions defining the "race" of the population; more specifically, the data for 1980 and 1990 represent individuals choosing American Indian in response to the census question on racial identification. This question required respondents to pick among specified categories and allowed only one response in both the 1980 and 1990 censuses. However, both censuses also asked a broader question on "ancestry." The 1990 census question—worded "What is this person's ancestry or ethnic origin?"—required respondents to write in their own response and permitted more than one ethnic identification. These "ancestry" data are thought to elicit a broader ethnic identification, including some with lesser degrees of attachment than the racial classification (Waters, 1990).

The ancestry data show a very large population that claims some degree of Indian ancestry—a much larger population than that choosing to identify with the American Indian in racial terms. In 1980, 6.8 million persons claimed American Indian ancestry, of which only 21 percent, or 1.4 million persons, chose to identify with the American Indian *racial* group (Table 4-3). Likewise, in 1990, only 22 percent of the 8.8 million people claiming American Indian ancestry identified as American Indian by race. Thus, there is very large pool of "potential" American Indians, i.e., persons with some American Indian ancestry who may or may not choose to identify as American Indian by race. In this context, the errors of closure in 1980 and 1990 represent very small fractions of the "potential" American Indian population—5 percent in 1980 and only 2 percent in 1990. Thus, the possibility exists for further large increases in the American Indian population in the future, if social, political, economic,

TABLE 4-3 American Indian Population by Race and Ancestry: 1990 and 1980 Censuses

American Indian Definition	1990 Census		1980 Census	
	Amount	Percent	Amount	Percent
By ancestry, total	8,798,000	100	6,766,000	100
By race				
Census count	1,959,000	22	1,420,000	21
Estimate from previous census	1,771,000	20	1,055,000	16
Error of closure	189,000	2	366,000	5
By ancestry, but not by race	6,839,000	78	5,346,000	79

and methodological factors continue to encourage the shifts in identification.

Age Patterns of Increase

Another demographic measure, the census survival ratio (CSR), offers a tool for ascertaining whether the large increases in the American Indian population over the last four decades are concentrated in specific age groups or cohorts. The CSR is a simple measure: it is the ratio of the population in a given age cohort in one census to the same group of people in the previous census, i.e., the age group 10 years younger in the census 10 years earlier:

$$CSR_{x,t} = P_{x,t}/P_{x-10,t-10}$$

where $CSR_{x,t}$ =   census survival ratio for age x at time t (e.g., ages 10–14 in 1990)

$P_{x,t}$ =   population aged x at time t (e.g., aged 10–14 in 1990)

$P_{x-10,t-10}$ =   population age x – 10 at time t – 10 (e.g., aged 0–4 in 1980).

Since the American Indian population experiences negligible immigration, the CSRs should all be less than 1.0 because the population in an age cohort can only *decrease* through mortality. If CSRs are greater than 1.0, they indicate movement into a cohort, in the case of American Indians through shifts in self-identification. The greater the CSR, the larger the shift into the population.

For the 1980 and 1990 censuses, the American Indian CSRs show a very strong age pattern of increases. For ages 10–19, the CSRs exceed 1.2, indicating increases of more than 20 percent in these cohorts as they aged from 0–9 in 1980 to 10–19 in 1990. In addition, all cohorts aged 30–59 have large CSRs, indicating sizeable increases at these ages. Thus, the figures for ages under 10 and 20–29 are consistent with data from the previous 10-year period, but other cohorts show increases that can be attributable only to "new" individuals identifying as American Indian. A virtually identical pattern shows up for the 1950–1960 and 1960–1970 decades (Figure 4-1). For 1970–1980, all of the CSRs are much higher than in other decades because the overall error of closure was much greater. For ages 10–49 in 1980, the CSRs exceed 1.40, indicating at least 40 percent increases in size beyond demographic changes.

Accompanying the large CSRs are, of course, numerical increases in cohort size that have occurred for all ages 10–59 in every census since 1960, with the exception of ages 20–34 in 1950. Particularly large in-

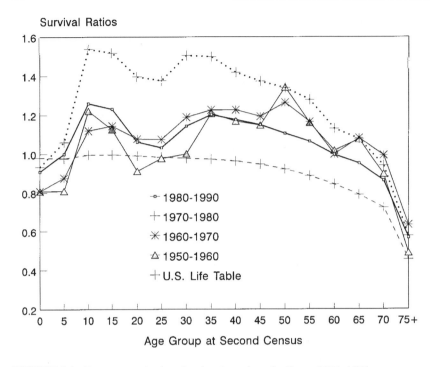

FIGURE 4-1 Census survival ratios for American Indians, 1950–1990.

creases occurred in the last two censuses for cohorts aged 10–49. Some actual numbers illustrate the striking character of these changes. For American Indians born in the 1940s, about 96,000 were enumerated in their first census, in 1950. By the time this group had reached their 40s in the 1990 census, they had more than doubled to 223,000. Those born in the 1950s showed an even greater increase in size, from 175,000 in 1960 (at ages 0–9) to 321,000 in 1990 (at ages 30–39). All birth cohorts of American Indians reaching adulthood in the post-World War II era have participated in the accretions from changing self-identification.

Birth Statistics

The exceptions to census survival ratios greater than 1.0 are the cohorts born in the decade before the census, i.e., at ages 0–9. Low CSRs are to be expected at these ages because young children are omitted from censuses at high rates, particularly in populations such as American Indians with large households, high poverty rates, and many difficult-to-enumerate situations (Robinson et al., 1992). Even for the 1970–1980 de-

cade, with its huge increases in self-identification, the CSRs for ages under 10 approximate the combined effects of undercoverage and mortality,
implying that the shifts in identification may not occur for young children. However, for American Indians, another definitional complication
arises in these early age groups.

In computing CSRs for ages under 10, births in the decade preceding
the census are compared with the census counts for ages 0–9. The birth
statistics are not collected in the census, but are compiled from registration data by the National Center for Health Statistics (NCHS). The system
used by NCHS to assign births to racial groups differs considerably from
that used in collecting census data. For every birth, NCHS collects information on the race of the mother and the race of the father, based on self-
identification.[5] Until 1989, births were assigned to race groups by a rule
that tended to favor assignment to racial minorities. Specifically, if only
one parent was white, the child was assigned the race of the nonwhite
parent; otherwise, the child was assigned the race of the father (if known).
Beginning in 1989, NCHS dropped its "old rule" for *official* classification
of births by race in favor of tabulations based only on the race of the
mother or the race of the father.

As Table 4-4 shows, the "old" NCHS classification scheme produced
numbers of American Indian births that are 20 percent or so higher than
those produced by either the "father" or "mother" classification. However, none of the three classification methods is consistent with the way
children were identified in the censuses of 1980 and 1990. In their first
census, the total number of young American Indian children (under age
10) was roughly comparable to the most inclusive classification method,
i.e., the "old" NCHS rule. However, by the time the 1970s birth cohorts
had reached their teens in 1990, even this rough comparability had disap-
peared as the 1990 census counts greatly exceeded the numbers of births.
Thus, registration data on births of American Indians from NCHS cannot
be considered comparable with decennial census figures and must clearly
be used with caution. Further analyses presented below extend these
cautions.

GEOGRAPHIC DISTRIBUTION

The American Indian population is not uniformly distributed across
the country; growth also has occurred differentially across states. American Indians are concentrated in the western region, which had 934,000
American Indians in 1990 (Table 4-5), or 48 percent of the U.S. total. The

---

[5]In some cases, the information is based on observation by hospital personnel.

TABLE 4-4 American Indian Births Based on Alternative Classification
Procedures: 1968–1989

Year or Period	Race Assignment Rule			Percent Difference from Old NCHS Rule	
	Old NCHS Rule	Mother Rule	Father Rule	Mother Rule	Father Rule
Annual data					
1989	49,267	39,478	38,667	−19.9	−21.5
1988	45,804	37,020	36,032	−19.2	−21.3
1987	43,595	35,222	34,379	−19.2	−21.1
1986	42,561	34,087	33,233	−19.9	−21.9
1985	42,521	33,936	33,338	−20.2	−21.6
1984	41,160	33,081	32,145	−19.6	−21.9
1983	41,269	32,774	32,518	−20.6	−21.2
1982	40,901	32,288	32,147	−21.1	−21.4
1981	37,000	29,517	29,594	−20.2	−20.0
1980	36,618	29,212	29,517	−20.2	−19.4
1979	34,021	27,305	27,567	−19.7	−19.0
1978	32,955	26,497	26,919	−19.6	−18.3
1977	30,460	24,764	25,172	−18.7	−17.4
1976	28,966	23,768	24,100	−17.9	−16.8
1975	27,531	22,684	23,048	−17.6	−16.3
1974	26,600	22,169	22,330	−16.7	−16.1
1973	26,420	22,255	22,084	−15.8	−16.4
1972	27,314	23,301	22,977	−14.7	−15.9
1971	27,110	23,222	22,754	−14.3	−16.1
1970	25,838	22,242	21,940	−13.9	−15.1
1969	23,938	20,830	20,670	−13.0	−13.7
1968	24,250	21,484	20,380	−11.4	−16.0
Five-Year Periods					
1985–1989	223,748	179,743	175,649	−19.7	−21.5
1980–1984	196,948	156,872	155,921	−20.3	−20.8
1975–1979	153,933	125,018	126,806	−18.8	−17.6
1970–1974	133,282	113,189	112,085	−15.1	−15.9
1970–1989	707,911	574,822	570,461	−18.8	−19.4

NOTES: Numbers rounded to hundreds; percents based on unrounded numbers. Alternative race assignment rules:

Old NCHS Rule—Race of birth is assigned to nonwhite parent in white/nonwhite couple; assigned Hawaiian if either parent is Hawaiian; otherwise, assigned race of father, if known.
Mother Rule—Race of birth is assigned to mother's race.
Father Rule—Race of birth is assigned to father's race, if known.

SOURCE: Unpublished tabulations from the National Center for Health Statistics.

south had the next largest number with 563,000, or 29 percent. Just a handful of states have large American Indian populations. Only four had more than 100,000 in 1990: Oklahoma (252,000), California (242,000), Arizona (204,000), and New Mexico (134,355). There were another nine states with 45,000–100,000 American Indians: Alaska (86,000), Washington 81,000), North Carolina (80,000), Texas (66,000), New York (63,000), Michigan (56,000), South Dakota (51,000), Minnesota (50,000), and Montana (48,000). These top 13 states had 72 percent of the 1990 total U.S. population of American Indians.

The 1,959,000 American Indians represent only 0.8 percent of the 1990 total U.S. population. In every state, the American Indian population constituted only a small minority of the population, with Alaska having the largest percentage at 15.6 percent. In only 7 other states did American Indians represent as much as 2 percent of the total population: New Mexico (8.9 percent), Oklahoma (8.0), South Dakota (7.3), Montana (6.0), Arizona (5.6), North Dakota (4.1), and Wyoming (2.1).

Errors of Closure for States

The geographic concentration of American Indians has actually decreased substantially over the last 40 years. In the 1950 census, 19 states plus Alaska had 3,000 or more American Indians and accounted for 93 percent of the total U.S. American Indian population. These states have represented a steadily decreasing percentage of the American Indian population since then: 90 percent in 1960, 84 in 1970, 81 in 1980, and only 78 percent in 1990. This deconcentration has occurred in part because of migration from the original 19 states to the other 31 (Eschbach, 1993). However, most of the deconcentration is actually attributable to changes in self-identification because increased reporting as American Indian, as measured by error of closure, has occurred disproportionately in the states that did not have large American Indian populations in 1950.

We first divide the states into two groups: 19 states that historically have had large American Indian populations, i.e., more than 3,000 American Indians in 1950, and are designated "Historical Indian" states[6] or simply "Indian states;" and the remaining 31 states plus the District of Columbia, which historically have not had large American Indian popu-

---

[6]The 19 states are New York, Michigan, Wisconsin, Minnesota, North Dakota, South Dakota, Nebraska, North Carolina, Oklahoma, Montana, Idaho, Wyoming, New Mexico, Arizona, Utah, Nevada, Washington, Oregon, and Alaska. California had more than 3,000 American Indians in 1950, but is excluded from the "Indian" states because it had very few organized tribes and a very different pattern of population change from that of the other 19 states over the 1950–1980 period.

TABLE 4-5 American Indian Population and Components of Change, for Regions, Divisions, and States: 1980–1990

Region, Division and State	Census Counts 1990	Census Counts 1980	Births 1980–1990	Deaths 1980–1990
U.S., Total	1,959,200	1,420,400	422,200	72,100
Indian States*	1,287,500	951,100	317,600	60,000
Non-Indian States	671,800	469,300	104,600	12,100
Northeast	125,100	79,000	15,600	2,900
Midwest	337,900	248,400	75,400	13,800
South	562,700	372,200	90,100	16,300
West	933,500	720,700	241,200	39,000
New England	32,800	21,600	5,000	800
Maine	6,000	4,100	1,200	200
New Hampshire	2,100	1,400	200	0
Vermont	1,700	1,000	100	0
Massachusetts	12,200	7,700	1,900	200
Rhode Island	4,100	2,900	800	200
Connecticut	6,700	4,500	700	100
Middle Atlantic	92,400	57,400	10,600	2,100
New York*	62,700	39,600	7,000	1,600
New Jersey	15,000	8,400	2,100	300
Pennsylvania	14,700	9,500	1,500	200
East North Central	149,900	105,900	24,100	4,300
Ohio	20,400	12,200	3,100	400
Indiana	12,700	7,800	1,100	100
Illinois	21,800	16,300	3,300	500
Michigan*	55,600	40,100	7,500	1,400
Wisconsin*	39,400	29,500	9,200	2,000
West North Central	188,000	142,500	51,300	9,500
Minnesota*	49,900	35,000	14,100	2,100
Iowa	7,300	5,500	1,600	200
Missouri	19,800	12,300	1,900	200
North Dakota*	25,900	20,200	8,500	1,600
South Dakota*	50,600	45,000	17,800	4,100
Nebraska*	12,400	9,200	3,600	800
Kansas	22,000	15,400	3,800	500

Average Annual Rate[a]		Estimated 1990 Population	Error of Closure (Implied Migration)	
Birth	Death		Amount	Percent[b]
25.0	4.3	1,770,600	188,700	9.6
28.4	5.4	1,208,700	78,700	6.1
18.3	2.1	561,800	110,000	16.4
15.2	2.9	91,700	33,500	26.8
25.7	4.7	310,000	27,900	8.3
19.3	3.5	446,000	116,700	20.7
29.2	4.7	922,900	10,600	1.1
18.2	3.0	25,700	7,100	21.5
23.8	4.3	5,100	900	15.4
11.8	1.3	1,500	600	28.1
7.0	0.5	1,100	600	36.9
19.4	2.3	9,500	2,800	22.7
24.2	6.1	3,500	500	13.3
12.1	2.4	5,100	1,600	23.7
14.2	2.8	65,900	26,400	28.6
13.7	3.1	45,000	17,600	28.1
17.8	2.9	10,100	4,800	32.2
12.4	1.7	10,800	4,000	27.0
18.8	3.4	125,700	24,300	16.2
18.9	2.5	14,900	5,500	26.8
10.8	0.6	8,900	3,800	30.2
17.1	2.7	19,000	2,800	12.9
15.7	2.9	46,200	9,500	17.0
26.6	5.7	36,700	2,700	6.9
31.1	5.7	184,400	3,600	1.9
33.1	5.0	47,000	2,900	5.9
25.6	3.9	6,800	500	6.8
11.9	1.3	14,000	5,800	29.2
36.8	6.7	27,100	−1,200	−4.5
37.2	8.5	58,700	−8,100	−16.0
33.6	7.1	12,100	300	2.8
20.4	2.7	18,700	3,300	15.0

TABLE 4-5 Continued

Region, Division and State	Census Counts 1990	Census Counts 1980	Births 1980–1990	Deaths 1980–1990
South Atlantic	172,300	118,700	23,700	4,900
Delaware	2,000	1,300	200	100
Maryland	13,000	8,000	1,500	100
District of Columbia	1,500	1,000	100	0
Virginia	15,300	9,500	1,300	200
West Virginia	2,500	1,600	100	0
North Carolina*	80,200	64,700	16,000	3,900
South Carolina	8,200	5,800	800	100
Georgia	13,300	7,600	900	100
Florida	36,300	19,300	2,800	400
East South Central	40,800	22,500	3,500	700
Kentucky	5,800	3,600	400	0
Tennessee	10,000	5,100	600	100
Alabama	16,500	7,600	600	100
Mississippi	8,500	6,200	1,800	500
West South Central	349,600	231,000	62,900	10,800
Arkansas	12,800	9,400	1,500	100
Louisiana	18,500	12,100	2,900	300
Oklahoma*	252,400	169,500	52,600	9,900
Texas	65,900	40,100	5,800	500
Mountain	480,500	364,400	135,200	23,600
Montana*	47,700	37,300	15,000	3,100
Idaho*	13,800	10,500	3,200	700
Wyoming*	9,500	7,100	3,100	600
Colorado	27,800	18,100	5,700	600
New Mexico*	134,400	106,100	37,600	6,500
Arizona*	203,500	152,700	58,600	10,300
Utah*	24,300	19,300	6,900	800
Nevada*	19,600	13,300	5,000	1,000
Pacific	452,900	356,400	105,900	15,400
Washington*	81,500	60,800	18,500	3,500
Oregon*	38,500	27,300	7,100	1,200
California	242,200	201,400	52,400	5,400
Alaska*	85,700	64,100	26,300	5,100
Hawaii	5,100	2,800	1,600	100

NOTE: All figures include Eskimos and Aleuts. Births projected for 1989–1990; deaths for 1988-1990.

*Indian states include all states with 3,000+ Indians in the 1950 census, except California.

aRates per 1,000 mid-period population.

bBase of percent is estimated 1990 population.

Average Annual Rate[a]		Estimated 1990 Population	Error of Closure (Implied Migration)	
Birth	Death		Amount	Percent[b]
16.3	3.3	137,600	34,700	20.1
11.3	4.5	1,400	600	28.6
14.7	1.2	9,400	3,500	27.2
5.2	2.6	1,100	400	27.5
10.5	1.5	10,600	4,700	30.8
4.9	0.6	1,700	800	31.0
22.1	5.3	76,800	3,400	4.2
12.1	1.3	6,500	1,700	21.0
9.0	0.8	8,500	4,900	36.5
10.0	1.5	21,600	14,700	40.5
11.0	2.1	25,300	15,500	38.0
9.1	1.0	4,000	1,800	30.9
8.5	0.8	5,700	4,400	43.4
4.8	0.7	8,100	8,400	51.1
25.1	6.5	7,600	1,000	11.4
21.7	3.7	283,100	66,500	19.0
13.9	1.3	10,800	1,900	15.2
19.1	1.9	14,700	3,900	20.8
24.9	4.7	212,200	40,200	15.9
10.9	0.9	45,400	20,500	31.1
32.0	5.6	476,000	4,500	0.9
35.3	7.2	49,200	−1,500	−3.1
26.5	5.9	13,000	800	5.5
37.8	6.7	9,700	−200	−2.0
25.0	2.6	23,200	4,600	16.5
31.2	5.4	137,200	−2,800	−2.1
32.9	5.8	201,100	2,500	1.2
31.8	3.9	25,300	−1,100	−4.3
30.6	6.0	17,400	2,300	11.6
26.2	3.8	446,900	6,100	1.3
26.0	4.9	75,800	5,700	7.0
21.6	3.7	33,200	5,300	13.8
23.6	2.5	248,400	−6,200	−2.6
35.1	6.8	85,300	400	0.4
40.6	3.3	4,200	900	16.9

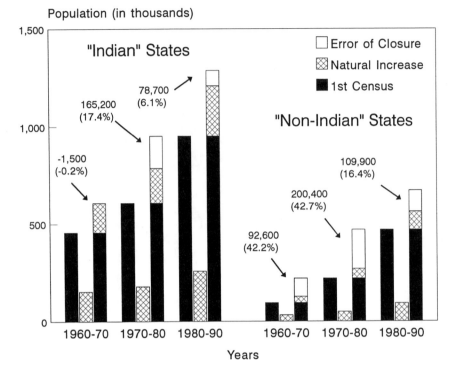

FIGURE 4-2 Error of closure by decade and state groups for American Indians, 1960–1990.

lations and are designated "non-Indian states." For each group of states, we can define error of closure as above. The measure is so large for many states that it must be interpreted as indicating changes in self-identification.

For the 1960–1970 decade, the "Indian" states had essentially no error of closure—actually a negative error of closure amounting to 1,500 persons, or 0.2 percent of the population (Figure 4-2). This magnitude indicates little change in reporting or possibly a small amount of out-migration from the "Indian" states. The remaining 32 "non-Indian" states, however, showed a growth exceeding natural increase (i.e., error of closure) of 93,000, or 42 percent of the 1970 population of these states. Thus, the large increase from changing self-identification in 1970 was completely confined to the states that historically had not had significant American Indian populations.

Similar patterns occurred in the next two decades, although not to the extreme shown in the 1960–1970 decade. For 1970–1980, the "Indian"

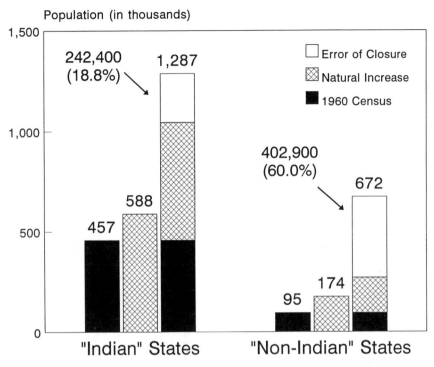

FIGURE 4-3 Error of closure by state groups for American Indians, 1960–1990.

states had an error of closure of 165,000 or 17 percent, whereas in the "non-Indian" states it amounted to 200,000, or fully 43 percent of the 1980 population in these states. The errors were more muted for 1980–1990: 79,000 or 6 percent in the "Indian" states and 110,000 or 16 percent in the "non-Indian" states. (See Table 4-5 for full detail on the 1980–1990 errors of closure.) Thus, the percentage errors for each decade are all smaller in the "Indian" states than for every decade in the "non-Indian" states. For the entire 30-year period, the error of closure in the "Indian" states is 242,000 or 19 percent of the 1990 population, whereas it is 403,000 or 60 percent in the "non-Indian" states (Figure 4-3). These patterns imply that shifts in identification are more likely to occur in areas without large concentrations of American Indians or significant reservation populations. In the "Indian" areas, which have reservations and large concentrations, identification as American Indian is more established by both self and community and so is less likely to change over time.

Births and Deaths

Crude birth and death rates demonstrate further the incompatibility of census and vital statistics data on American Indians. Direct observation of substantial inconsistencies in race reporting on matched birth and infant death certificates has been reported (Hahn et al., 1992). The crude rates also show inconsistencies and changes in racial identification of American Indians over time. Crude birth (and death) rates are measured as births (deaths) divided by population. The birth (death) data are collected by NCHS using its own data collection method and classification for racial identification. To the extent that changes in self-identification are captured in the census and not in vital statistics, birth and death rates will be excessively low in areas where there is a great deal of overreporting as American Indian in the census. In other words, the census figures will be inflated relative to the vital statistics in those areas.

Figure 4-4 shows the differences in crude birth and death rates between "Indian" and "non-Indian" states for 1970, 1980, and 1990. Birth rates in "Indian" states are substantially higher than in the remaining "non-Indian" states, which have American Indian birth rates approximating (but slightly higher than) the rates for the total population. This pattern does not, by itself, prove that there are data inconsistencies. Birth rates in the "non-Indian" states may simply be lower than the rates in the "Indian" states. However, taken together with the patterns of crude death rates, the birth rates do support the data inconsistency hypothesis.

The patterns of crude death rates are much more extreme and striking than those of the birth rates. In fact, the death rates are not consistent with simple demographic differences across the states. The death rates in "Indian" states are higher—a great deal higher—than those for American Indians in the "non-Indian" states. In fact, the death rates in "non-Indian" states are so low that they suggest serious underidentification in the vital statistics (numerator) or overreporting as American Indian in the census data (denominator). The patterns across time and across the groups of states provide another strong indication of increasing identification as American Indian in the "non-Indian" states, as well as substantial differences in identification between the census and vital statistics systems.

The strong influence of the denominator (i.e., the census count) in the vital rates can be demonstrated in another way. In the United States, high crude birth rates in states are normally associated with low crude death rates and vice versa, because of age-structure effects. In other words, the high crude birth rates usually lead to a relatively young population with large concentrations of children and adults of child-bearing age, i.e., low-death-rate age groups. Such age structures tend to have low

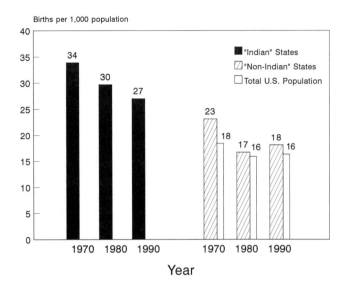

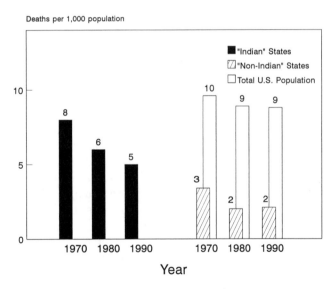

FIGURE 4-4 Crude birth and death rates by state groups for American Indians, 1970–1990.

crude death rates. Conversely, states with high crude death rates tend to have high percentages of elderly persons and thus low crude birth rates. Utah (crude birth rate of 24.0 per thousand total population and crude death rate of 5.6 in the 1980s) and Florida (crude birth rate of 14.2 and crude death rate of 10.6) provide extreme examples of this negative relationship. Overall, the negative relationship between crude birth rates and crude death rates for the total population at the state level is very strong, with a correlation coefficient of –0.73 for the 1980s.

The American Indian population by state, however, shows just the opposite—a strong direct relationship between American Indian birth and death rates in the 1980s (shown in Table 4-5). The correlation coefficient between the two is extraordinarily high at +0.85. The "Indian" states have high American Indian birth and death rates, whereas the other states are low on both. (See Figures 4-5 and 4-6 for the strongly contrasting patterns in the relationship between crude birth rates and crude death rates for the total population and American Indians.) This pattern, so contrary to demographic expectations, must be driven by the size of the denominator (i.e., the census count), rather than the age structure and demographic behavior of the population. The very large denominators in "non-Indian" states artificially lower the computed crude birth rates and crude death rates because of the fundamental inconsistency between census data and vital statistics.

CONCLUSION

In general, the 1990 census data on American Indians appear to capture the basic demographic features of this population, such as the age structure and size, but shifts in self-identification suggest some caution in analyses of this population. The 1990 census data are somewhat more consistent with vital statistics and the previous census than in other decades, but some inconsistencies still remain. Although there were some changes in self-identification as American Indian over the 1980–1990 decade, the shifts were smaller, both absolutely and proportionately, than in the previous two decades. Even with these smaller shifts, however, individuals identifying as American Indian were much more likely to be associated with organized American Indian groups (e.g., tribes, recognized bands, Alaska Native villages) in some areas (e.g., "Indian" states) than in others. Similarly, community recognition of individuals as American Indian was more likely to agree with the individual's response to the census in these same areas.

In sum, the different patterns of population growth and change in "Indian" and "non-Indian" states imply a need for some caution in interpreting census data, but do not rule out the utility of the data for assessing the social, demographic, and economic situation of the American Indian population. Recognized inconsistencies between 1990 census data on American Indians, on the one hand, and vital statistics or the previous census, on the other, point to the desirability of restricting some analyses to certain areas and groups or proceeding with care and conducting spe-

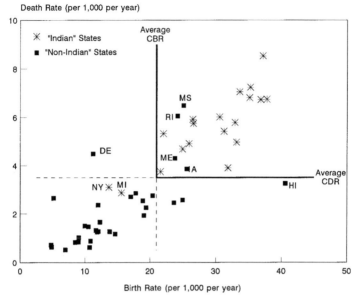

FIGURE 4-5 Birth and death rates by state for American Indians, 1980–1990. NOTE: Populations based on census counts.

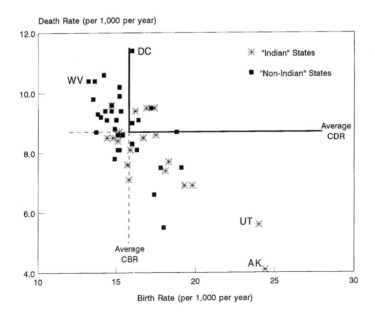

FIGURE 4-6 Birth and death rates by state for total population, 1980–1990.

cific analyses to address data compatibility issues. However, for the areas with the largest concentrations of American Indians, the data should be extremely useful for analyzing socioeconomic and demographic conditions of different American Indian populations and other racial groups.

REFERENCES

Eschbach, K.
   1993   Changing identification among American Indians and Alaska Natives. *Demography* 30(4, November):635–652.
Fix, M., and J.S. Passel
   1994   *Immigration and Immigrants: Setting the Record Straight.* Washington, D.C.: The Urban Institute.
Hahn, R. A., J. Mulinare, and S. M. Teutsch
   1992   Inconsistencies in coding of race and ethnicity between birth and death in U.S. infants. *Journal of the American Medical Association* 267:259–263.
Harris, D.
   1994   The 1990 Census count of American Indians: What do the numbers really mean? *Social Science Quarterly* 75 (September):580–593.
Passel, J. S.
   1976   Provisional evaluation of the 1970 Census count of American Indians. *Demography* 13:397–409.
Passel, J. S.
   1992   The growing American Indian population, 1960–1990. Unpublished paper presented at the annual meetings of the American Statistical Association, Boston, MA, August.
Passel, J. S., and P. A. Berman
   1986   Quality of 1980 Census data for American Indians. *Social Biology* 33:163–182.
Robinson, J. G., B. Ahmed, P. Das Gupta, and K. A. Woodrow
   1992   Estimation of Coverage in the 1990 United States Census Based on Demographic Analysis. Unpublished paper of the Population Division, U.S. Bureau of the Census, Washington, D.C.
Snipp, C. M.
   1989   *American Indians: The First of This Land.* New York: Russell Sage Foundation.
Waters, M. C.
   1990   *Ethnic Options.* Berkeley: University of California Press.

5
Tribal Membership Requirements and the Demography of "Old" and "New" Native Americans

Russell Thornton

INTRODUCTION

After some 400 years of population decline beginning soon after the arrival of Columbus in the Western Hemisphere, the Native American population north of Mexico began to increase around the turn of the twentieth century. The U.S. census decennial enumerations indicate a Native American population growth for the United States that has been nearly continuous since 1900 (except for an influenza epidemic in 1918 that caused serious losses), to 1.42 million by 1980 and to over 1.9 million by 1990.[1] To this may be added some 740,000 Native Americans in Canada in 1986 (575,000 American Indians, 35,000 Eskimo [Inuit], and 130,000 *Metis*), plus some additional increase to today and perhaps 30,000 Native Americans in Greenland. The total then becomes around 2.75 million in North America north of Mexico—obviously a significant increase from the perhaps fewer than 400,000 around the turn of the century, some 250,000 of which were in the United States. However, this 2.75 million remains far less than the estimated over 7 million circa 1492 (see Thornton, 1987a). It is also but a fraction of the total current populations of the United States (250 million in 1990) and Canada (over 25 million in 1990) (see Thornton, 1994a, 1994b).

---

[1]Changing definitions and procedures for enumerating Native Americans used by the U.S. Bureau of the Census also had an effect on the enumerated population size from census to census during this century.

The population recovery among Native Americans has resulted in part from lower mortality rates and increases in life expectancy as the effects of "Old World" diseases and other reasons for population decline associated with colonialism have diminished (see Thornton, 1987a; Snipp, 1989). For example, life expectancy at birth increased from 51.6 years in 1940 to 71.1 years in 1980, compared with an increase from 64.2 to 74.4 years among whites during the same period (Snipp, 1989). The population recovery has also resulted from adaptation through intermarriage with non-native peoples and changing fertility patterns during the twentieth century, whereby American Indian birth rates have remained higher than those of the average North American population. In 1980, for example, married American Indian women aged 35 to 44 had a mean number of children ever born of 3.61, in comparison with 2.77 for the total U.S. population and only 2.67 for whites. Intermarried American Indian women generally had lower fertility rates in 1980 than American Indian women married to American Indian men; however, intermarried American Indian women still had higher fertility than that of the total U.S. population (Thornton et al., 1991).

"OLD" AND "NEW" NATIVE AMERICANS

The twentieth-century increase in the Native American population reflected in successive U.S. censuses can also be attributed to changes in the identification of individuals as "Native American." Since 1960, the U.S. census has relied on self-identification to ascertain an individual's race. Much of the increase in the *American Indian* population—excluding Eskimo (Inuit) and Aleuts—from 523,591 in 1960 to 792,730 in 1970 to 1.37 million in 1980 to over 1.8 million in 1990 resulted from individuals not identifying themselves as American Indian in an earlier census, but doing so in a later one.[2] One might estimate, for example, that these changes in identification account for about 25 percent of the population "growth" of American Indians from 1960 to 1970, about 60 percent of the "growth" from 1970 to 1980, and about 35 percent of the "growth" from 1980 to 1990 (see Passel, 1976; Passel and Berman, 1986; Thornton, 1987a; Harris, 1994;

---

[2]The 1980 U.S. census obtained information that some 7 million Americans had some degree of Native American ancestry. Native American ancestry ranked tenth among the total United States population in 1980. In descending order, the ten leading ancestries were English, German, Irish, Afro-American, French, Italian, Scottish, Polish, Mexican, and Native American.

[3]Put in other words, the "error of closure"—the difference between natural increase and the enumerated population from one time period to another (assuming no migration)—was 8.5 percent in the 1970 census count, 25.2 percent in the 1980 census count, and 9.2 percent in the 1990 census count (see Passel, 1976; Passel and Berman, 1986; Harris, 1994).

Eschbach, 1995).[3] Why did this occur? The political mobilization of Native Americans in the 1960s and 1970s, along with other ethnic pride movements, may have removed some of the stigma attached to a Native American racial identity. This would be especially true for persons of mixed ancestry, who formerly may have declined to disclose their Native American background for this reason. Conversely, however, individuals with only minimal Native American background may have identified themselves as Native American out of a desire to affirm a marginal ethnic identity and their "romanticized" notion of being Native American (see, for example, Eschbach, 1995).

TRIBAL MEMBERSHIP REQUIREMENTS

Many different criteria may be used to delimit a population. Language, residence, cultural affiliation, recognition by a community, degree of "blood," genealogical lines of descent, and self-identification have all been used at some point in the past to define both the total Native American population and specific tribal populations. Of course, each measure produces a different population, and the decision about which variables to use in defining a given population is an arbitrary one. The implications of the decision for Native Americans can be enormous, however.

Native Americans are unique among ethnic and racial groups in their formal tribal affiliations and in their relationships with the U.S. government. Today, 317 American Indian tribes in the United States are legally recognized by the federal government and receive services from the U.S. Bureau of Indian Affairs (U.S. Bureau of Indian Affairs, 1993). (There are some tribes recognized by states but not by the federal government.) In addition, there are some 125-150 tribes seeking federal recognition and dozens of others that may do so in the future (U.S. Bureau of Indian Affairs, personal communication).[4]

Contemporary American Indians typically must be enrolled members of one of the 317 federally recognized tribes to receive benefits from either the tribe or the federal government. To be considered enrolled members, they must in turn meet various criteria for tribal membership, which vary from tribe to tribe and are typically set forth in tribal constitutions approved by the U.S. Bureau of Indian Affairs. Once recognized as members, individuals are typically issued tribal enrollment (or registration) numbers and cards that identify their special status as members of a particular American Indian tribe.

---

[4]Criteria used to establish whether a Native American group can become a federally recognized tribe are presented in Porter (1983).

The process of enrollment in a Native American tribe has historical roots that extend back to the early nineteenth century. As the U.S. government dispossessed native peoples, treaties established specific rights, privileges, goods, and money to which those party to a treaty—both tribes as entities and individual tribal members—were entitled. The practices of creating formal censuses and keeping lists of names of tribal members evolved to ensure an accurate and equitable distribution of benefits. Over time, Native Americans themselves established more formal tribal governments, including constitutions, and began to regulate their membership more carefully, especially with regard to land allotments, royalties from the sale of resources, distributions of tribal funds, and voting. In the twentieth century, the U.S. government established additional criteria for determining eligibility for such benefits as educational aid and healthcare. The federal government also passed the Indian Reorganization Act of 1934, under which most current tribes are organized. These tribes typically have written constitutions that contain a membership provision (Cohen, 1942).[5] Generally, these constitutions were either first established or, if already in place, modified after the act of 1934.

A variety of court cases have tested tribal membership requirements. From the disputes, American Indian tribal governments have won the right to determine their own membership: "The courts have consistently recognized that in the absence of express legislation by Congress to the contrary, an Indian tribe has complete authority to determine all questions of its own membership" (Cohen, 1942:133).[6]

Individuals enrolled in federally recognized tribes also receive a Certificate of Degree of Indian Blood (referred to as a CDIB) from the Bureau of Indian Affairs, specifying a certain degree of Indian blood, i.e., a blood quantum. The Bureau of Indian Affairs uses a blood quantum definition—generally one-fourth Native American blood—and/or tribal membership to recognize an individual as Native American. However, each tribe has its own set of requirements—generally including a blood quantum—for membership (enrollment) of individuals. Typically, blood quantum is established by tracing ancestry back through time to a relative or relatives on earlier tribal rolls or censuses that recorded the relative's

---

[5]The Pueblo of Taos, for example, has no written constitution; rather, it has what it calls "a traditional form of government" (Pueblo of Taos, personal communication).

[6]As Cohen (1942:133) notes, the ability of an American Indian tribe to determine its own membership "is limited only by the various statutes of Congress defining the membership of certain tribes for purposes of allotment or for other purposes, and by the statutory authority given to the Secretary of the Interior to promulgate a final tribal roll for the purpose of dividing and distributing tribal funds."

proportion of Native American blood. In such historical instances, the proportion was more often than not simply self-indicated.

Enrollment criteria have sometimes changed over time; often, the change has been to establish minimum blood quantum requirements. For instance, in 1931, the Eastern Band of Cherokee Indians established a one-sixteenth blood quantum requirement for those born thereafter (Cohen, 1942). Sometimes the change has been to establish more stringent requirements: the Confederated Salish and Kootenai Tribes have tightened their membership requirements since 1935 and in 1960 established that only those born with a one-quarter or more blood quantum could be tribal members (Trosper, 1976). Conversely, tribes may reduce their blood quantum requirements, sometimes even eliminating a specified minimum requirement. Cohen (1942:136) states: "The general trend of the tribal enactments on membership is away from the older notion that rights of tribal membership run with Indian blood, no matter how dilute the stream. Instead it is recognized that membership in a tribe is a political relation rather than a racial attribute."

Blood quantum requirements for membership in contemporary tribes vary widely from tribe to tribe (U.S. Bureau of Indian Affairs, unpublished data). Some tribes, such as the Walker River Paiute, require at least a one-half Indian (or tribal) blood quantum; many, such as the Navajo, require a one-fourth blood quantum; some, generally in California and Oklahoma, require a one-eighth, one-sixteenth, or one-thirty-second blood quantum; and many have no minimum blood quantum requirement, but require only a documented tribal lineage (see Thornton, 1987a, 1987b; Meyer and Thornton, 1991). A summary of this information is given in Table 5-1.

TABLE 5-1 Blood Quantum Requirements of American Indian Tribes by Reservation Basis and Size

	Blood Quantum Requirement		
	More than 1/4	1/4 or Less	No Minimum Requirement
Number of tribes	21	183	98
Reservation based	85.7%	83.1%	63.9%
Median size	1022	1096	1185

NOTE: Information not available on 15 tribes.

SOURCES: Thornton (1987b); U.S. Bureau of Indian Affairs (unpublished tribal constitutions and tribal enrollment data obtained by the author).

Around one-fourth of American Indians in the United States live on 278 reservations (or pueblos or rancherias) or associated "tribal trust lands," according to the Census Bureau. The largest of these is the Navajo Reservation, home to 143,405 Native Americans and 5,046 non-Indians in 1990 (Thornton, 1994a).[7] American Indian tribes located on reservations tend to have higher blood quantum requirements for membership than those located off reservation. As indicated in Table 5-1, over 85 percent of tribes requiring more than a one-quarter blood quantum for membership are reservation based, as compared with less than 64 percent of those having no minimum requirement. Tribes on reservations have seemingly been able to maintain *exclusive* membership by setting higher blood quanta, since the reservation location has generally served to isolate the tribe from non-Indians and intermarriage with them. Tribes without a reservation basis have maintained an *inclusive* membership by setting lower blood quanta for membership, since their populations have interacted and intermarried more with non-Indian populations.

As additionally indicated in Table 5-1, tribes with more restrictive blood quantum requirements tend to be somewhat smaller than those with less restrictive requirements, although the differences are not particularly striking. Obviously, requiring a greater percentage of American Indian blood limits the potential size of the tribal population more than requiring a smaller percentage.

In the early 1980s, the total membership of federally recognized tribes was about 900,000 (U.S. Bureau of Indian Affairs, unpublished data). Therefore, many of the 1.37 million individuals identifying themselves as American Indian in the 1980 census were not actually enrolled members of federally recognized tribes. In fact, only about two-thirds were. In the late 1980s, the total membership of these tribes was somewhat over 1 million (U.S. Bureau of Indian Affairs, unpublished data); hence, only about 60 percent of the 1.8+ million people identifying themselves as

---

[7]Around 60 percent of the Native American population of Alaska lives in "Alaska Native Villages." The Bureau of Indian Affairs recognizes 222 Native American villages, communities, and other entities (U.S. Bureau of Indian Affairs, 1993). Alaskan Eskimo (Inuit) and Aleuts present a somewhat different picture than American Indians. Most of the 50,555 enumerated in the 1980 census were tied closely to small, local communities, representing ancestral grounds rather than government reservations. For example, there were approximately 100 Eskimo (Inuit) villages, each having 600 or fewer people. About one-third of the slightly more than 8,000 Aleuts in Alaska in 1980 lived in the 12 surviving villages of the Aleutian and Pribilof islands; the others lived in either rural communities or urban areas (Osborn, 1990). Typically, membership is expressed in terms of a "common bond of living together," and all living in the village may be members.

American Indian in the 1990 census were actually enrolled in a federally recognized American Indian tribe (Thornton, 1987b, 1994a).

Such discrepancies vary considerably from tribe to tribe. Most of the 158,633 Navajos enumerated in the 1980 census and the 219,198 Navajos enumerated in the 1990 census were enrolled in the Navajo Nation; however, only about one-third of the 232,344 Cherokees enumerated in the 1980 census and the 308,132 Cherokees enumerated in the 1990 census were actually enrolled in one of the three Cherokee tribes (the Cherokee Nation of Oklahoma, the Eastern Band of Cherokee Indians [of North Carolina], or the United Keetoowah Band of Cherokee Indians of Oklahoma) (see Thornton, 1990, 1994a). Thus the Navajo Nation is the American Indian tribe with the largest number of enrolled members, but more individuals self-identifying as Native American identified themselves as "Cherokee" in the 1980 and 1990 censuses than as members of any other tribe.

IMPLICATIONS OF URBANIZATION AND INTERMARRIAGE

Urbanization and associated increases in intermarriage have resulted in new threats to Native Americans in the last half of the twentieth century.

The 1990 census indicated that 56.2 percent of Native Americans lived in urban areas (U.S. Bureau of the Census, 1992; Thornton, 1994b). Cities with the largest Native American populations were New York City, Oklahoma City, Phoenix, Tulsa, Los Angeles, Minneapolis-St. Paul, Anchorage, and Albuquerque.

In 1900, only 0.4 percent of Native Americans in the United States lived in urban areas. This percentage increased gradually during the early decades of the century. At mid-century, still only some 13.4 percent of Native Americans in the United States lived in urban areas. During subsequent decades, however, more rapid increases in urbanization occurred; the 1980 census indicated that for the first time in history over one-half of all Native Americans lived in urban areas.

The above-described trend toward requiring low percentages of Indian blood for tribal membership and dealing with the federal government to certify it may be seen in part as a result of "a demographic legacy of 1492." As the numbers of Native Americans have declined and Native Americans have come into increased contact with whites, blacks, and others, Native American peoples have increasingly married non-Indians. As a result, they have had to rely increasingly on formal certification as proof of their Indian identity. This pattern has accelerated as urbanization has increased the numbers of non-Native Americans encountered by American Indians and other Native Americans and thus increased intermarriage rates. Today, almost 60 percent of all American Indians are married to non-Indians (Sandefur and McKinnell, 1986; Thornton, 1987a; Snipp, 1989; Eschbach, 1995). Moreover, it has been argued that the "new Native Americans" who have changed their census self-identification, as discussed above, are more likely to be intermarried (Eschbach, 1995; see also Nagel, 1995).

Urbanization has also seemingly brought about some decreased emphasis on Native American tribal identity. For example, overall, about 20 percent of American Indians enumerated in the 1970 census reported no tribe, but only about 10 percent of those on reservations reported no tribe versus about 30 percent of those in urban areas (Thornton, 1987a). (Comparable data from the 1980 and 1990 censuses are not available; the 1980 census indicated that about 25 percent reported no tribal affiliation [Thornton, 1987a], while the figure in the 1990 census was about 15 percent [computed from data available in U.S. Bureau of the Census, 1994].) As indicated in the 1990 census, only about one-fourth of all American Indians speak an Indian language at home; however, census enumerations also indicate that urban residents are far less likely than reservation residents to speak an Indian language or even participate in tribal cultural activities (see Thornton, 1987a; U.S. Bureau of the Census, 1992).

If these trends continue, both the genetic and tribal distinctiveness of the total Native American population will be greatly lessened. A Native American population comprising primarily "old" Native Americans strongly attached to their tribes will change to a population dominated by "new" Native American individuals who may or may not have tribal attachments or even tribal identities. Indeed, it may make sense at some future time to speak of Native Americans mainly as people of Native American ancestry or ethnicity.

Taking into account the high rates of intermarriage, it has been projected that within the next century, the proportion of those with a one-half or more blood quantum will decline to only 8 percent of the American Indian population, whereas the proportion with less than a one-fourth blood quantum will increase to around 60 percent (see U.S. Congress, 1986). Moreover, these individuals will be increasingly unlikely to be enrolled as tribal members. Even if they are tribal members, a traditional cultural distinctiveness may be replaced by mere social membership if language and other important cultural features of American Indian tribes are lost. Certainly the total Native American population as a distinctive segment of American society will be in danger. Moreover, if individuals who identify themselves as Native American cannot meet established blood quantum enrollment criteria, they will have no rights to the associated benefits. Stricter requirements will operate to restrict the eligible Native American population, as well as, ultimately, the number of federally recognized Native American entities. As long as reservations exist, there will undoubtedly be a quite distinct—genetically and culturally— segment of the Native American population that is very different from the total U.S. population. However, for the U.S. government, decreasing blood quanta of the total Native American population may be perceived as meaning that the numbers of Native Americans to whom it is obligated have declined.

CONCLUSIONS

Native American peoples in the United States (and Canada) have experienced a population recovery during the twentieth century. However, new demographic and tribal threats may be faced during the twenty-first century. Intermarriage with non-Native Americans may continue to undermine the basis of the Native American population as a distinctive racial and cultural group. In the next century, tribal membership may well be the criterion for determining who is distinctively Native American, irrespective of how that membership may be determined. Tribes with high blood quantum requirements may find themselves with a shrinking population base unless they manage to control marriages between tribal members and non-Native Americans (or even Native American non-tribal members)—or, of course, unless they lower their blood quantum requirements. Continued urbanization is likely not only to result in increased intermarriage as more and more Native Americans come in contact with non-Native peoples, but also to diminish further the identity of Native Americans as distinctive tribal peoples tied to specific geographical areas.

REFERENCES

Cohen, F.
   1942   *Handbook of Federal Indian Law.* Washington, D.C.:   U.S. Government Printing Office.
Eschbach, K.
   1995   The enduring and vanishing American Indian: American Indian population growth and intermarriage in 1990. *Ethnic and Racial Studies* 18:89-108.
Harris, D.
   1994   The 1990 Census count of American Indians: What do the numbers really mean. *Social Science Quarterly* 75:580-593.
Meyer, M.L., and R. Thornton
   1991   The blood quantum quandary.   Unpublished paper presented at the 1991 Annual Meeting of the American Historical Association (Pacific Coast Branch), Kona, HI.
Nagel, J.
   1995   Politics and the resurgence of American Indian ethnic identity. *American Sociological Review* 60:947-965.

Osborn, K.
 1990   *The Peoples of the Arctic.* New York: Chelsea House.
Passel, J.S.
 1976   Provisional evaluation of the 1970 census count of American Indians. *Demography*
        13:397-409.
Passel, J.S., and P.A. Berman
 1986   Quality of 1980 census data for American Indians. *Social Biology* 33:163-182.
Porter, F.W. III, ed.
 1983   *Nonrecognized American Indian Tribes: An Historical and Legal Perspective.* Occasional
        Paper Series No. 7. Chicago, IL: D'Arcy McNickle Center for the History of the
        American Indian, The Newberry Library.
Sandefur, G.D., and T. McKinnell.
 1986   American Indian intermarriage. *Social Science Research* 15:347-371.
Snipp, C.M.
 1989   *American Indians: The First of This Land.* New York: Russell Sage.
Thornton, R.
 1987a *American Indian Holocaust and Survival: A Population History Since 1492.* Norman,
        OK: University of Oklahoma Press.
 1987b Tribal history, tribal population, and tribal membership requirements: The cases
        of the Eastern Band of Cherokee Indians, the Cherokee Nation of Oklahoma, and
        the United Keetoowah Band of Cherokee Indians in Oklahoma. *Towards a
        Quantative Approach to American Indian History*, Occasional Papers Series No. 8.
        Chicago, IL: D'Arcy McNickle Center for the History of the American Indian, The
        Newberry Library.
 1990   *The Cherokees: A Population History.* Lincoln, NE: University of Nebraska Press.
 1994a Population. Pp. 461-464 in Mary B. Davis, ed., *Native Americans in the 20th Century:
        An Encyclopedia.* New York: Garland.
 1994b Urbanization. Pp. 670-672 in Mary B. Davis, ed., *Native Americans in the 20th Cen-
        tury: An Encyclopedia.* New York: Garland.
Thornton, R., G.D. Sandefur, and C.M. Snipp.
 1991   American Indian fertility history. *American Indian Quarterly* 15:359-367.
Trosper, R.L.
 1976   Native American boundary maintenance: The Flathead Indian Reservation, Mon-
        tana, 1860-1970. *Ethnohistory* 3:256-274.
U.S. Bureau of the Census
 1992   *Census of the Population: General Population Characteristics, American Indian and Alas-
        kan Native Areas, 1990.* Washington, D.C.: U.S. Government Printing Office.
 1994   *1990 Census of Population: Characteristics of American Indians by Tribe and Language.*
        Washington, D.C.: U.S. Government Printing Office.
U.S. Bureau of Indian Affairs
 1993   Indian entities recognized and eligible to receive services from the United States
        Bureau of Indian Affairs. *Federal Register* 58:54364-54369.
U.S. Congress (Office of Technology Assessment)
 1986   *Indian Health Care.* OTA-H-290. Washington, D.C.: U.S. Government Printing
        Office.

6

Problems in Sampling the Native American and Alaska Native Populations

Eugene P. Ericksen

INTRODUCTION

Statisticians drawing samples of African Americans can create efficient plans using well-known strategies (Ericksen, 1976). They can take advantage of residential segregation to select blocks with many blacks at higher rates than blocks with fewer. They can instruct interviewers to code the race of "door answerers" by observation, and to subselect African American households within their sampled blocks. Because African Americans are thought to be culturally homogeneous, estimates for subgroups defined by cultural factors are not needed. Instead, estimates for the usual subclasses defined by variables such as age, sex, education, and income are sufficient. Since these subclasses tend not to be geographically concentrated, a national design providing precise estimates for all African Americans is likely to provide precise estimates for these subgroups as well.

These strategies are not likely to work as well for the Native American and Alaska Native populations. Native Americans and Alaska Natives are neither as segregated nor as concentrated as blacks. While the average black in a typical American city might live on a block where 75 percent of the population is African American, such concentrations of population occur only for Native Americans living on certain reservations or for Alaska Natives living in certain rural areas. Only small proportions of Native Americans and Alaska Natives live in such areas (Beals et al., 1994).

At the same time, there is great cultural diversity among Native Americans and Alaska Natives. Their distinctive cultures are more likely to be maintained on reservations and in other areas where Native populations are concentrated. These cultural subgroups tend to live in separate areas, e.g., Navajos in Arizona, Eskimo and Aleuts in Alaska, Sioux in the Northern Great Plains. When a national survey is taken, most respondents from any one of these subgroups are likely to live in just a few areas. The result is a highly clustered subsample producing imprecise subgroup estimates. If the cultural patterns associated with different tribal groups are related to the survey subject of interest, e.g., health practices, this clustering will reduce the precision of national estimates as well. For example, the designers of the Strong Heart Study (Lee et al., 1990) thought rates of heart disease varied greatly among different groups in different geographic areas. The importance of local cultures may decrease the efficiency of a clustered sample, necessitating a larger sample and creating tougher choices between designs maximizing precision for overall estimates and those more likely to improve the precision of subclass estimates.

Beals et al. (1994) found that over 300 tribal groups are recognized formally by the federal government, and there may be as many as 500 groups in the United States today. These groups have diverse histories, and to the extent that they have maintained their traditional identities, combining groups as separate as Seminole and Sioux into one category called "Indian" seems little different than combining Polish Jews and Scottish Protestants into one category called "European." While political arrangements and economic opportunities may have lessened the need for separate cultural identities within the large categories of Indian and European, the apparent surge in Native American identity that has occurred over the past 30 or 40 years makes this less likely for them.

Finally, while blacks can usually be identified by visual inspection, this is more difficult for the Native American population. Generations of intermarriage and cultural mixing have blurred the distinctions between Native and other Americans, and it seems likely that many persons who would identify themselves as Native American in one situation might select a different racial identity in another situation. This creates the serious problem of how to estimate the total size of the population we are trying to study (see also Passel, in this volume).

This paper does not present an easy solution to the problem of how to sample the Native American and Alaska Native populations, and the correct statistical design will surely differ depending on the objectives of each study. Rather, the paper describes in some detail the three problems above, and attempts to explain decisions that need to be made with regard to each. The discussion begins with the most serious problem, defining the population, then turns to the issue of cultural subgroups, and finally to strategies for sampling. First, however, we look briefly at two examples of surveys of Native Americans as context for the discussion that follows. The final section of the paper presents concluding remarks.

TWO EXAMPLES OF SURVEYS OF THE NATIVE AMERICAN POPULATION

The Survey of American Indians and Alaska Natives (SAIAN) (Cunningham, 1995) and the Strong Heart Study (Lee et al., 1990) are two examples of surveys that include important elements of the Native American population, but do not provide complete coverage. The SAIAN surveyed those persons eligible for coverage by the Indian Health Service (IHS), i.e., Native Americans or Alaska Natives in federally recognized tribes living in IHS service areas. This population, while national, included only 906,000 persons, just under half the nearly 2 million Native Americans and Alaska Natives counted in the 1990 census. To increase the cost-efficiency of the sample, the SAIAN excluded counties with fewer than 400 American Indians or Alaska Natives, and 2.8 percent of the otherwise eligible population lived in these counties. The SAIAN also excluded "sampling segments," i.e., individual blocks or census enumeration districts, that were located in the eligible counties, but had less than 0.5 percent Native American or Alaska Native population.

The total sample size was 6,500, permitting useful national comparisons based on age, perceived health status, income, and place of residence. However, the sampling design resulted in two problems. First, there were no comparisons by tribal group or geographic area. Thus cultural factors unique to individual tribal groups that are crucial to understanding healthcare usage could not be studied with the SAIAN design. More important, there could be no generalizations from the study population to the million or so persons identifying themselves as Native American on the census who were not eligible for IHS services.

The Strong Heart Study attempted to overcome the first of these problems by focusing on three large and important groups: (1) the Gila and Salt River Pima/Maricopa Indian communities of Arizona, who were thought to be a low-risk population for cardiovascular diseases (Stoddart et al., n.d.); (2) seven tribes living off reservation in southwestern Oklahoma, thought to be a moderate-risk population; and (3) three Sioux tribes living in South and North Dakota, thought to be a high-risk population.

Each of these groups was sampled from tribal rolls, with about 1,500 persons being selected in each group. This design made tribal comparisons possible. It did not, however, overcome the second problem with the SAIAN design since the Strong Heart sample, selected from tribal rolls, permitted no generalization to those Indians not included in a federally recognized tribal group. The SAIAN and Strong Heart study populations were both more likely than other Native Americans to live on reservations or in other areas of concentrated Native American population. These groups may be more important to government policies than their more assimilated brethren living in cities, suburbs, and other "non-Native" areas. Moreover, their Native American or Alaska Native identity is likely to be more distinct.

Another possibility for studying the Native American population is to use samples drawn for very large government surveys and to add some questions pertinent to Native concerns. For example, Eschbach and Supple (1995) report that a 1993 edition of the Current Population Survey included 1700 American Indians living in 758 households. The problem with this design, in addition to an imprecise definition of the covered population, is that the distributions of the Native American and total Current Population Survey populations are quite different: where one is sparse, the other tends to be numerous. The Current Population Survey design is likely to produce large numbers of Native American respondents in certain clusters; thus a substantial share of this subsample will appear in just a few locations, and the clusters will be quite different from one another. To the extent that place-to-place and group-to-group variations are important, this design reflects the inefficiencies of using a sample designed to produce precise estimates for the total population rather than for uniquely distributed subpopulations like Native Americans and Alaska Natives.

PROBLEMS OF DEFINITION

Passel (1976) observed the rapid and discrepant growth of the Native American population from 1960 to 1970. Using "best estimates" of the numbers of Native American births and deaths between 1960 and 1970 and assuming that international migration was negligible, he found that Native American population growth could not be accounted for by demographic factors. Even with plausible assumptions about errors in the estimated numbers of births or deaths or changes in the net undercounting of the Native American populations in the 1960 and 1970 censuses, the estimated increase in numbers of Native Americans was still implausible. The only reasonable explanation was that people who had not identified themselves as Native American in 1960 had done so in 1970.

This trend accelerated (Table 6-1) after 1970. Whereas the counted population of Native Americans and Alaska Natives had remained at between 300,000 and 400,000 from 1930 through 1950 and grown to just

TABLE 6-1 Census-Counted Populations of Native Americans and Alaska Natives

Birth Cohort	Counted Population (thousands)			Growth Rates (%)		
	1970	1980	1990	1970-1980	1980-1990	1970-1990
1980-1990	—	—	429	—	—	—
1970-1980	—	296	388	—	31	—
1960-1970	212	326	367	54	13	73
1950-1960	198	274	338	38	23	71
1940-1950	127	191	231	50	21	82
1930-1940	93	127	143	37	13	54
1915-1930	104	131	126	26	−4	21
Before 1915	94	75	43	−20	−43	−54
Total	828	1,420	2,065	71	45	149

SOURCE: 1970 census data are from U.S. Bureau of the Census (1970:Part 1, Tables 48 and 190, and Part 3, Table 139); 1980 and 1990 data are from U.S. Bureau of the Census (1993b:Table 1).

over 600,000 in 1960, it tripled in the next 30 years, reaching 828,000 in 1970, 1.42 million in 1980, and 2.06 million in 1990.

We can perhaps focus more easily on the problem by considering those persons identified as Native American or Alaska Native who were born between 1930 and 1970 and were aged 0 to 40 in 1970, 10 to 50 in 1980, and 20 to 60 in 1990. They numbered 630,000 in the 1970 census, but in spite of the deaths that surely occurred between 1970 and 1990, grew to 918,000 in 1980 and to 1,079,000 in 1990. The growth from 1970 to 1980 was 46 percent, from 1980 to 1990 18 percent, and for the full 20-year period 71 percent. Such extreme growth has not been limited to this particular group. In 1980, there were 296,000 persons identified as Native American or Alaska Native who were aged 0 to 9; by 1990 there were 388,000 aged 10 to 19, an increase of 31 percent.

To understand this growth and its application to our sampling problem, we must look at the way racial data are obtained on the census. The person filling out the form, intended to be the head or spouse of head of household, indicates the race of every person living in the household. In cases of persons with mixed racial identities, the respondent uses judgment, and these judgments have apparently changed over time. There seem to be many people with some Native ancestry who must choose an identity, usually between white and Native American/Alaska Native, but often between black and Native American/Alaska Native. These choices can be influenced by factors such as what group is dominant in the area where the household is located, political and economic opportunities that may be limited to persons identifying as Native American or Alaska Native, or just a psychological desire to choose a particular identity. For example, a child with a Native American father who grew up living with a white or black mother and perhaps with some of the mother's relatives in a household where the father was absent may decide to identify as Native American upon becoming an adult.

In many ways, the problem of Native American identity is similar to that of Hispanic identity. In both cases, persons of mixed ancestry are asked to choose one racial identity in a way that takes their individual situation into account. Studies by the U.S. Bureau of the Census (1979) showed that about 10 percent of persons identifying themselves as Hispanic on various surveys identified themselves as non-Hispanic upon being reinter-viewed. The likelihood of consistent responses was greater for those with a shorter generational gap between themselves and their immigrant ancestors: while 99 percent of persons born in a Hispanic country reported themselves to be of Spanish origin in the 1970 census, this percentage fell to 73 percent for the third generation and to 44 percent for the fourth generation. Similarly, where there were Spanish ancestors on both sides of the family (mother and father), 97 percent reported being of Spanish origin on the census; only 21 percent did so when there were Spanish ancestors on just one side of the family.

One of the studies on which the Census Bureau reported was a special 1974 census taken in Gallup, New Mexico, where large numbers of Hispanics and Native Americans live. A reinterview study showed that 91.7 percent of those who had listed themselves as "American Indian" on the census did so again on a follow-up reinterview. The comparable proportion for Hispanic persons in Gallup was 89.2 percent.

In a way, Hispanic or Native American identity can be thought of as an attitude (Yancey et al., 1976). It can be subject to the local context, i.e., whether the person is living among others who are Hispanic or Native American, or the perceived political or economic opportunities that might result from selecting a particular identity. As people move from one place to another or as the economic or political climate changes, self-identification may change as well. At the same time, it seems likely that those whose ancestry is not mixed or who live on or near a reservation are more likely to identify themselves consistently.

The importance of context is also evident in the way parents assign racial identities to children living in mixed-race families. Passel (1991) examined the racial identities of children included in the 1970 census in households where the father and mother were of different races. In cases where one parent was black or white, the race of the father was dominant

TABLE 6-2   Proportions of Children Living with Both
Parents Assigned Race of Father and Race of Mother
When These Two Races Are Different, 1970 Census

Race of Father	Race of Mother	Percent Other	Percent White	Percent Black
Other	White	48.7	51.3	X
White	Other	23.3	76.7	X
Other	Black	36.4	X	63.6
Black	Other	14.0	X	86.0
White	Black	X	53.3	46.7
Black	White	X	25.4	74.6

SOURCE: Passel (1991).

(Table 6-2), being assigned 66 percent of the time. The particular race of
the mother and father also mattered: where the father was black and the
mother white or other, children were more likely than average (77 percent) to be assigned the father's race; where the mother was black and the
father white or other, the likelihood of being assigned the father's race
was considerably less (51 percent). Of the three groups examined in this
study—black, white, and other (predominantly Asian and Native American)—parents who were other were least likely to live with children assigned to the same race. Where the father was other and the mother white
or black, only 48 percent of children were identified as other; where the
mother was other and the father white or black, only 23 percent of children were identified as other.

Passel's study reflects a racial dynamic that existed in 1970. Were the
study to be repeated for 1990 or 2000, the patterns might well be different.
In 1970, having a black parent increased the chance of a mixed-race child
being called black, and to a lesser degree having a white parent increased
the chances of being called white. To the extent that Asian or Native
American identities have become more powerful predictors of racial identity since 1970, this pattern may have changed. In addition, there may be
more mixed-race families, or the racial identities of fathers and mothers
may be changing. All of these factors could contribute to a rapid growth
of Native American and Alaska Native populations that cannot be accounted for simply by counting births and deaths. This complexity reflects the social-psychological nature of racial identities, as well as the
effects of specific situations in which people live. And it leads to a vexing
problem for surveys.

In 1990, the census counted over 2 million Native Americans and
Alaska Natives on the basis of the race question on the short form admin-

istered to all households. It is not clear how many of these individuals would be counted as Native American or claimed as members by any tribal group. Nor is it clear how many of those who identified themselves as Native American or Alaska Native on the census would so identify themselves to a survey interviewer. It may be that many of these people consider themselves to be "Indian" or "Eskimo" only for the purpose of what they put down when filling out the census form. Their answer may have neither political implication nor cultural meaning for them and may be irrelevant to their economic prospects. They may not be included in tribal rolls and may be unimportant for purposes of developing policy for the Native American and Alaska Native populations. Whether the correct number for public policy is the total claimed by tribal groups, the 2 million counted on the census, or some number in between is not clear.

People with a limited attachment to a Native group may also be difficult for a survey interviewer to identify as such. Interviewers are typically uncomfortable asking respondents to state their race, and such information is usually obtained by inspection. This approach suffices when the goal is to identify blacks, whites, and perhaps Asians, and to distinguish them from each other. Under such a scheme, less-numerous groups are likely to be undercounted. Between 1972 and 1993, over 29,000 persons aged 18 and over were interviewed for the General Social Survey (Davis and Smith, 1993). Information on race was obtained by inspection unless the interviewer was uncertain, in which case (s)he was supposed to ask. During this period, only 131 Native Americans or Alaska Natives were identified, about 0.4 percent of all samples. This is below the population proportion obtained by the census, which increased from 0.4 percent in 1970 to 0.7 percent in 1990. This difference of (0.7 − 0.4 =) 0.3 percent sounds minimal; however, if a sampling rate were specified assuming that the 0.7 percent figure was correct, the shortfall in sample size would be $100\% \times (1 - 0.4/0.7) = 43$ percent. While some of this gap is probably due to undercounting—i.e., the interviewers never found some Native Americans who should have been included in the sample—much of it probably results from persons who call themselves "Native American" or "Alaska Native" not being identified as such by the interviewers.

The issue is complicated by a separate result from the 1990 census. One of the questions included on the long form administered to a sample of households asked people to indicate their ancestry, and more than one answer was allowed. The U.S. Bureau of the Census (1993a:Table 56) reports that 8.7 million people indicated Native American ancestry on the form. This suggests that if people are asked directly whether they have Native American or Alaska Native ancestry, a larger number will reply "yes" than if they are asked to make this choice from a list of presented alternatives.

Considering Native American or Alaska Native identity as an attitude, as suggested above, is perhaps a new way of conceptualizing the demographic classification. Especially with increasing rates of intermarriage, racial and ethnic identity is ambiguous for more and more people in the United States. It thus becomes important to focus on how questions about a person's racial identity are asked, because different ways of asking can lead to different answers. For example, if a person were asked to choose a race among black, white, Asian, Native American, or other, the answer might be different than it would be on the Current Population Survey. On the latter, a person is asked to choose an ethnic identity from a long list that includes groups such as German, English, Italian, Mexican-American, Chicano, Puerto Rican, Afro-American (black, Negro), or "another group not listed," but omits white, Native American, and Alaska Native. Still other results might be obtained in answer to a direct question, such as "Do you consider yourself to be a Native American or Alaska Native?"

It is also likely that answers given will vary with particular circumstances. For example, a person trying to register for a government program may feel that self-identifying in a certain way will affect his/her chances of being eligible. Similarly, a person might self-identify in one way, whereas someone else, perhaps a relative filling out a death certificate, might identify that person differently. Moreover, we cannot assume that all persons who are included on tribal rolls or are eligible for the IHS will indicate themselves to be "American Indian" on the census, nor, as is now obvious, can we assume the opposite—that all Native Americans or Alaska Natives who are eligible for the IHS can be found on tribal rolls.

In conclusion, people who want to survey Native Americans and Alaska Natives need to decide on a definition. If the decision is to include only persons on tribal rolls or those with specified numbers of Native American or Alaska Native parents or grandparents, it is likely that the total population will be substantially less than the 2 million counted by the census. If the definition includes persons who would identify themselves as Native American or Alaska Native on a survey when offered the full range of racial identities used by the census, then 2 million is probably the accurate population size. In this latter case, skilled interviewing is needed to find people who might have reason to identify themselves as Native American or Alaska Native in some situations, but as members of different groups in other situations.

THE PROBLEM OF CULTURAL SUBGROUPS

Native Americans and Alaska Natives are culturally diverse, a conclusion based on both general understanding and reports of people who have worked with them (e.g., Beals et al., 1994). Thus, grouping them may create the same problem that occurs when the Census Bureau groups all persons of Hispanic origin to publish aggregated statistics. As a result of such aggregation, the extreme poverty of Puerto Ricans living in some Northeastern cities is disguised by the middle-class nature of other Hispanics (Ericksen, 1985); the affluence of Cubans is combined with the poverty of Mexican Americans and the even greater poverty of Puerto Ricans to create aggregate statistics that represent none of the subgroups.

Just as a survey of the Hispanic population will be more meaningful if separate statistics are published for Puerto Ricans, Mexican Americans, and Cubans, a survey of the Native American and Alaska Native populations will be more meaningful if separate statistics can be published for key subgroups. The problem is to decide what the subgroups should be. Two of them should no doubt be Native Americans and Alaska Natives. The problem is that the first of these groups is nearly 20 times larger than the second. If we want separate estimates of equal reliability for Native Americans and Alaska Natives, substantial oversampling of the latter population will be required, increasing total survey costs. Similarly, we must oversample further if we desire separate estimates for individual tribal groups (e.g., Navajo) or combined groups (e.g., southwestern Indians).

Alternatively, separate estimates may be desirable for those living on or off reservations. Sampling only those who live on reservations would be wrong for at least two reasons. One is that only a minority of the population, by any definition, lives on a reservation. The second is that even among those who would be certain to identify their race as Native American or Alaska Native, the reservation population is probably very different from the nonreservation population. Their jobs, living standards, and even laws are likely to differ. It also seems likely that health conditions among the reservation and nonreservation populations differ greatly.

Whether a study focuses on reservations or not, the cultural diversity among the various tribal groups needs to be considered. While Census Bureau reports and other commentaries frequently describe Native Americans as one group, there are important cultural and historical differences among Native groups. Whether the similarities outweigh the differences is a matter for substantive judgment. Moreover, once the differences have been recognized, even more expert judgment is required to determine how the various tribal groups might be combined to compute subclass estimates. Unless one has the resources for a very large sample, it is likely that only a small number of subgroups, perhaps four to six, can be recognized. How this determination is made—whether by Native Americans versus Alaska Natives, by reservation versus nonreservation populations, by identification of certain very large groups (such as the Navajo), or by regional separation of populations—is an important issue with policy implications. While the statistician can point out the need to make these judgments, the judgments themselves must be made by subject matter experts. Because the number and types of subclasses of interest affect the overall sample size, we need to specify these subclasses as part of the survey planning process.

A SAMPLING STRATEGY

Once the population has been defined and important subclasses identified, we can turn our attention to how to construct the sample. Geographic dispersion creates a substantial sampling problem. Using the Census Bureau definition, the Native American and Alaska Native populations combined comprise 0.8 percent of the total U.S. population. Most of these people live in areas where their population is sparse, i.e., where Native Americans and Alaska Natives comprise a small share of the total population. Out of a population of 2 million, only 579,000, fewer than one-third, live in counties where they comprise at least 10 percent of the total population. The household screening necessary to find eligible respondents could vastly increase survey costs.

To understand this problem, it helps to recognize the statistical principle of *optimal allocation*. By this rule, if a population can be divided into strata, the rate at which we should sample among the various strata should be proportional to the reciprocal of the costs of obtaining the average interview in each stratum. For example, if the costs in one stratum were four times greater than the costs in a second stratum, we would sample the first stratum at half the rate of the second. Use of optimal allocation to determine sampling rates within strata maximizes the precision of sample estimates for a fixed total cost. In other words, if we have x dollars to spend on data collection, we know how to allocate the sample across the strata to minimize the standard errors of the sample estimates. Given that we have a fixed amount of money to spend on data collection, optimal allocation tells us what the sampling rate and therefore sample sizes should be in the various strata to minimize sampling error.

For a survey of Native Americans and Alaska Natives, costs would be determined largely by screening rates. Screening involves contacting each sample household and determining whether an eligible respondent lives there. For a limited screening task, such as whether an eligible Native person lives at a particular address, it is reasonable and consistent with past experience to assume that the cost of screening is about one-tenth the cost of obtaining a complete interview. The optimal sampling plan that would result if the ratio of screening to interviewing costs were as high as one-fifth or as low as one-twentieth is not greatly different from the plan that would result with a ratio of one-tenth.

In an area where everyone was eligible, say, on a reservation, the cost per interview would be 1.1C, where C is the cost of actually going through the questionnaire with one respondent. In an area where 50 percent of the households included an eligible respondent, the cost would be 1.2C, since there would be two screenings per interview; where 10 percent of the households were eligible, the cost would be 2.0C; and where 1 percent of the households (close to the national average) were eligible, the cost would be 11.0C. For these four examples, if we set the sampling rate in the area where everyone was eligible at f, then the optimal sampling rates in the other areas would be .96f, .74f, and .32f, respectively. In other words, the sampling rates in areas where 50 or 100 percent of the population was Native American or Alaska Native would be almost the same (f and .96f); where only 10 percent of the population so qualified, the sampling rate would be a little bit less (.74f); but where only 1 percent of the population so qualified, it would be a great deal less (.32f). Table 6-3 shows a larger set of examples.

Looking at it another way, costs are reasonably consistent in areas where the proportion eligible varies from 10 to 100 percent, but they increase sharply when the proportion eligible falls below 10 percent and especially when it falls below 5 percent. Because there are clear advan-

TABLE 6-3 Sampling Rates Determined by Optimal Allocation for Areas of Different Population Concentrations

Percent Native American or Alaska Native	Cost[a] per Interview[b]	Optimal Sampling Rate
100	1.1C	f
50	1.2C	.96f
25	1.4C	.89f
10	2.0C	.74f
5	3.0C	.61f
4	3.5C	.56f
3	4.33C	.50f
2	6.0C	.43f
1	11.0C	.32f
0.5	21.0C	.23f
0.1	101.0C	.10f

[a]By optimal allocation, the sampling rate is proportion to the reciprocal of the square root of cost.

[b]The cost of screening one household is assumed to be 10 percent of the cost of one interview.

TABLE 6-4 Sizes of Native American and Alaska Native Populations Living in Counties Where at Least 10 Percent of the Population is Native American or Alaska Native, by State, 1990

State	Size of Eligible Population in Designated Counties[a]	Percentage of County Populations Native American or Alaska Native
Alaska	59,421	38
Arizona	128,044	40
Colorado	2,141	11
Montana	31,205	35
New Mexico	105,578	37
North Carolina	49,429	30
North Dakota	15,500	50
Oklahoma	138,770	17
Oregon	2,674	20
South Dakota	33,755	54
Utah	9,194	26
Washington	3,597	11
Total, 12 States	579,308	28

[a]Designated counties are those where at least 10 percent of the 1990 census-counted populations are Native American or Alaska Native.

SOURCE: U.S. Bureau of the Census, U.S. Census of Population, 1990.

tages to area sampling where this strategy is feasible, its use can be recommended in areas where the proportion eligible is at least 10 percent. Where the proportion is between 5 and 10 percent, we might consider use of area sampling, but in areas where the proportion eligible is less than 5 percent, we should probably adopt other strategies.

Table 6-4 shows the distribution of counties by state where Native Americans and Alaska Natives are concentrated. For example, in Colorado there is one county, Montezuma, where at least 10 percent of the population is Native American or Alaska Native; the eligible population totals 2,141. The calculations in Table 6-4 indicate that over the total United States, about 29 percent of Native Americans and Alaska Natives live in counties where they are at least 10 percent of the population. In these counties they are 28.3 percent of the total, so the costs of screening would be moderate. If we dropped the limit to 5 percent of the county's population to try to capture some of the remaining 71 percent, it is doubtful that we would increase the proportion of eligible counties greatly or capture much of the remaining population. A better strategy would be to substitute smaller geographic areas for counties. In other words, we would use area sampling in all towns, townships, and census enumeration districts where at least 10 percent of the population is Native American or Alaska Native. This set of areas might well include half of the Native population, but a substantial number would still be omitted.

Supplementing the area sample would be difficult. One strategy would be to use tribal rolls, adding all listed persons who lived outside the designated set of places where area sampling was used. This process would be costly and error prone. Listed addresses, especially in rural areas, are often inexact, and some may be out of date as well. Moreover, it would be expensive to get even a sample of tribal rolls from the different tribes, and their quality is likely to be uneven.

A second alternative strategy is "multiplicity sampling." This strategy can take many forms, but one version would work as follows. We would take a sample of persons living on reservations or in concentrated areas. In each case, we would obtain a list of designated relatives, perhaps parents, grown children, and siblings. Addresses would be obtained for each of these designated persons, and a subset of those living in places other than where area sampling was used would be added to the sample. We would need to be careful to account for differential probabilities of sampling. If we included all relatives in the sample, a person with six designated relatives living in "Native areas" would have a higher chance of selection than a person with one such relative. Judicious subsampling, fastidious record keeping, and high-quality interviews providing the correct list of relatives and their addresses would be needed for multiplicity sampling to work well.

The proposed strategy has several disadvantages: (1) careful interviewing is sometimes difficult to maintain; (2) it would be difficult to obtain an equal probability sample given the variation in the numbers of living relatives; (3) even if we kept careful records, the costs of traveling to and interviewing those living away from concentrations of eligible persons would still be high; (4) Native Americans and Alaska Natives with no relatives living in the designated areas would be left out of the survey; and (5) interviewing so many relatives of persons already interviewed would increase sampling errors because the clusters of selected relatives would be more similar to each other than two randomly selected respondents would be, increasing the "design effects" due to cluster sampling and thus decreasing the efficiency of the sample.

CONCLUDING REMARKS

Both area sampling supplemented by lists and multiplicity sampling are complex and risky procedures. They have the potential to limit the biases due to omitting Native persons living away from areas of population concentration, but increase cost as well as risk. Since the bias is not eliminated entirely and since the question of how to define the population of concern remains ambiguous, it is not obvious that the advantages are worth the added cost and risk.

Given the diversity of the Native American and Alaska Native cultures, the sparse distribution of their populations, problems in identifying the population of concern, and the varying objectives of different surveys, no one sampling plan will suffice for all surveys. Rather than trying to devise such a plan, it may be more useful to indicate some of the key decisions the survey taker must make.

One is to decide whether to use list or area sampling. List sampling simplifies many aspects of the survey as the population is readily defined to be list members; addresses are given; and, as was the case in the Strong Heart Study, we can select large enough samples from each list to permit explicit comparisons of cultural groups. The major disadvantage of the list sampling approach is that unlisted persons are omitted, and most persons identifying as Native American or Alaska Native on the 1990 census are not included on any tribal roll.

The second decision is how to identify the population of concern. One choice is including persons on tribal lists, as was done by the SAIAN and the Strong Heart Study. This has the advantage of providing a clear definition, but excludes many people who may be of concern to meet the study goals. The alternative to this approach is self-identification, including either those who select Native American or Alaska Native from a list of proffered racial alternatives or those who say "yes" when asked if they have Native ancestry. On the other hand, self-identification involves problems of unreliability; for example, people who identify with a particular race on one survey may not do so again when offered the same choice at a later date. The approach will lead to an enlarged Native population, but this will be an advantage only if Native persons not included on tribal lists really matter to the study.

A third decision is how to define subgroups of interest. Explicit tribal comparisons must be limited in number for any survey with a small enough sample to be accomplished within a budget that would be realistic for most studies. As discussed before, this is a decision for substantive experts, and unless individual tribes are to be compared, the grouping of similar tribes will presumably be based on geographic, economic, or cultural similarities.

All of these decisions are conditioned in part by the need to define the population of interest. The population of persons included on tribal rolls and served by an agency such as the IHS is much smaller than the population of persons identifying as American Indian on a survey. It seems reasonable to advise that before good decisions can be made on the three issues just identified, study directors must decide whether to focus on persons included on a tribal list or those who identify as Native American or Alaska Native.

REFERENCES

Beals, J., E.M. Keane, and S.M. Manson,
   1994   Population Studies of Older American Indians and Alaska Natives. Unpublished paper. National Center for American Indian and Alaska Native Mental Health Research, Denver, CO.
Cunningham, P.J.
   1995   Health Care Access, Utilization and Expenditures for American Indians and Alaska Natives Eligible for the Indian Health Service. Unpublished paper presented at the National Academy of Sciences workshop on the Demography of American Indians and Alaska Natives, May 22-23.
Davis, J.A., and J.W. Smith
   1993   *General Social Surveys (1972-1993): Cumulative Codebook.*   Chicago, IL: National Opinion Research Center.
Ericksen, E.P.
   1976   Sampling a rare population: A case study. *Journal of the American Statistical Association* 71:816-822.
Ericksen, E.P., ed.
   1985   *The State of Puerto Rican Philadelphia.*   Philadelphia, PA: Institute for Public Policy Studies, Temple University.
Eschbach, K., and K. Supple
   1995   Employment, Household Structure, and the Health Insurance Coverage of American Indians, whites and blacks. Unpublished paper presented at the National Academy of Sciences workshop on the Demography of American Indians and Alaska Natives, May 22-23.
Lee, E.T., T.K. Welty, R.R. Fabsitz, L.D. Cowan, A.L. Ngoc, A.J. Oopik, A.J. Cucciara, P.J. Savage, and B.V. Howard
   1990   The strong heart study—A study of cardiovascular disease in American Indians: Design and methods. *American Journal of Epidemiology* 132:6, 1141-1155.
Passel, J.
   1976   Provisional evaluation of the 1970 census count of American Indians. *Demography* 13:398-409.
   1991   Demographic Analysis: A Report on Its Utility for Adjusting the 1990 Census. Unpublished paper submitted to U.S. Secretary of Commerce Robert Mosbacher. (June).
Stoddart, M.K., B. Jarvis, B. Blake, R.R. Fabsitz, B.V. Howard, E.T. Lee, and T.K. Welty.
   no   Recruitment of American Indians in Epidemiologic Research: The Strong Heart
   date   Study. Unpublished paper, Center for Epidemiologic Research, Oklahoma City, OK.
U.S. Bureau of the Census
   1970   *1970 Census of Population: Characteristics of the Population.* Volume 1. Washington, D.C.: U.S. Bureau of the Census.
   1979   Coverage of the Hispanic population in the 1970 census. *Current Population Reports*, Series P-23, No. 82. Washington, D.C.: U.S. Department of Commerce.
   1990   1990 census of population, supplementary reports, detailed ancestry groups for states. (1990 CP-S-1-2) Series 1-2. Washington, D.C.: U.S. Department of Commerce.

1993a *Statistical Abstract of the United States: 1993* (113th edition). Washington, D.C.: U.S. Department of Commerce.

1993b *Current Population Reports, P25: U.S. Population Estimates, by Age, Race, & Hispanic Origin: 1980 to 1991.* Washington, D.C.: U.S. Department of Commerce.

Yancey, W.L., E.P. Ericksen, and R.L. Juliani

1976 Emergent ethnicity: A review and reformulation. *American Sociological Review* 41:391-403.

III

Social and Economic Conditions

7

The Individual Economic Well-Being of Native American Men and Women During the 1980s: A Decade of Moving Backwards

Robert G. Gregory, Annie C. Abello, and Jamie Johnson

INTRODUCTION

The decade of the 1980s was one of the best ever for U.S. employment growth. Between 1979 and 1989, the employment-population ratio increased from 59.9 to 63.0 percent to reach the highest level since World War II. A commonly noted characteristic of the U.S. and other wealthy economies is that when job opportunities grow quickly, the least skilled and those who are disadvantaged in labor markets are able to do better (Okun, 1973). There is a strong up-draft effect. Low hourly earnings tend to increase relative to the median, and unemployment falls. Native Americans have always been disadvantaged in the labor market, and on the basis of aggregate job growth over the 1980s, their economic position should have improved.

The 1980s, however, were unusual. Despite strong job growth, the labor market conditions for low-skilled, low-paid men deteriorated. Real hourly earnings and employment fell (Katz and Murphy, 1992; Freeman and Katz, 1994). In such an environment, it might be thought that Native American men would fare badly. They tend to be overrepresented among the unskilled and have always found it difficult to find employment. In addition, the U.S. government reduced income support for Native American people during most of the period, and this, too, must have affected Native American incomes (Levitan and Miller, 1991). It is an interesting question whether, on balance, the income opportunities of Native Ameri-

Thanks to E. Klug for providing excellent research support.

133

can men improved in response to stronger aggregate job growth or deteriorated in response to the declining income opportunities of the less skilled and reduced government support.

The employment growth of the 1980s particularly favored women; their share of total employment increased from 41.7 to 45.2 percent. They, too, were subject to a widening hourly earnings and income gap between those with labor market skills and those with less education and labor market experience. However, by 1989, white women from all parts of the income distribution had moved up the income ladder relative to men. Another issue, therefore, is whether Native American women shared in these gains.

This paper is organized as follows. The next section reviews in broad terms the change in the ratio of the means of individual Native American and white incomes. The story is clear, stark, and generally depressing. At the beginning of the 1980s, the average income of a Native American male was just 62.5 percent of the average white male income. By the end of the decade, the income ratio had fallen to 54.4 percent. There is a similar story for women. At the beginning of the 1980s, Native American women reported incomes that were on average 77.0 percent of white female incomes. By 1989, the ratio had fallen to 69.8 percent. In economic terms, one of the most disadvantaged groups in the United States moved backwards.

The third section of the paper examines the components of the income ratio change in terms of changes in annual earnings, annual hours worked, and earnings per hour. Native Americans have lost ground on all dimensions, but the greatest losses have been in terms of earnings per hour, followed by annual hours worked.

The fourth section presents estimates-of-income equations for Native Americans and whites, which are the counterparts to human capital hourly earning equations. These equations summarize quite well the different outcomes for Native Americans and whites and enable us to focus on the effects of education, experience, marital status, and location on the shifting income relationship between the two groups. The fifth section then applies the same model to explain the income shifts in terms of changes in annual hours worked and earnings per hour.

The sixth section draws some of the threads of the discussion together, while the last offers concluding comments.

A SIMPLE METHOD OF ANALYSIS AND
DATA PRESENTATION

The data for this analysis are drawn from the 5 percent public-use sample from the 1980 and 1990 U.S. censuses and include all respondents who identified as white[1] or Indian (American) in response to the race question. Native American people are a small proportion of the U.S. population—approximately 0.5 percent—but their population is increasing quickly as a result of high fertility levels, declining death rates, reduced underenumeration in census collections, and increased self-identification.[2] Note that in the present discussion, we do not address the issues that arise from increased self-identification and from the economic, social, regional, and tribal diversity of different groups of Native Americans.

We begin with the income data, which represent aggregate annual income from all sources as reported by men and women aged 16-64 in the calendar years of 1979 and 1989. The data are often presented as the ratio of the means of the individual incomes of Native Americans and whites. The income ratio is a summary measure incorporating Native American-white differences in employment rates, hours of work, hourly earnings, welfare payments, and other income. We prefer to work with an income ratio in the first instance, even though hourly earnings is the usual focus of economic analysis. The income ratio is a better measure of well-being as it includes income from all sources and the effects of different employment rates.

To help in understanding why average income is so different for Native Americans and whites and why the income ratio changed over the decade, the first method of analysis proceeds in two steps. The method is rather mechanical, but it provides a useful technique for focusing on aggregate changes, describing the data, and assessing the effects of changes in income dispersion on the mean income ratio. The changing economic circumstances of Native Americans have not been extensively analyzed, and it is useful to spend some time on basic summary statistics. The method is supplemented by a more detailed analysis in the next section.

The method is described in the context of the male income ratio. The first step is to determine the *position* of Native American men on the white male income distribution ladder. That position will depend on individual

---

[1]White includes white Hispanics.

[2]Changing levels of self-identification and underenumeration in the census illustrate that population definition is a complex issue (Snipp, 1989:Chapter 3). The population of Native Americans, as measured by the U.S. census, increased 79 percent over the decade 1969-1979. About 60 percent of this growth is attributable to either increased self-identification on the census form or inadequate correction for underregistration of Native American births (Passel and Berman, 1986). Over the decade 1979-1989, the Native American population increased a further 38 percent. Very little is known as to whether the increased self-identification imparts a bias to income and employment statistics. Our best guess is that for our purposes, the bias is small, but such a guess is based on little information.

human capital characteristics, such as education and labor market experience, and the rate of return to those characteristics. Thus, on average, Native American men may be lower down the white income ladder because their average human capital characteristics are lower relative to whites or because their human capital delivers a lower rate of return.

The second step is to determine the change in income *compression*, that is, the extent to which the white male income distribution ladder changes over the period. Other things being equal, the average income of those at the bottom of the income ladder will fall relative to white mean income if the income distribution among whites becomes less compressed. The change in the white income ladder can be thought of as a summary measure of economy-wide influences on income compression.

More formally, we proceed as follows. White males at each date are ranked by reported income levels and the population divided into deciles. Native American men are then placed in each of these deciles according to their income. Then the income ratio, $\overline{Y}^I / \overline{Y}^W$, is written as the sum of ten terms, each the product of three components, where superscripts I and W represent indigenous (Native American) and white, respectively.

$$\overline{Y}^I / \overline{Y}^W = \sum_{i=1}^{10} \Pi_i \Phi_i \, \overline{X}_i^W / \overline{\overline{X}}^W \tag{1}$$

The first two components are used to provide measures of the position of indigenous men on the white income ladder; Π_i is the proportion of indigenous men whose income falls in the ith white income decile, and Φ_i is the ratio of the indigenous to the white male income mean within each white income decile $\overline{X}_i^I / \overline{X}_i^W$. The third component, $\overline{X}_i^W / \overline{X}_i^W$, measures white male mean income in each decile as a ratio of the overall white male mean income and is used to calculate income compression.

Applying the above method, we find that in 1979, 19.1 percent of Native American men aged 16-64 received income that placed them in the same income range as the bottom decile of the white male income distribution (column 1 of Table 7-1). At the other end of the income ladder, 3.5 percent of Native Americans were in the same income bracket as the top 10 percent of white males. Native American men are disproportionately concentrated at the bottom of the income ladder and underrepresented at the top.

By 1989, the ladder position of Native American men had further deteriorated (column 2 of Table 7-1). The proportion of Native American men in the top decile of the white distribution had fallen 25 percent, while the proportion in the bottom decile had increased 13 percent. Native American men lost income because they slipped down the income ladder.

TABLE 7-1 Percentage of Native American Men and White and Native American Women Classified by White Male Income Deciles, 1979 and 1989 (percent)

White Male Income Deciles	Male Native Americans		Female White Americans		Female Native Americans	
	1979	1989	1979	1989	1979	1989
1st	19.1	21.6	32.8	24.6	36.2	30.0
2nd	16.0	17.2	18.4	18.0	21.7	23.7
3rd	14.9	14.8	16.0	14.9	17.9	17.3
4th	13.7	11.5	14.0	12.3	12.1	11.1
5th	8.7	9.4	7.9	9.8	5.6	7.0
6th	7.3	7.1	4.8	7.3	2.9	4.4
7th	6.3	6.2	2.7	5.3	1.7	3.0
8th	5.6	5.2	1.7	3.8	1.0	1.9
9th	4.9	4.3	1.0	2.4	0.6	1.1
10th	3.5	2.6	0.7	1.5	0.3	0.4

SOURCE: Census of Population and Housing 1980 and 1990. Public Use Microdata Sample (5 percent).

In 1979, the Native American male with median income was positioned opposite a white male ranked at the 30th percentile. By 1989, the Native American male with median income had shifted to the 27th percentile of the white distribution.

The combined effect of position on the income ladder and compression determines the income ratio, which is presented in Table 7-2. The entries along each diagonal are the actual income ratios in 1979 and 1989. Thus the row 1, column 1 entry is the 1979 actual male income ratio, 62.5. The off-diagonal term is a hypothetical income ratio that allows us to determine the effects of ladder and compression changes. Row 2, column 1 places Native American and white males in their 1989 ladder position and calculates the income ratio this would produce at the 1979 level of income compression. Thus, if income compression had not changed, the income ratio would have fallen from 62.5 to 57.4 percent. Native Americans lost 5.1 percentage points of relative income because they slipped down the white ladder. The remaining change from 57.4 to 54.4 percent is the result of the changed compression of the white income ladder. Native Americans lost 3.0 percentage points because the income distribution of whites widened.

The slip down the ladder accounts for two-thirds of the decline in the income ratio.[3] This suggests that influences particular to Native Ameri-

---

[3]This assumes that ladder positions and compression are independent.

TABLE 7-2 Native American and White Income Ratios, 1979 and 1989

Income Compression

Ladder Position	Native American Men/White Men		White Women/ White Men		Native American Women/White Men		Native American Women/White Women		Native American Women/ Native American Men	
	1979	1989	1979	1989	1979	1989	1979	1989	1979	1989
1. 1979	62.5		35.8		28.3		77.0		45.2	
2. 1989	57.4	54.4	49.0	45.4	34.2	31.7	69.7	69.8	59.5	58.2

cans are more important than the general influences that were changing the degree of compression of the white income distribution. Even after accounting for growing inequality in the United States, there is a large Native American relative income decline that needs to be accounted for.

Columns 3 and 4 of Table 7-1 document the large move up the white male income ladder that occurred among white females over the 1979-1989 decade. The proportion of white women who received income in the top decile of the white male income distribution increased from 0.7 to 1.5 percent, while the proportion in the bottom decile decreased from 32.8 to 24.6 percent. In 1979, the white woman who received median income for her group was placed at the 19th percentile of the white male distribution; by 1989, her ranking had moved up to the 25th percentile.

Native American women also made gains. Columns 5 and 6 indicate that although they occupied the lowest ladder positions, they, too, unlike Native American men, moved up the ladder. The proportion of Native American women who received income in the top decile of the white male income distribution increased from 0.3 to 0.4 percent, while the proportion in the bottom decile fell from 36.2 to 30.0 percent.

Columns 3 to 6 of Table 7-2 apply our simple technique to white and Native American women. For both groups, the move up the white male ladder increased their income relative to white males by a significant amount: from 35.8 to 49.0 for white women (row 1, column 3 to row 2, column 3) and from 28.3 to 34.2 for Native American women (row 1, column 5 to row 2, column 5). As remarked earlier, Native American women have made significant strides up the white male income ladder, especially when compared with Native American men, who slipped in ladder position.

Both white and Native American women are still disproportionately positioned in the bottom half of the white male income ladder. They gained income from moving up the ladder relative to white males during the period, but the widening income distribution of the white male income ladder took some of those gains away. The size of these losses is quite significant: 49.0 to 45.4 for white women and 34.2 to 31.7 for Native American women. The change in the income ratio therefore understates quite considerably the gains women made relative to men in similar circumstances to themselves at the beginning of the decade. Women have been making economic progress, but this has been hampered because they have been "swimming upstream" against the increased inequality of the 1980s (Blau and Kahn, 1994).

Columns 7 and 8 of Table 7-2 describe the position of Native American women relative to their white counterparts. The Native American-white female income ratio was 77.0 in 1979, but had fallen to 69.8 by 1989. Although Native American women made significant gains relative to white men, they did not keep pace with white women. Columns 9 and 10 of Table 7-2 show the change for Native American women relative to Native American men. Native American women made income gains of 28.8 percent relative to Native American men, a gain similar to that made by white women relative to white men. The economic balance is shifting between the genders as women of both groups are increasing their income share.

ANNUAL INCOME, ANNUAL EARNINGS, ANNUAL HOURS WORKED, AND HOURLY EARNINGS

The decline in the annual income ratio could come from many sources. A comparison of rows 1 and 2 of Table 7-3 allows us to apportion the income ratio change to employment and nonemployment income, and a comparison of rows 3 and 4 then enables us to apportion the change in employment earnings into the change in annual hours worked and average earnings per hour employed.[4] Each of the variables for Native Americans and whites—annual income, annual earnings, annual hours worked, and average earnings per hour—is divided by its respective working-age population, aged 16-64; the individual means of both groups are then expressed as a ratio. We also include the employment-population ratio at the time of the census (row 5) and the proportion of the population employed some time during the year (row 6).

The lower annual income of Native American men arises from all three sources: lower income from nonemployment, fewer hours worked per year, and lower average earnings per hour. Native American and white men receive the same proportion of their income (8 percent) from nonemployment sources, and consequently the income ratio (row 1) and the earnings ratio (row 2) are approximately the same. Within the employment income category, the lower income for Native men is accounted for in roughly equal proportions between fewer hours worked per year and lower average earnings per hour. During 1979, Native American men worked 23 percent fewer hours during the year and were paid, on average, 19 percent less per hour.

The proportions of earned and nonearned income are slightly different for women. Native American women received 16 percent of their 1979 income from nonemployment sources; for white women, the ratio is

---

[4]It is noticeable that the total income ratio is lower than the ratios in each education category. This occurs because Native Americans are disproportionately represented in the low-income, low-education groups; see Appendix Tables 1 and 3 for the original data.

a little less, at 14 percent. The difference between the income and earnings ratio therefore is quite small, 2 to 3 percentage points.

The largest differences in income between white and Native American women also arise within the employment income category. Relative to their white counterparts, Native American women were employed in the labor market for 16 percent fewer hours per year and in 1979 received hourly earnings that were 11 percent less. As with men, the largest difference between Native American and white women is annual hours worked, rather than earnings per hour.

We now turn to our primary concern, the change in the income ratio over the decade. There has been no change in the relationship between male income and earnings ratios and only a marginal shift for women. Therefore, the income ratio change between 1979 and 1989 arises almost completely from changes in annual hours worked and hourly earnings, rather than changes in nonemployment income. For both groups, the decline in relative earnings is more important.

The data in Table 7-3 suggest that to explain changes in the income ratio, we should focus our attention on annual hours worked and earnings per hour and not on income from nonemployment. Since annual earnings, annual hours, and earnings per hour are linked by an identity, we could estimate equations for two variables and combine them to explain changes in the third. Alternatively, we could fit equations to explain all three variables and ignore the relationship between them.

It seemed best to estimate an income equation consistent with the data of Tables 7-1 and 7-2; this we do in the next section. Then in the following section, we estimate equations for individual earnings per hour and annual hours worked. The advantage of this approach is that parameter estimates and their significance levels can be directly observed for all variables.

There remains the question of model choice. We could have emphasized locational aspects, industry, and occupation of employment, but chose a simple methodology that seemed particularly appropriate given the paucity of economic research on the determinants of Native American income, employment, and earnings. We adopted a human capital model that stresses the role of education and labor market experience and, in the interest of parsimony, puts aside industry and occupation of employment.[5] The models also use the same explanatory variables in each equation. We see this as an advantage as it consistently maps simple relationships that may point to relevant directions for the future.

---

[5]This is obviously a simplification. It is not difficult to show there are industry and occupational effects on wages over and above the effects of human capital characteristics (see Dickens and Katz, 1987).

TABLE 7-3 Income, Earnings, Annual Hours, Hourly Earnings, and
Employment/Population Native American-White Ratios, 1979 and 1989

| | 1979 | | | | |
	No High School	High School	Some College	College	Total
Men					
Income	0.67	0.70	0.77	0.75	0.62
Earnings	0.67	0.71	0.77	0.74	0.62
Annual Hrs	0.75	0.81	0.88	0.91	0.77
Hrly Earnings	0.89	0.88	0.87	0.82	0.81
Emp/pop 1	0.75	0.83	0.88	0.93	0.78
Emp/pop 2	0.89	0.93	0.95	0.97	0.89
Women					
Income	0.82	0.89	0.94	0.97	0.77
Earnings	0.75	0.90	0.95	1.02	0.75
Annual Hours	0.80	0.94	1.03	1.08	0.84
Hourly Earnings	0.93	0.96	0.92	0.95	0.89
Emp/pop I	0.79	0.92	0.96	1.00	0.82
Emp/pop 2	0.91	0.99	1.03	1.04	0.90

NOTES: All ratios computed based on mean values for working-age population
(aged 16-64). See Appendix Table 1 for base data.

Income	= earnings + unearned income
Earnings	= hourly earnings × annual hours
Annual Hours	= weeks worked in the year × usual hours worked per week

THE INCOME EQUATION

A fuller development of the human capital model is found in Mincer
(1974). But very briefly, the model explains individual hourly earnings in
terms of formal education, labor force experience, and family attributes.
When undertaking formal education, the student forgoes contemporane-
ous earnings in the labor market, which are thought of as an investment
that subsequently receives a rate of return. It is the return to this investment that leads to higher income for workers with more education.

With respect to the relationship between earnings and labor force
experience, workers are thought of as investing in on-the-job training, for
which they receive lower earnings when they are young; the gap between
the lower earnings per hour during on-the-job training and the alternative market wage is further investment in human capital. More-experi-

1989					Percent Change 1979-1989				
No High School	High School	Some College	College	Total	No High School	High School	Some College	College	Total
0.67	0.64	0.70	0.68	0.55	1	−8	−9	−9	−12
0.67	0.65	0.70	0.68	0.55	0	−8	−10	−9	−12
0.75	0.77	0.86	0.90	0.74	0	−5	−3	−1	−3
0.89	0.85	0.81	0.76	0.73	0	−4	−7	−8	−9
0.73	0.81	0.87	0.94	0.77	−2	−2	−1	1	−1
0.86	0.92	0.93	0.96	0.88	−4	−1	−2	−1	−1
0.84	0.80	0.85	0.90	0.70	4	−10	−10	−8	−9
0.74	0.77	0.84	0.91	0.67	−1	−14	−11	−11	−10
0.78	0.86	0.94	1.03	0.81	−3	−8	−9	−4	−4
0.95	0.90	0.90	0.89	0.83	2	−6	−3	−7	−7
0.75	0.86	0.92	1.00	0.81	−5	−6	−5	1	−1
0.85	0.94	0.97	1.00	0.88	−6	−5	−6	−4	−3

Hourly Earnings = annual earnings/annual hours
Emp/pop 1 = no. of employed/population
Emp/pop 2 = no. employed anytime within the year/population

enced workers receive higher wages than those less experienced, part of which is a return to earlier investment. On-the-job training leads to a positive slope of the experience-earnings profile until the depreciation of human capital (represented by a quadratic or nonlinear component) begins to dominate the returns to investment, and the experience-earnings profile peaks and then declines.

Finally, family variables, such as marital status, are included in the model. The link between these variables and human capital is not usually developed in any detail. Family variables can be thought of as reflecting motivation in the labor market and willingness to invest in on-the-job training (which is typically not measured in these data sets) and serving as proxies for interrupted labor force experience (which is also not measured in these data sets).

A similar human capital analysis can be applied to decisions to seek employment and to choose hours of work. Those who are better educated and have more labor force experience are likely to receive higher hourly earnings/wages and, in the absence of any significant income effects, to participate more in the labor market and work longer hours. Employment and hours decisions should reinforce human capital effects on hourly earnings, and as a result, the returns to education and labor market experience in the income equation should be larger than in the hourly earnings equation.

To estimate the model, we add white and Native American income equations together as

$$E_i = \sum_{j=1}^{k} B_j X_{ij} + \sum_{j=1}^{k} G_j^I X_{ij}^I + U_i. \tag{2}$$

where E_i is the log of the income of the ith person, and X_j are formal education, labor force experience, family variables, and location of all individuals. We refer to the values of the X variables as characteristics. The superscript I refers to Native Americans. Consequently, white males earn B_j for each attribute and Native Americans $(B_j + G_j)$. U_i is an error term.

Results for 1979 and 1989 of fitting equation (2) to men aged 16-64 with real annual income of at least \$500 are given in columns 1 and 2 of Table 7-4. The constant term measures the average log of income of a white male who completed high school, has never been married, and lives outside a metropolitan area. Other coefficients are interpreted as percent changes in income in response to a one-unit increase in the value of the independent variable. Those variables without a Native American superscript estimate the additional pay-off for white men over and above the constant term. Thus, an estimate of average income of a white male college graduate, with all other attributes included in the constant term, is given by addition of the constant term to the estimated coefficient, B, attached to the degree variable. The estimated income of a Native American college graduate, with all the other attributes of the constant term, is given by the addition of the constant term to the sum of the degree coefficients B and G. By presenting the data in this way, the t-statistics for the G's indicate whether Native American coefficients are significantly different from white coefficients. Definitions of variables are given in Appendix Table 2.

Each of the major propositions derived from human capital theory holds very well in the income equations, and coefficient estimates reflect what might be expected of a human capital model. The male income equations explain between 37.6 and 40.3 percent of the variance of the log of income.

Consider first the education results for white males. Additional education is associated with additional income, and the coefficients exhibit a high degree of statistical significance. The average income penalty for a white male from not completing high school in 1979 is a 38.5 percent loss of income relative to a white male who completes high school. The average income gain to completing a college degree relative to completing high school is 45.2 percent.[6]

In 1979, Native American men of all education categories received less income than whites. There are two noticeable features. First, although more education is associated with higher income among Native American men, in much the same way as for white men, there is a considerable mark-down in each education category, ranging from 20.5 to 27.1 percent. Second, the process of acquiring more education does not narrow the income gap within each education category. Obtaining a college degree rather than not completing high school does not move the income of a Native American closer to that of his white counterpart in the higher education category.

From 1979 to 1989, the income returns to education for whites increased markedly. Returns to a college degree holder relative to those who completed high school increased from a premium of 45.2 to 63.4 percent. The return to those who failed to complete high school relative to those who completed high school fell from –38.5 to –47.5 percent. The Native American mark-downs across education levels increased marginally in two of the education groups, but fell for those who did not complete high school. These changes, however, did not offset those among whites, and thus the widening returns to education among whites extended to Native Americans. The average additional income to a Native American from completing a college degree relative to completing high school increased from 38.7 to 60.6 percent.[7] A given dispersion of education qualifications among Native American men became associated with a greater dispersion of income, not primarily because of changes specific to Native American education, but as a result of general influences in the economy.

We now turn to the labor force experience-income profiles. The slope of the experience-income profile is positive over most white age groups.

---

[6]Our interpretation of these coefficients is an approximation. The percentage change in income as a dummy variable changes from zero to unity is e^x-1. This transformation, however, has a negligible effect on the coefficients of Tables 7-4, 7-5, and 7-6, with the possible exception of the marital status variable in the income equation. The estimated coefficient for the 1979 married white male is 55.2 percent. The adjusted coefficient is 73.7 percent.

[7]The additional returns to a Native American man from moving from high school completion to college degree completion in 1979 are given as 45.2 - 27.1 + 20.6 = 38.7. For 1989, the ratio is 63.4 – 26.8 + 24.0 = 60.6.

TABLE 7-4 Native American and White Income Equations, 1979 and 1989

Explanatory Variable	Men		Women	
	1979	1989	1979	1989
Constant	8.418 (1480.9)	8.254 (1985.7)	8.185 (1099.5)	8.042 (1585.6)
Education				
No high school	-0.385 (-89.7)	-0.475 (-151.8)	-0.325(-60.2)	-0.417(-106.2)
Some college	0.126 (27.7)	0.158 (53.7)	0.145 (26.6)	0.223 (66.6)
College degree	0.452 (98.5)	0.634 (203.2)	0.470 (74.7)	0.693 (178.4)
NA × no high school	-0.240 (-12.2)	-0.182 (-12.2)	-0.252 (-9.9)	-0.138 (-7.9)
NA × high school	-0.206 (-10.5)	-0.240 (-16.5)	-0.124 (-5.0)	-0.134 (-7.9)
NA × some college	-0.205 (-9.2)	-0.241 (-15.0)	-0.100 (-3.7)	-0.108 (-6.0)
NA × college degree	-0.271 (-9.4)	-0.268 (-12.3)	-0.069 (-1.9)	-0.061 (-2.5)
Experience				
Experience	0.076 (159.8)	0.078 (222.4)	0.060(105.1)	0.066 (165.1)
Experience squared	-0.001(-134.3)	-0.001 (-182.3)	-0.001(-90.7)	-0.001(-144.5)
NA × experience	-0.005 (-2.5)	-0.013 (-9.2)	0.011 (4.7)	0.000[a] (-0.2)
NA × experience sqd.	0.000[b] (0.1)	0.000[c] (6.7)	0.000[d](-5.2)	0.000[e] (0.8)

Marital Status			
Married	0.552 (116.1)	0.474 (147.0)	-0.062 (-10.3)	-0.028 (-6.9)
Other married	0.289 (41.4)	0.191 (41.6)	0.217 (30.1)	0.189 (39.4)
NA × married	0.040 (2.1)	0.087 (6.7)	0.122 (5.1)	0.010 (0.6)
NA × other married	-0.002 (-0.1)	0.047 (2.8)	-0.047 (-1.7)	-0.122 (-6.9)
Location				
Metropolitan area	0.120 (27.3)	0.195 (64.2)	0.194 (34.0)	0.244 (66.7)
NA × metropolitan area	0.066 (4.7)	0.050 (5.0)	-0.085 (4.8)	-0.032 (-2.8)
R-squared	0.376	0.403	0.158	0.224
Sample Size				
Native American	13,863	29,047	11,481	27,296
White	229,971	509,191	183,713	433,746

NOTES: T-statistics are given in parentheses next to coefficients. Sample includes those aged 16-64 with real annual income > $500 (1982-1984 prices). See Appendix Table 2 for definitions and Appendix Table 3 for variable means.

[a] 0.0004
[b] 0.00001
[c] 0.00021
[d] 0.00027
[e] 0.00003.

Experience is measured as age minus years of schooling minus 6. The coefficient for 1979 indicates a 7.6 percent increase in log income for each additional year of male labor force experience and a nonlinear component of –0.001 percent, which implies that the experience-income profile peaks at 30 years of labor force experience.

For 1979, there is a statistically significant but slight difference in the experience-income profile of whites and Native Americans. By 1989, however, there are substantial adjustments to be made to the white experience-income profile to represent the experience-income relationship for Native Americans. The relationship for Native Americans has become flatter. Native American males in the middle age groups did not share in the income increases that accrued to whites.

Family variables are also important and exert slightly different influences across the two groups. Married white men received income well above that of never-married men, as did the group other married, which includes those divorced, widowed, or separated. A similar marriage premium is observed among Native American men, but the additional income is a little higher. Among Native Americans, a married man, *ceteris paribus*, received 59.2 percent more income than an unmarried man. There was little change in these relationships over the decade for Native Americans, but it does appear that the marriage premium among whites may have fallen.

Finally, other things being equal, white males who resided in metropolitan areas received on average 12.0 percent more income than those in rural areas. The premium for Native American males is larger at 18.6 percent in 1979.

These results suggest a number of tentative conclusions, which will be examined in more detail later. First, the very large and consistent mark-downs associated with the Native American education variables suggest that there is some uniform determinant of Native American income that is missing from these equations. The model explains reasonably well the variance in income among Native Americans, but does not do that well in explaining the income gap between Native American and white men. The 20.5 to 27.1 percent education mark-down in 1979 is essentially operating as a Native American dummy variable in the equation, explaining approximately two-thirds of the income gap. The second point is that the widening of the income dispersion among white and Native American males is clearly evident in the increased dispersion of the income returns to education. On average, Native Americans have less education than whites, and as a result their relative income will fall.

Columns 3 and 4 of Table 7-4 present the regression results for women. The equations have considerably less explanatory power for women than for men. This is probably because the proxy for labor force experience is less satisfactory, as women may spend considerably more time out of the labor force.[8]

Among white women, higher education levels are strongly associated with higher income, in much the same manner as for males. Once again there was a significant widening of the rate of return to education over the decade. The return to a college degree relative to completing high school increased from 47.0 to 69.3 percent.

Native American women also gain extra income from additional education, but it is notable that in every education category, the mark-down for Native Americans is again large, ranging in 1979 from 25.2 percent for those who did not complete high school to 6.9 percent for a college degree holder. Among Native American women, the mark-down falls as the education level increases. Among Native American men, the mark-down is not consistently related to education categories. Higher education levels narrow the income gap between white and Native American women, but leave the gap among men unchanged. In the next section, we attempt to determine whether the difference arises from the hourly earnings or the average hours equation.

The experience-income profile for white women is flatter than that of white men, but both the linear and quadratic terms are significant for 1979. The white women's experience-income profile does not significantly change over the decade. The profile for Native American women is not the same as for whites. It is considerably steeper for 1979, suggesting that this may be an important contributor to the income gap, but it is not significantly different from that of whites for 1989.[9]

The metropolitan area premium for white women is larger than that for men, and it increases between 1979 and 1989, whereas for Native American men and women it falls slightly.

The above results suggest that we may have already made significant progress toward understanding the reasons for the change in the income ratio. For men it appears that the economy-wide changes in the income returns to education are likely to be more important than any change in the Native American-white return within each education category. It is more difficult to conjecture as to the effects of the other variables. We now turn to the analysis of annual hours and average earnings.

---

[8] There are methods that can be used to attempt to estimate a better proxy for labor force experience, but they do not work particularly well.

[9] There are differences in the Native American-white relationships between marital status and income. The marital status variables indicate that white married women received 6.2 percent less income than single women in 1979 and 2.8 percent less in 1989. The income loss associated with marriage fell. In 1979, a married Native American woman received 6.0 percent more than a single Native American woman, while in 1989 the loss was 1.8 percent.

EQUATIONS FOR HOURLY EARNINGS AND
ANNUAL HOURS WORKED

To summarize the relationships between hourly earnings and human capital variables, we adopt identical equations to those fitted to the annual income data. Columns 1 and 2 of Table 7-5 list the results for 1979 and 1989 earnings per hour for men aged 16-64 who reported positive employment earnings.

The qualitative results for whites are similar to those from the income equation discussed earlier and from hourly earnings equations found in other studies (Murphy and Welch, 1992; Juhn et al., 1993), and we will not spend too much time on detailed description of those results here. For white men, there are positive relationships between hourly earnings and education and hourly earnings and labor force experience. There was also an increase in the hourly earnings return to education over the 1979-1989 period. The return to a college degree relative to high school completion increased from 38.1 to 53.1 percent. The reduction in hourly earnings from not completing relative to completing high school increased from 20.6 to 25.8 percent.

The data presented above in Table 7-3 show that on average, the hourly earnings of Native American men are 10-12 percent below those of whites. When other factors such as location, age, and marital status are taken into account, as in the regression equations reported in Table 7-5, this relationship changes, and Native American men, in all except the college degree category, receive higher earnings per hour than their white counterparts. There is a positive education premium for Native American men. Thus in 1979, *ceteris paribus*, a never-married Native American man who did not complete high school and who lived outside a metropolitan area earned on average 11.1 percent more per hour than his white counterpart.

The positive education premiums, over and above the white education coefficients, are surprising. For other labor market minorities, such as blacks or women, the education premiums relative to whites are always negative. We have tried different specifications for the hourly earnings equations, and it is clear that the estimated education premiums change as the variables included in the regression change. The key variable seems to be location. If location is excluded from the regression, the education premiums become negative as the contribution of the negative coefficient—NA × metropolitan area—is transferred to the Native American education premiums. If the data are divided into two groups, those who live in cities and those who do not, the hourly earnings premiums are negative and statistically significant for city dwellers and positive (but not generally significant) for non-city dwellers.[10]

Other studies of Native American hourly earnings have found positive education premiums. On the basis of data from the 1976 Survey of Income and Education, Sandefur and Scott (1983) comment that "Indians receive more favorable returns to education and marital status than whites," but they do not investigate the source of this result. We do not pursue this matter further. Our current concern is the exploration of changes in the income ratio over the decade, and the adjustment in the equations to account for location does not affect our conclusions. A complete study of Native American incomes, however, must come to grips with the relationships between location and hourly earnings.[11]

There are changes in the education premiums received by Native Americans over the period, but economy-wide returns (as indicated in the coefficients for whites) dominate and carry over to Native Americans. Thus for Native Americans who have not completed high school, earnings per hour remains much the same relative to earnings per hour for a high school graduate, but earnings per hour for a Native American with a college degree increases from 35.7 to 51.3 percent. As Native Americans are disproportionately represented among the less educated, the increased hourly earnings for more-educated men will ensure that the income ratio falls.

The experience-earnings profile is similar among Native American and white men, and a change in this relationship does not appear to be part of the large income changes that occurred over this period. Finally, for both groups, the marriage premium is declining, but the changes do not affect the income ratio to a significant degree.

The female hourly earnings equations are similar to the male equations. For white women, the return to education widened over the period by much the same amount as for white men. As with Native American men, there are positive education premiums for Native American women for both years, and the education premiums tend to fall as the education level rises. There have been some changes in the premiums by 1989, but they do not offset the changes in the education return for whites. The

---

[10]If the equations are restricted to full-year full-time workers, the coefficients become negative for high school graduates and above and increase with the level of education. These equations are available from the authors. Different equations affect the interpretation of the education coefficients, but they do not affect our conclusions about the factors underlying the changes in the income ratio.

[11]Some studies have focused on the different geographical distribution of Native Americans and whites, but they do not address this issue systematically.

TABLE 7-5 Native American and White Hourly Earnings Equations, 1979 and 1989

Explanatory Variable	Men 1979		Men 1989		Women 1979		Women 1989	
Constant	1.500	(308.2)	1.278	(369.4)	1.378	(250.0)	1.199	(327.0)
Education								
No high school	-0.206	(-55.1)	-0.258	(-97.1)	-0.153	(-36.3)	-0.204	(-68.2)
Some college	0.101	(26.2)	0.138	(56.2)	0.130	(32.3)	0.178	(73.0)
College degree	0.381	(97.3)	0.531	(204.4)	0.416	(89.5)	0.573	(204.6)
NA × no high school	0.111	(6.5)	0.163	(12.9)	0.084	(4.3)	0.110	(8.1)
NA × high school	0.064	(3.8)	0.109	(8.9)	0.069	(3.7)	0.047	(3.7)
NA × some college	0.051	(2.6)	0.041	(3.0)	0.032	(1.6)	0.029	(2.2)
NA × college degree	-0.024	(-1.0)	-0.018	(-1.0)	0.035	(1.3)	0.030	(1.7)
Experience								
Experience	0.040	(94.6)	0.043	(142.3)	0.026	(58.8)	0.030	(99.9)
Experience squared	-0.001	(-68.9)	-0.001	(-97.9)	-0.000[a]	(-42.9)	0.000[b]	(-73.4)
NA × experience	-0.002	(-0.9)	-0.002	(-1.9)	0.005	(2.4)	0.002	(1.3)
NA × experience sqd.	-0.000[c]	(-0.1)	0.000[d]	(1.9)	-0.000[e]	(-2.6)	0.000[f]	(-0.7)

Marital Status								
Married	0.216	(52.2)	0.206	(75.5)	0.001	(0.1)	0.020	(6.9)
Other married	0.113	(18.5)	0.071	(18.1)	0.040	(7.1)	0.038	(10.5)
NA × married	-0.055	(-3.3)	-0.086	(-7.7)	-0.026	(-1.4)	-0.024	(-2.1)
NA × other married	-0.040	(-1.8)	-0.057	(-3.8)	-0.042	(-1.9)	-0.043	(-3.1)
Location								
Metropolitan area	0.130	(34.0)	0.174	(67.9)	0.151	(35.1)	0.195	(72.1)
NA × metropolitan area	-0.094	(-7.5)	-0.141	(-16.6)	-0.128	(-9.3)	-0.149	(-17.2)
R-squared	0.218		0.289		0.112		0.194	
Sample Size								
Native American	12,439		26,425		9,548		22,859	
White	213,709		481,847		160,926		395,520	

NOTES: T-statistics are given in parentheses next to coefficients. Sample includes those aged 16-64 with positive annual hours and hourly earnings. See Appendix Table 2 for definitions and Appendix Table 3 for variable means.

[a] 0.00043
[b] 0.00049
[c] 0.00001
[d] -0.00005
[e] -0.00012
[f] 0.00002

change in the rate of return to education among white women has therefore extended to Native American women.

Table 7-6 lists the equations for annual hours employed. Among
white males there is a clear association between education level and hours
worked. In 1979, for example, never-married men who failed to complete
high school and lived in a nonmetropolitan area worked 17.4 percent
fewer hours over the year than high school graduates. Over the decade
there was a widening of the education-hours worked relationship in much
the same way that there was a widening in the education-hourly earnings
relationship. Those with college degrees were working more hours, and
those who did not complete high school were working less.

There is a very large Native American effect on hours worked. Although Native Americans with more education worked more hours than
those with less education, it is noticeable that in all education categories,
Native Americans worked less than their white male counterparts. Never-
married Native Americans who did not complete high school and lived in
a nonmetropolitan area worked 36.8 percent fewer hours than whites
who did not complete high school. Native Americans with a college
degree worked 24.8 percent fewer hours than whites with a degree.

Between 1979 and 1989, the gap in hours worked for whites of different education levels widened. For Native American men there was a
substantial decline in hours worked relative to whites, but this decline
was spread evenly across all education categories. As a result, the change
in the white education-hours relationship extends into the Native American labor market, and there is a wider dispersion of hours worked. There
is also an important location effect on annual hours worked. Native
Americans in metropolitan areas work significantly more hours than Native Americans in nonmetropolitan areas.

Hours of work are influenced by labor market experience. There is a
strong nonlinear relationship so that among men, hours of work increase
with experience, peak at year 26, and then decline. In 1979 there was no
significant difference between whites and Native Americans. By 1989,
however, the relationship had changed so that Native American men
with less experience worked marginally fewer hours than their white
counterparts.[12]

---

[12]Married men work more hours per year than single men, and this is especially so for
Native Americans. The hours gap between married and single whites is narrowing, but
this is not the case for Native Americans. There is no consistent pattern between hours of
work and location for whites. In 1979, white residents of metropolitan areas worked fewer
annual hours than those who lived outside metropolitan areas, but in 1989 the relationship
was reversed. However, Native Americans who live in metropolitan areas work substantially more hours, and the hours gap relative to nonmetropolitan areas has increased.

Columns 3 and 4 of Table 7-6 list the results for women. The responsiveness of hours of work to education levels is greater for women and especially so for Native Americans. More-educated women work more hours. Once again there is a large Native American-white gap in average hours worked, especially among the least educated.

Marriage also affects the two groups differently. Married white women work fewer hours over the year than never-married white women. Native American women work more hours than their never-married counterparts, but the gap is narrowing.

PULLING THE THREADS TOGETHER

We begin by applying Oaxaca decompositions to the income, hourly earnings, and annual hours worked equations (Oaxaca, 1973). This technique can be used to divide the income, hours, and hourly earnings ratio changes between 1979 and 1989 into changes generated by changes in regression coefficients and those generated by changes in characteristics (Table 7-7).

We begin with the income equation for men. First, the income ratio is predicted from the regression equations of each year.[13] Thus, row 1, column 1 and row 2, column 2 list the predicted income ratios from the male income equation for 1979 and 1989, respectively (65 and 59). These ratios indicate an 11 percent decline in the income ratio.[14] The 1979 Native American and white characteristics are then combined with the 1989 regression coefficients to calculate a "hypothetical income ratio" for 1989, row 1, column 2 (60). A comparison of this calculation with the predicted 1989 income ratio will reveal the contribution of the change in characteristics over the decade.

We find that the "hypothetical income ratio" falls over the period by almost the same amount as the ratio predicted from the regression equation (60 and 59). The male income ratio change can therefore be explained by regression coefficient changes and not by the change in the relative human capital characteristics of Native Americans and whites. A comparison of hypothetical and predicted ratios for hours worked and hourly earnings—moving down columns 1 and 2 of Table 7-7—indicates that this

---

[13]We predict income by multiplying the regression coefficients by mean values of the explanatory variables to calculate the predicted log income by race and gender. The ratio of the antilog values is then computed. The income ratios are predicted dollar incomes (or hourly earnings), rather than ratios of the predicted log income (or hourly earnings).

[14]These ratios differ from actual ones because the predicted means of logarithmic equations are not the same as the actual means of the raw data.

TABLE 7-6 Native American and White Annual Hours Equations, 1979 and 1989

Explanatory Variable	Men		Women	
	1979	1989	1979	1989
Constant	6.813 (1372.6)	6.801 (1910.0)	6.607 (808.2)	6.614 (1280.8)
Education				
No high school	-0.174 (-45.5)	-0.258 (-94.7)	-0.212 (-33.9)	-0.293 (-69.7)
Some college	0.002 (0.5)	0.001 (0.2)	0.017 (2.9)	0.039 (11.4)
College degree	0.053 (13.2)	0.069 (25.9)	0.073 (10.7)	0.127 (32.2)
NA × no high school	-0.368 (-21.0)	-0.470 (-36.2)	-0.476 (-16.3)	-0.462 (-24.2)
NA × high school	-0.276 (-15.9)	-0.430 (-34.1)	-0.260 (-9.4)	-0.297 (-16.4)
NA × some college	-0.247 (-12.6)	-0.362 (-26.0)	-0.196 (-6.7)	-0.238 (-12.8)
NA × college degree	-0.248 (-9.8)	-0.342 (-18.2)	-0.141 (-3.5)	-0.124 (-4.9)
Experience				
Experience	0.046 (106.6)	0.051 (163.3)	0.041 (61.3)	0.046 (108.5)
Experience squared	-0.001 (-97.2)	-0.001 (-153.5)	-0.001 (-47.0)	-0.001 (-92.0)
NA × experience	-0.001 (-0.5)	-0.006 (-4.3)	0.018 (6.3)	0.007 (3.9)
NA × experience sqd.	0.000[a] (0.0)	0.000[b] (4.2)	-0.000[c] (-4.9)	0.000[d] (-1.0)

	(1)		(2)		(3)		(4)	
Marital Status								
Married	0.351	(83.2)	0.280	(99.8)	−0.052	(−7.7)	−0.044	(−10.6)
Other married	0.229	(36.6)	0.157	(39.0)	0.149	(17.9)	0.121	(23.8)
NA × married	0.099	(5.8)	0.174	(15.1)	0.154	(5.6)	0.052	(3.1)
NA × other married	0.027	(1.1)	0.094	(6.1)	0.056	(1.7)	−0.066	(−3.4)
Location								
Metropolitan area	−0.008	(−2.0)	0.035	(13.1)	0.076	(12.0)	0.096	(25.3)
NA × metropolitan area	0.134	(10.5)	0.200	(22.9)	−0.028	(−1.4)	0.078	(6.4)
R-squared	0.196		0.195		0.066		0.084	
Sample Size								
Native American	12,439		26,425		9,548		22,859	
White	213,709		481,847		160,926		395,520	

NOTES: T-statistics are given in parentheses next to coefficients. Sample includes those aged 16-64 with positive annual hours and hourly earnings. See Appendix Table 2 for definitions and Appendix Table 3 for variable means.

[a] 0.000001
[b] 0.00012
[c] 0.00033
[d] −0.00004

TABLE 7-7 Decomposition Results from Regressions on Income, Hourly Earnings, and Annual Hours (Native American-White Ratios), 1979 and 1989

	Coefficients					
	Men			Women		
Characteristics	1979	1989	1989W 1979NA	1979	1989	1989W 1979NA
Income Equations						
1979 characteristics	65	60		80	71	
1989 characteristics	65	59	62	84	73	79
Hourly Earnings Equations						
1979 characteristics	83	79		90	84	
1989 characteristics	82	78	79	90	85	87
Annual Hours Equations						
1979 characteristics	80	75		88	79	
1989 characteristics	81	75	80	94	84	93

NOTES:

1. Change in characteristics: For any one column, compare ratios in rows 1 and 2, 3 and 4, or 5 and 6 to assess the effect of the change in characteristics from 1979 to 1989 (when applied to 1979 or 1989 coefficients).

2. Change in coefficients: For any one row, compare ratios in columns 1 and 2 or columns 4 and 5 to assess the effect of the change in coefficients from 1979 to 1989 (when applied to 1979 or 1989 characteristics).

3. Subcomponents of changes in coefficients:

• Native-specific: For any one of rows 2, 4, or 6, compare columns 2 and 3 or columns 5 and 6, to assess the effect of the change in Native-specific coefficients from 1979 to 1989 (taking White coefficients for 1989 as fixed).

• Economy-wide: For any one of rows 2, 4, or 6, compare columns 1 and 3 or columns 4 and 6, to assess the effect of the change in economy-wide or White coefficients from 1979 to 1989 (taking Native American coefficients for 1979 as fixed).

is a general conclusion. The changes in average education levels, marital status, labor force experience, and location of Native American and white men over the decade do not explain a significant proportion of the decline in annual income, annual hours worked, and hourly earnings ratios.

Having determined that it is coefficient changes which matter most, we can go one step further. The coefficient changes can be divided into two groups: white coefficient changes, which we think of as economy-wide influences that affect whites and Native Americans alike, and the adjustments to produce the Native American coefficient changes, which we identify as Native American-specific effects. Thus in row 2, column 3, we take the 1989 characteristics of whites and Native Americans and calculate an income ratio keeping the Native American coefficients fixed at 1979 levels and setting the white coefficients at 1989 levels. The difference between row 2, column 3 and row 2, column 1 estimates the economy-wide changes. The difference between row 2, column 2 and row 2, column 3 estimates the Native American-specific effects.

Economy-wide changes (65-62) and Native American-specific effects (62-59) have adversely affected the income ratio of Native American men by 3 percentage points each. The Native American-specific effects indicate that within an increasingly adverse environment, as measured by the change in white coefficients, Native Americans have fallen behind whites who in 1979 would have received similar income. These results bring us back to the beginning of the chapter, where we demonstrated that not only has the white income ladder changed in ways that disadvantage all Americans with low income—the compression effects—but Native Americans have also slipped down the ladder—the position effect.

When we undertake the same analysis for hourly earnings and hours worked, an interesting pattern emerges. As indicated earlier, all the changes in the hourly earnings ratio occur because of coefficient changes, but it is the change in white coefficients that makes the major contribution (82-79). Thus, the changes in Native American hourly earnings have been determined primarily by changes in the white hourly earnings structure.

For hours worked, it is also the coefficient changes that drive the ratio change, but in this instance, the change in Native American coefficients is the principal determinant of the change in hours worked (80-75), rather than economy-wide coefficient changes (81-80). An interesting issue yet to be determined is whether this is a demand or supply side effect.

Among Native American women, the pattern is a little more complicated. Their income ratio has increased because of improved characteristics (80-84), but adverse coefficient changes (84-73) have dominated and overwhelmed the characteristics effect. Thus, the source of the income ratio decline relative to white women is the change in coefficients and not the change in characteristics. The effect of coefficient changes is shared equally between economy-wide changes (84-79) and changes specific to Native Americans (79-73).

The changes in the characteristics of Native American women do not affect the hourly earnings ratio. Approximately half the changes are the result of economy-wide coefficient changes (90-87) and half the result of Native American-specific coefficient changes (87-85). The changes in characteristics exert all their effect through the annual hours equation, where, other things being equal, they have increased annual hours worked by Native American women (88-94). The annual hours worked by Native American women have not been adversely affected to a significant degree by economy-wide influences relative to white women (94-93). All the decline in the annual hours ratio is the result of Native American-specific effects (93-84).

CONCLUDING COMMENTS

The economic circumstances of Native Americans are very poor. They have low income, work fewer annual hours, and receive lower hourly earnings than whites. Our primary focus has not been on explaining these gaps, but on showing that according to census data, the economic circumstances of Native American men and women further deteriorated relative to white men and women during the period 1979-1989.[15]

Native American men have been most affected. Relative to white men, their income ratio fell 12 percent during 1979-1989, their average hourly earnings ratio fell 9 percent, and their annual hours worked fell 3 percent. These declines translate into even larger declines in real income over the decade. Thus, for Native American men who had not completed high school, average real income fell 22 percent. For those who had completed high school, real income fell 12 percent. Only those with college degrees experienced real income increases over the decade.

Perhaps the first point that should be made is that these changes did not occur because human capital characteristics of Native American men deteriorated relative to white men. In terms of adding to their education and labor market experience, Native American men more or less kept pace with their white counterparts. Native Americans improved their education levels quite markedly over the decade, but the change did not map into relative income gains because white men also increased their education and skill levels.

The major adverse change originated from the changing valuation placed by the labor market on the human capital characteristics of men. Over this period, the least skilled and least educated were rewarded less for their human capital characteristics and found it more difficult to remain employed. Native Americans are disproportionately represented in this group, and hence their income fell.

The change in the income ratio can be divided into changes in average hourly earnings and annual hours worked. Almost all the adverse trends in average hourly earnings for Native American men can be attributed to changes in economy-wide hourly earnings structures (with the least skilled being paid less), and there is no specific Native American effect.

---

[15]There is an interesting contrast with indigenous Australians, who have made large gains over the last decade as a result of considerable government support; see Gregory and Daly (1994).

With regard to the large decline in relative annual hours worked, most of the change is specific to Native Americans. Our research has provided no indication of how to interpret this Native American-specific effect. It could be because Native Americans are last hired and first fired, or it could be an indication of a supply response to large wage declines.

The changing economic circumstances for women have been better. Native American women lost significant income relative to white women during the period—a 9 percent loss in the income ratio, a 7 percent loss in average hourly earnings, and a 4 percent loss in annual hours worked—but they gained income relative to Native American and white men. With the exception of those who had not completed high school, they experienced real income gains. Among Native American women with college degrees, for example, the increase in real income over the decade was 29 percent. Most of this increase is attributable to an increase in annual hours worked.

The change in the economic circumstances of women is also largely attributable to changes in the labor market valuation of human capital characteristics. Thus, most of the changes in hourly earnings can be explained by economy-wide effects, while the opposite is true of hours worked.

An important finding of this research is the role of economy-wide relative to Native-specific effects on the economic outcomes for Native Americans. The pattern is similar for both genders. Approximately half of the decline in the income ratio is attributable to changes in economy-wide coefficients and half to Native American-specific effects. The economy-wide effects dominate the change in hourly earnings, while the Native American-specific effects dominate the change in annual hours worked.

With the exception of the effect on annual hours worked by women, changes in the education levels or labor market experience of Native Americans have exerted little influence on relative incomes. This result suggests that closing the income gap for Native Americans, or reversing the decline of the last decade, is not going to be easy. The need for Native Americans to increase their education, skill, and labor market experience if they wish to increase income levels seems even greater than in the past. If returns to the low-skilled continue to fall, Native Americans will need to improve their human capital characteristics substantially relative to whites just to maintain their relative income level.

The large economic changes that occurred over the decade seem to suggest a new range of pressures on Native Americans. For example, what are the implications for the structure of Native American families when for women, income and hours worked are increasing considerably, while for men, income and hours worked are declining by very large amounts? What are the implications for the geographic dispersion of Native Americans as the income premium from living in metropolitan areas increases?[16]

The economy-wide effects on the distribution of American wages over the decade have been well documented, although the exact importance of different sources of these changes is not known. Some authors suggest that reduced trade union power, increased international trade, increased levels of low-skilled immigrants, and technological changes biased against the low-skilled have all made a contribution to reducing the income of the low-skilled (Freeman and Katz, 1994). It is not possible to forecast future changes, but it is not clear what will reverse these trends. If these trends continue, the economic fortune of Native Americans relative to their white counterparts is likely to continue to deteriorate.

Snipp (1989) concludes his study of the Native American data from the 1980 census with the following comment:

> Despite these hardships, the future of the American Indian population is in some ways brighter today than it has been for a long time. Whether this will continue in the future is impossible to predict but the 1990 census will provide some very important clues.

Those clues, at least with regard to the economic circumstances of Native Americans as a group, are rather depressing for men, but much brighter for women. On the basis of the 1990 census, we cannot say for Native Americans as a group that "the (economic) future of the American Indian population is brighter today than it has been for a long time." One lesson is that we need to comment differently for men and women. Another is that judgments cannot be made on the basis of looking at Native Americans alone. To a considerable degree, the economic future of Native Americans is being determined by economy-wide changes and not just by changes that are specific to them, particularly with respect to the changes in hourly earnings. Whether some of the changes in annual hours are indeed Native American-specific effects or evidence of employment discrimination (the effect of which has increased with changes in the

---

[16]As noted frequently throughout this volume, there is considerable economic variation among Native American peoples. This chapter treats Native Americans as a group. There should be considerable gains in understanding the large changes that are occurring once we begin to disaggregate the data. On average, those who live on reservations receive lower incomes than those employed in cities, mainly because job opportunities for the latter are limited (Snipp, 1989). Those who speak only a native language typically receive 40 percent less income than those who speak only English. Among families in which one spouse is Native American, median family income is 23 percent higher than when both family members are Native American. This chapter makes none of these or many other interesting distinctions. There would be considerable value in disaggregating the data further, but doing so would lead to a much larger study.

economy) has yet to be determined. Of course, in the future there will be economic gains for Native Americans from gambling casinos and particular development projects, but the general changes that are currently occurring in the U.S. economy seem adverse for the majority of Native American men.

REFERENCES

Blau, F.D., and L.M. Kahn
   1994   Rising wage inequality and the U.S. gender gap. *The American Economic Review* 84(2):22-28.
Dickens, W., and L. Katz
   1987   Inter-industry wage differences and industry characteristics. Pp. 48-89 in K. Lang and J. Leonard, eds., *Unemployment and the Structure of Labor Markets.* New York: Basil Blackwell.
Freeman, R.B., and L.F. Katz
   1994   Rising wage inequality: The United States versus other advanced countries. Pp. 29-62 in R.B. Freeman, ed., *Working Under Different Rules.* New York: Russell Sage Foundation.
Gregory, R.G., and A.E. Daly
   1994   Welfare and economic progress of indigenous men of Australia and the U.S., 1980-1990. Centre for Economic Policy Research Discussion Paper 318.
Juhn, C., K.M. Murphy, and B. Pierce
   1993   Wage inequality and the rise in returns to skill. *Journal of Political Economy* 101(3):410-442.
Katz, L.F., and K.M. Murphy
   1992   Changes in relative wages 1963-87: Supply and demand factors. *Quarterly Journal of Economics* 107(Feb):35-78.
Levitan, S.A., and E.I. Miller
   1991   *The Equivocal Prospects for Indian Reservations.* Washington, D.C.: Center for Social Policy Studies, The George Washington University.
Mincer, J.
   1974   *Schooling, Experience and Earnings.* New York: National Bureau of Economic Research.
Murphy, K., and F. Welch
   1992   The structure of wages. *Quarterly Journal of Economics* 107(1):215-326.
Oaxaca, J.R.
   1973   Male-female wage differentials in urban labour markets. *International Economic Review* 14:693-709.
Okun, A.M.
   1973   Upward mobility in a high-pressure economy. Pp. 207-261 in A.M. Okun and G.L. Perry, eds., *Economic Activity* Volume 1. Washington, D.C.: The Brookings Institution.
Passel, J.S., and P.A. Berman
   1986   Quality of 1980 census data for American Indians. *Social Biology* 33:163-182.
Sandefur, G.D., and W.J. Scott
   1983   Minority group status and the wages of Indian and black males. *Social Science Research* 12:44-68.
Snipp, C.M.
   1989   *American Indians: The First of This Land.* New York: Russell Sage Foundation.

APPENDIX TABLE 1A Income, Earnings, Annual Hours, Hourly Earnings and Employment/Population (1982-1984 = $100)

	1979		1989		NA/White		Percent change
	White	Native Am.	White	Native Am.	1979	1989	1979-1989
Men, N	251,862	16,346	559,977	34,592			
Total income	20,817	12,911	22,480	12,330	0.62	0.55	-12
No high school	13,365	8,903	10,312	6,956	0.67	0.67	1
High school	19,346	13,499	18,400	11,857	0.70	0.64	-8
Some college	20,700	15,865	21,455	14,985	0.77	0.70	-9
College degree	31,719	23,646	38,948	26,465	0.75	0.68	-9
Earnings	19,220	11,910	20,650	11,278	0.62	0.55	-12
No high school	11,749	7,837	8,907	5,969	0.67	0.67	0
High school	17,908	12,707	16,960	11,039	0.71	0.65	-8
Some degree	19,200	14,825	19,872	13,846	0.77	0.70	-10
College degree	29,795	22,184	35,942	24,420	0.74	0.68	-9

Annual hours	1,704	1,307	1,765	1,314	0.77	0.74	-3
No high school	1,315	982	1,135	852	0.75	0.75	0
High school	1,788	1,440	1,815	1,394	0.81	0.77	-5
Some college	1,762	1,559	1,848	1,580	0.88	0.86	-3
College degree	1,954	1,777	2,089	1,880	0.91	0.90	-1
Hourly Earnings	11.28	9.11	11.70	8.59	0.81	0.73	-9
No high school	8.94	7.98	7.85	7.01	0.89	0.89	0
High school	10.01	8.82	9.35	7.92	0.88	0.85	-4
Some college	10.90	9.51	10.75	8.76	0.87	0.81	-7
College degree	15.25	12.48	17.20	12.99	0.82	0.76	-8
Emp/pop 1[a]	0.80	0.62	0.81	0.63	0.78	0.77	-1
No high school	0.65	0.48	0.59	0.43	0.75	0.73	-2
High school	0.83	0.69	0.82	0.67	0.83	0.81	-2
Some college	0.82	0.72	0.84	0.73	0.88	0.87	-1
College degree	0.90	0.84	0.92	0.86	0.93	0.94	1
Emp/pop 2[a]	0.88	0.79	0.89	0.78	0.89	0.88	-1
No high school	0.75	0.67	0.73	0.62	0.89	0.86	-4
High school	0.91	0.84	0.90	0.83	0.93	0.92	-1
Some college	0.93	0.89	0.94	0.87	0.95	0.93	-2
College degree	0.95	0.92	0.96	0.93	0.97	0.96	-1

NOTE: Sample includes working-age population (16-64 years).
[a]See Appendix Table 2 for definitions.

APPENDIX TABLE 1B Income, Earnings, Annual Hours, Hourly Earnings and Employment/Population (1982-1984 = $100)

	1979		1989		NA/White		Percent change
	White	Native Am.	White	Native Am.	1979	1989	1979-1989
Women, N	266,954	16,823	578,086	36,029			
Total income	7,709	5,936	10,192	7,154	0.77	0.70	−9
No high school	4,475	3,652	4,130	3,489	0.82	0.84	4
High school	7,191	6,418	8,228	6,581	0.89	0.80	−10
Some college	8,599	8,058	10,825	9,180	0.94	0.85	−10
College degree	12,906	12,559	18,123	16,234	0.97	0.90	−8
Earnings	6,671	5,016	9,158	6,173	0.75	0.67	−10
No high school	3,450	2,584	3,199	2,382	0.75	0.74	−1
High school	6,330	5,667	7,338	5,659	0.90	0.77	−14
Some degree	7,593	7,191	9,872	8,287	0.95	0.84	−11
College degree	11,315	11,529	16,602	15,136	1.02	0.91	−11

Annual hours	944	796	1,164	942	0.84	0.81	−4
No high school	618	496	616	480	0.80	0.78	−3
High school	983	920	1,139	980	0.94	0.86	−8
Some college	1,064	1,091	1,298	1,217	1.03	0.94	−9
College degree	1,173	1,261	1,472	1,516	1.08	1.03	−4
Hourly Earnings	7.07	6.30	7.87	6.55	0.89	0.83	−7
No high school	5.59	5.21	5.19	4.96	0.93	0.95	2
High school	6.44	6.16	6.44	5.77	0.96	0.90	−6
Some college	7.14	6.59	7.60	6.81	0.92	0.90	−3
College degree	9.65	9.14	11.28	9.98	0.95	0.89	−7
Emp/pop 1[a]	0.56	0.45	0.65	0.52	0.82	0.81	−1
No high school	0.38	0.30	0.40	0.30	0.79	0.75	−5
High school	0.57	0.52	0.63	0.54	0.92	0.86	−6
Some college	0.62	0.60	0.72	0.66	0.96	0.92	−5
College degree	0.71	0.70	0.80	0.80	1.00	1.00	1
Emp/pop 2[a]	0.66	0.59	0.75	0.66	0.90	0.88	−3
No high school	0.47	0.43	0.52	0.44	0.91	0.85	−6
High school	0.66	0.66	0.72	0.68	0.99	0.94	−5
Some college	0.75	0.77	0.83	0.80	1.03	0.97	−6
College degree	0.79	0.83	0.86	0.87	1.04	1.00	−4

NOTE: Sample includes working age population (16–64).
[a]See Appendix Table 2 for definitions.

APPENDIX TABLE 2 Definitions of Variables Used in the Regressions

Dependent Variables	
Income	Total income from all sources, 1979 and 1989, in real terms,[a] for those with real annual income greater than or equal to $500.
Hourly Earnings	Annual earnings divided by annual hours, in real terms, for those with positive annual hours and positive hourly earnings in said years.
Annual hours	Weeks worked in 1979 and 1989, multiplied by usual hours worked per week in 1979 and 1989, for those with positive annual hours and positive hourly earnings in said years.
Independent Variables	
Education	
No high school	DV: One if in or finished 11th grade or lower.
High school	DV: One if in or finished 12th grade.
Some college	DV: One if in or finished 1-3 years in college/beyond high school.
College degree	DV: One if in or finished 4th year of college or higher.
Experience	Age minus years of schooling minus 6.
Marital Status	
Single	DV: One if never married.
Married	DV: One if now married.
Other married	DV: One if widowed, separated, or divorced.
Location: MSA	DV: One if county groups located within standard metropolitan statistical areas (SMSAs) or mixed SMSA/non-SMSA areas.

NOTE: DV = (1,0) Dummy variable.

[a]Deflated using CPI base year 1982-1984 (U.S. President, 1995. Economic Report of the President. Washington, D.C.: U.S. Government Printing Office, p. 341).

APPENDIX TABLE 3 Variable Means for Income, Hourly Earnings and Annual Hours Regressions, 1979 and 1989

Variables*	Men 1979 White	Men 1979 NA	Men 1989 White	Men 1989 NA	Women 1979 White	Women 1979 NA	Women 1989 White	Women 1989 NA
N								
Income eq.	229,971	13,863	509,191	29,047	183,713	11,481	433,746	27,296
Hourly earnings eq.	213,709	12,439	481,847	26,425	160,926	9,548	395,520	22,859
Annual hours eq.	213,709	12,439	481,847	26,425	160,926	9,548	395,520	22,859
Ln Income	9.65	9.20	9.68	9.13	8.90	8.68	9.05	8.73
Education								
No high school	0.22	0.36	0.15	0.26	0.19	0.35	0.13	0.24
High school	0.34	0.34	0.32	0.37	0.39	0.35	0.34	0.35
Some college	0.22	0.21	0.29	0.28	0.24	0.22	0.32	0.32
College degree	0.22	0.09	0.24	0.09	0.17	0.07	0.21	0.09
Experience								
Experience	18.34	16.62	18.94	17.71	18.38	16.44	18.76	17.79
Experience sqd	538.74	455.18	526.83	467.20	552.04	451.80	527.42	472.52
Marital S.								
Married	0.66	0.59	0.63	0.53	0.58	0.49	0.58	0.46
Single	0.26	0.29	0.27	0.32	0.23	0.26	0.24	0.27
Other married	0.08	0.12	0.10	0.15	0.19	0.26	0.19	0.27
Location								
MSA	0.78	0.61	0.83	0.66	0.79	0.61	0.83	0.65

continued on next page

APPENDIX TABLE 3 Continued

	Men				Women			
	1979		1989		1979		1989	
Variables[a]	White	NA	White	NA	White	NA	White	NA
Ln Hrly Earnings	2.22	2.02	2.19	1.91	1.82	1.71	1.85	1.68
Education								
No high school	0.20	0.33	0.14	0.24	0.16	0.29	0.11	0.19
High school	0.34	0.36	0.32	0.37	0.40	0.38	0.34	0.35
Some college	0.23	0.22	0.29	0.29	0.26	0.25	0.33	0.35
College degree	0.23	0.09	0.25	0.10	0.18	0.08	0.22	0.10
Experience								
Experience	17.21	15.28	17.89	16.44	16.36	14.30	17.35	16.34
Experience sqd	482.25	389.70	474.08	406.83	453.05	353.24	455.92	401.55
Marital S.								
Married	0.66	0.59	0.62	0.53	0.59	0.52	0.58	0.50
Single	0.26	0.30	0.28	0.33	0.25	0.27	0.25	0.27
Other married	0.08	0.12	0.10	0.15	0.16	0.21	0.17	0.23
Location								
MSA	0.79	0.61	0.83	0.67	0.80	0.61	0.84	0.66

Ln Hours	7.41	7.17	7.43	7.16	6.99	6.87	7.11	6.96
Education								
No high school	0.20	0.33	0.14	0.24	0.16	0.29	0.11	0.19
High school	0.34	0.36	0.32	0.37	0.40	0.38	0.34	0.35
Some college	0.23	0.22	0.29	0.29	0.26	0.25	0.33	0.35
College degree	0.23	0.09	0.25	0.10	0.18	0.08	0.22	0.10
Experience								
Experience	17.21	15.28	17.89	16.44	16.36	14.30	17.35	16.34
Experience sqd	482.25	389.70	474.08	406.83	453.05	353.24	455.92	401.55
Marital S.								
Married	0.66	0.59	0.62	0.53	0.59	0.52	0.58	0.50
Single	0.26	0.30	0.28	0.33	0.25	0.27	0.25	0.27
Other married	0.08	0.12	0.10	0.15	0.16	0.21	0.17	0.23
Location								
MSA	0.79	0.61	0.83	0.67	0.80	0.61	0.84	0.66

[a]Income, hourly earnings, and annual hours data are in logs. Education, marital status, and location variables present the proportion of the sample in that category. Experience and experience squared are in years.

8

American Indian Poverty on Reservations, 1969-1989

Ronald L. Trosper

INTRODUCTION

This chapter uses census data to describe changes in poverty and income on 23 Indian reservations over a 20-year period, 1969-1989. The principal conclusion is that the percentage of American Indian families living in poverty fell significantly in the 10-year period 1969-1979, but that these gains were eroded over the subsequent decade. In 1969, approximately one in three American Indian families was living in poverty throughout the nation. By 1979, this fraction had fallen to just less than one in four. Beginning around 1980, however, the position of many American Indian families deteriorated, so that by 1989, the number of American Indian families in poverty had risen to 27 percent.

On the 23 reservations for which we have 20 years of data, the pattern was similar. In 1969, 57 percent of the families on these reservations were below the poverty threshold. By 1979, this number had fallen to 43 percent. In the next decade, poverty increased, and in 1989 over half of the American Indian families on these reservations were in poverty. Although the reservations began the period with large differences in pov-

I would like to thank the staff of the Institute for Native Americans at Northern Arizona University, Bill Hildred for discussions on gaming, Michael Yellow Bird and other participants in the workshop for helpful comments, the anonymous reviewers, and the National Indian Policy Center for 1980 and 1990 census data extracts in its Indian Country Data System.

erty rates and levels of income, the broad trend described above affected nearly all of them. Family poverty rates decreased on all but 2 of the 23 reservations in the first decade, and increased on all but 3 in the second decade. Other measures of well-being, such as per capita income, median family income, the unemployment rate, and the labor force participation rate, followed similar patterns. Casual observation suggests that these trends parallel trends in real federal expenditures on Indian reservations.

DATA

The national censuses of 1970, 1980, and 1990 allow comparisons over time using data that were collected in a relatively consistent manner for 23 reservations. The 1970 census subject report on American Indians (U.S. Bureau of the Census, 1973) determined the selection of reservations for comparison in the present analysis. Although later census data provide extensive coverage of reservations, the data in the 1970 census are essential if one wishes to examine changes over time. Comparisons are made for two measures of income, two measures of poverty, and two measures of labor market conditions. Median family income and per capita income, converted to 1989 dollars using the consumer price index, allow for a comparison of changes in income levels. The U.S. Bureau of the Census held the definition of poverty constant in real terms over the 20-year period, and the percentages of families and individuals in poverty provide evidence of changes in the living standards of the poorest Indians. While incomplete as measures of economic activity, the unemployment rate and the labor force participation rate both provide a glimpse of the condition of labor markets.[1]

DESCRIPTIVE RESULTS

Table 8-1 provides national data on the key measures for all Americans, whites, blacks, and American Indians. For median family income, changes for the total U.S. population, for whites, and for blacks are similar. Median family income increased about 5-6 percent for each of the

---

[1]The 1980 census provided a special survey of Indians. Because the questions used in the special survey of reservations to collect income data were not the same as those used in 1970 and 1990, data for 1980 in this paper come from the state reports, which are consistent with the other two censuses, rather than from the special report on Indian reservations, which is not. A reader cross-checking the data for 1980 provided in this paper with those provided for 15 reservations in Snipp (1989) will find that the numbers are different for this reason.

TABLE 8-1 National Data on American Indians Compared with Whites and Blacks

Population	Median Family Income in 1989 dollars			Percentage Change	
	1969	1979	1989	1969-1979	1979-1989
Total U.S.	31,863	33,404	35,225	0.05	0.05
Whites	33,095	34,944	37,152	0.06	0.06
Blacks	20,158	21,129	22,429	0.05	0.06
American Indians	19,377	23,017	21,750	0.19	-0.06

Population	Per Capita Income in 1989 dollars			Percentage Change	
	1969	1979	1989	1969-1979	1979-1989
Total U.S.	10,429	12,240	14,420	0.17	0.18
Whites	11,011	13,095	15,687	0.19	0.20
Blacks	6,040	7,623	8,859	0.26	0.16
American Indians	5,226	7,844	8,328	0.50	0.06

Population	Percent of Families in Poverty		
	1969	1979	1989
Total U.S.	10.7	9.6	10.0
Whites	8.6	7.0	7.0
Blacks	29.8	26.5	26.3
American Indians	33.3	23.7	27.0

SOURCES: U.S. Bureau of the Census (1972, 1983, 1993b). All dollar values are adjusted by use of CPI-U (Consumer Price Index, All Urban Consumers) from the Bureau of Labor Statistics, reported in Table 8-4.

decades. Indians show a dramatic difference: an increase of 19 percent for the first decade and a decline of 6 percent for the second. These trends are even more dramatic for per capita income, also shown in Table 8-1. The total U.S. population had an increase of 17 percent for the 10 years between 1969 and 1979 and of 18 percent in 1979–1989. Indians had a 50 percent increase in the first decade and only a 6 percent increase in the second.

A similar pattern exists for the percentage of families in poverty. Changes are relatively small for the total U.S. population, for whites, and

TABLE 8-2 Summary of Results for 23 Reservations

	Number of Reservations			
	1970-1980		1980-1990	
	Improved	Deteriorated	Improved	Deteriorated
Median family income (+)	21	2	1	22
Per capita income (+)	23	0	5	18
% of families in poverty (–)	21	2	3	20
% of persons in poverty (–)	21	2	2	21
Unemployment				
Male	9	14	1	22
Female	9	14	6	17
Labor force participation (+)				
Male	21	2	10	13
Female	22	1	11	12

SOURCE: U.S. Bureau of the Census: (1973, 1983, 1993a, 1993b, 1993c); Stinson and Plantz (1986).

for blacks. All groups show a decrease in poverty from 1969 to 1979, most dramatically American Indians. But *only* Indians had a major increase in poverty rates in the second decade.

Table 8-2 presents summary results for the 23 reservations for which data are available for 1970, 1980, and 1990. For each of the measures of Indian income and poverty, it gives the number of reservations for which the measure improved or deteriorated from 1970 to 1980 and 1980 to 1990. Nearly every reservation had an increase in income and a decrease in poverty during 1970-1980 and a decrease in income and an increase in poverty in 1980-1990. As shown in Table 8-3, although 5 reservations had an increase in per capita income in the second decade, 2 of these 5 had an increase in poverty rates among families during that same time.

The patterns for unemployment and for labor force participation are not as dramatic as for income and poverty, but are similar: more improvements in the first decade of comparison than in the second. Unemployment among men and women increased on 14 reservations during the period 1970–1980. Unemployment among men increased on 22 reservations in the decade 1980–1990 and among women increased on 17 of the

TABLE 8-3 Poverty and Income on Selected Reservations, 1969-1989

Name of Reservation	Percent of Families Below Poverty Threshold			Percent Change		Per Capita Income in 1989 Dollars			Percent Change	
	1969	1979	1989	1969-1979	1979-1989	1969	1979	1989	1969-1979	1979-1989
Blackfeet Reservation	47.8	29.2	45.7	-0.39	0.57	3612	5523	4718	0.53	-0.15
Cheyenne River Reservation	54.8	47.5	57.2	-0.13	0.20	3050	4299	4077	0.41	-0.05
Crow Reservation	40.0	29.6	45.5	-0.26	0.54	3223	5050	4243	0.57	-0.16
Eastern Cherokee Reservation	52.2	31.6	30.0	-0.39	-0.05	3435	5142	6382	0.50	0.24
Flathead Reservation	32.4	34.4	31.8	0.06	-0.08	5027	5248	6428	0.04	0.22
Fort Apache Reservation	53.3	39.7	49.9	-0.25	0.26	2911	3873	3805	0.33	-0.02
Fort Peck Reservation	46.7	26.8	41.8	-0.43	0.56	3857	5481	4778	0.42	-0.13
Gila River Reservation	58.6	44.4	62.8	-0.24	0.41	2701	4037	3176	0.49	-0.21
Hopi Reservation	61.8	51.0	47.7	-0.17	-0.06	2768	4210	4566	0.52	0.08
Laguna Pueblo	24.4	11.6	27.7	-0.52	1.38	4469	7416	6085	0.66	-0.18
Menominee Reservation	38.0	14.9	48.8	-0.61	2.27	3585	5333	4738	0.49	-0.11
Navajo Reservation	62.1	47.3	54.2	-0.24	0.15	2578	4049	3817	0.57	-0.06

Northern Cheyenne Reservation	39.8	41.7	46.4	0.05	0.11	3834	4213	4479	0.10	0.06
Papago Reservation	78.1	49.5	62.8	-0.37	0.27	1954	3639	3113	0.86	-0.14
Pine Ridge Reservation	54.3	48.4	59.5	-0.11	0.23	3462	3705	3121	0.07	-0.16
Red Lake Reservation	43.0	26.3	50.3	-0.39	0.91	3379	6886	4287	1.04	-0.38
Rosebud Reservation	62.9	48.3	54.4	-0.23	0.13	2811	4166	4005	0.48	-0.04
San Carlos Reservation	62.3	45.9	59.8	0.26	0.30	2283	3794	3173	0.66	-0.16
Standing Rock Reservation	58.3	44.2	54.9	-0.24	0.24	3329	4364	3421	0.31	-0.22
Turtle Mountain Reservation	50.2	37.7	53.7	-0.25	0.43	3263	5600	5138	0.72	-0.08
Wind River Reservation	42.0	35.2	47.8	-0.16	0.36	4040	4891	4340	0.21	-0.11
Yakima Reservation	45.5	25.4	42.7	-0.44	0.68	3542	6366	4904	0.80	-0.23
Zuni Pueblo	56.7	41.8	47.4	-0.26	0.13	3253	3542	3904	0.09	0.10
Joint Use Area						1568				
Maximum in Column				0.06	2.27				1.04	0.24
Minimum in Column				-0.61	-0.08				0.04	-0.38
Number Increasing				2	20				23	5
Number Decreasing				21	3				0	18
Weighted averages for all reservations	57.3	42.7	51.0			2904	4341	4018		

reservations. Labor force participation improved on most reservations in the first decade (which may have contributed to the increase in unemployment rates during the period), but declined on a majority of reservations in the second decade.

Comparisons of Poverty Rates

The first five columns of Table 8-3 report changes in the percentage of families in poverty on each of the reservations during the two decades 1969-1979 and 1979-1989. Relative to the national poverty rates of 10 percent in each of the three observation years, Indians were extremely poor. The proportion of all families on these reservations that were in poverty in 1969 was 57 percent; this figure fell to 43 percent in 1979 and rose to 51 percent in 1989.

The range of poverty rates across reservations was great in each of the observation years. In all three years, the Laguna Pueblo had the lowest poverty rate: 24 percent in 1969, 12 percent in 1979, and 28 percent in 1989. In accordance with the general pattern, the poverty rate on the Laguna Pueblo fell in 1979 and rose in 1989, in this case to higher than it was in 1969. On some reservations, such as the Eastern Cherokee, the poverty rate in 1989 did not exceed that in 1969.

Although the reservation with the highest poverty rate among families was different in each of the three years, the Papago Reservation appears to have been the poorest reservation overall. In 1969, it had a poverty rate of 78.1 percent, which was exceeded only by that of the Navajo-Hopi Joint Use Area, 79.3 percent. In 1979, the Papago Reservation's poverty rate of 49.5 percent was exceeded by that of the Hopi Reservation, which was 51 percent; the Papago Reservation, however, was second in that year. The Hopi Reservation's increased poverty rate from 1969 to 1979 may have been influenced by the division of the Navajo-Hopi Joint Use Area, which occurred in 1977. In 1989, the Gila River Reservation and the Papago Reservation tied for the highest poverty rate at 62.8 percent.

The pattern of changes among reservations is complicated. The size of some of the changes is most impressive. The Blackfeet had a decrease of 39 percent in their poverty rate from 1969 to 1979, followed by an increase of 57 percent to return the rate nearly to where it started. The Flathead Reservation had a modest increase in its poverty rate from 1969 to 1979, followed by a modest decrease. This rather different pattern may have resulted from a large increase in the rental received by the Salish and Kootenai Tribes from Kerr Dam.

Although 20 reservations experienced an increase in the rate of family poverty from 1979 to 1989, only 10 had an increase over the entire 20 years from 1969 to 1989: Cheyenne River, Crow, Gila River, Laguna Pueblo, Menominee, Northern Cheyenne, Pine Ridge, Red Lake, Turtle Mountain, and Wind River. Although the poorest area in 1969—the Joint Use Area—was incorporated into both the Navajo and Hopi reservations, neither of these reservations had an overall increase in poverty rates for the 20-year period.

Although individual reservation data are not provided here, the pattern of change for persons in poverty is similar to that for families in poverty. The Flathead and Northern Cheyenne reservations were the only ones to have an increase in poverty rates in the first decade. In the second decade, the Flathead and Hopi had a decrease in the percentage of persons in poverty, as well as of families in poverty. The Eastern Cherokee Reservation, which had a decrease in the percentage of families in poverty, had a 3 percent increase in the percentage of persons in poverty.

The above discussion compares rates of poverty, not absolute numbers of families or people in poverty. It is important to note that although rates fell overall, the numbers of families and persons in poverty increased during the period. The number of families in poverty increased from just under 15,000 to just under 28,000, while the number of persons in poverty increased from 88,000 to 139,000.

Comparisons of Income

The last five columns of Table 8-3 report the changes in per capita income on the 23 reservations for the period under consideration. All 23 had an increase in per capita income between 1969 and 1979. There were 5 reservations—Eastern Cherokee, Flathead, Hopi, Northern Cheyenne, and Zuni—that had an increase between 1979 and 1989. Of these, only Eastern Cherokee, Flathead, and Hopi had a decrease in the percentage of families in poverty, and only Eastern Cherokee and Flathead had an increase in per capita income greater than the national average of 18 percent. Thus the general pattern of improvement in the 1970s followed by a decline in the 1980s is shown in the per capita income data as well.

DISCUSSION

What factors were responsible for the above complex patterns of changing poverty rates? To answer this question, one needs to identify factors that moved in opposite directions in the 1980s compared with the 1990s. Such factors would then have a positive or negative correlation with the turn-around in reservation poverty observed in the census data. If we look for a single cause, any variable that was constant or moved in the same direction in both periods should be viewed skeptically. If we look for a combination of causes, some explicit modeling of possible inter-actions among variables will be necessary. The following discussion be-gins with attention to single-variable effects; the discussion ends with two linear regressions that provide a start on multivariate analysis.

Spatial Variations in Income and Poverty

The data in Table 8-3 show that reservations varied tremendously in their poverty rates and levels of per capita income in each of the years under consideration. The scope of this discussion does not include con-sideration of the causes of different levels of income across reservations at any one time. The amount and quality of land per person on each reser-vation are the result of its particular history, especially in relation to imple-mentation of the allotment acts as reported by McDonnell (1991). Sutton (1985) and Geisler (1995) provide further discussion of the effects of land taking. Cornell and Kalt review the literature on the causes of economic development on reservations (see Cornell and Kalt, 1992: Kalt and Cornell, 1994); they find that simple explanations based on external opportunity and internal assets are not easy to identify. In their explanations for different levels of income, they include variables such as the characteris-tics of the tribal government in relationship to the culture of reservations (Cornell and Gil-Swedberg, 1995). Some Indian cultural values do not support maintenance of high levels of income as conventionally defined, since many traditional Indians believe in having a minimal impact on ecosystems. Others give away much of their wealth to other community members (Michael J. Yellow Bird, personal communication, 1995). Con-sequently, spatial analysis would need to include variations in cultural characteristics as well.

With a sample of only 23 reservations and a list of more than 23 possible determinants of spatial variation in income levels, a cross-sec-tional analysis would be very difficult, if not impossible. Remarkably, although these 23 reservations started the two decades with great dispari-ties in income and poverty, they followed similar paths of change during 1969-1979. This overall similarity deserves investigation.

Business Cycle Factors

Because of cycles in the levels of economic activity, any comparison of particular years may be distorted by the national business cycle. One could show high growth rates by comparing the trough of one business cycle with the peak of the next. One could show low growth rates with the opposite maneuver: comparing a peak of one cycle with the trough of another. Fortunately, each of the three census years used here for income

TABLE 8-4 General Economic Indicators

Indicator	1969	1979	1989
Bureau of Labor Statistics, unemployment			
Total	3.5	5.8	5.3
Men > 20 yrs	2.1	4.2	4.5
Women > 20 yrs	3.7	5.7	4.7
White	3.1	5.1	4.5
Black	NA	12.3	11.4
Business cycle, reference dates			
Trough	Feb. 1961	Mar. 1975	Nov. 1982
Peak	Dec. 1969	Jan. 1980	July 1990
Consumer Price Index— all urban consumers	36.9	73.1	122.6
Gini coefficients of inequality			
All workers	0.466	0.464	0.467
All families	0.349	0.365	0.401

SOURCES: Bureau of Economic Analysis, U.S. Department of Commerce (1992); Sacks and Larrain (1993); Levy and Murnane (1992); Nelson (1994).

data occurred just before the peak of the respective business cycle. The dates of the cycles are given in Table 8-4. In each case, the economy was on the verge of a downturn. The peaks occurred in December 1969, January 1980, and July 1990. This similarity suggests that comparisons of the census income data will not be biased by differences in timing in relation to business cycle activity.

There are differences, however, in the character of the business cycles in question. The 1969 peak was extreme, caused by the expansion of the Vietnam War. That expansion created inflationary pressure that was exacerbated by the subsequent OPEC oil price shock. By 1980, national policymakers were very concerned about high inflation and had started holding unemployment rates up in order to hold inflation in check. Thus, even in the peak employment years of 1979 and 1989, unemployment rates were high by post-World War II standards. The inflation pattern is evident in the consumer price index: it increased by 3-1/3 times from 1969 to 1979, but only by 1-2/3 times in the next 10 years.

The increase in national unemployment rates in 1979 compared with 1969 is reflected on the reservations: as noted above, 14 of the 23 reservations had an increase in unemployment rates during this period. In contrast, while the national unemployment rate in 1989 was slightly lower than in 1979 (5.3 versus 5.8 percent), there was an increase in unemployment among men on 22 of the reservations and an increase among women on 17. Thus the pattern of unemployment on reservations in the second decade is not consistent with the national business cycle.

Migration and Changes in Self-identification

Two of the most important candidate trends for explaining the changes in poverty rates are migration and changes in self-identification, which cannot be distinguished in census data. To examine these changes, disaggregation of population data by age cohorts is helpful. With regard to population totals, births of young people and deaths of older people can be distinguished from within-cohort changes due to migration and changes in self-identification. Table 8-5 provides cohort populations for all 23 reservations combined. Births during the 20 years are shown for the four youngest cohorts. Deaths show clearly in the cohort for individuals aged 70 and older.

Cohort sizes fell in 1990 for persons aged 20 to 24 and 25 to 29. A similar pattern occurred in 1980, in which the number of persons in their 20s declined (these people were in their 30s in 1990). Having passed high school age, many persons leave their reservations to attend college and for other reasons, and the data for the cohorts aged 30–39 in 1989 show they did not return in the numbers in which they left. Although the directions of change are similar in the two decades, during 1980 to 1990 there was a greater decline among those aged 20 to 29 as compared with the similar age group during 1970–1980. All cohorts other than those post-high school showed increases in population, which suggests either positive migration to reservations, an increase in self-identification, or better census procedures in locating American Indians.

What would be the effects on income and poverty of the differences in migration rates and self-identification? If we assume that persons in their 20s are typically lower-income earners than older persons, then the greater decline in their numbers in the second decade should tend to increase per capita income, other things being held constant. On the other hand, examination of the cohorts that were in their 30s in 1980 shows that there was a greater increase in people of this age in the first decade than in the 1980s. Assuming people in their 30s are higher-than-average income earners, this would drive income up in 1979 more than in 1989. This is consistent with what was observed.

Comparison of the last two columns of Table 8-5 shows that percentage increases in cohorts tended to be higher in the 1970s than the 1980s.

How could in-migration or increases in self-identification during these periods have affected the patterns of income change discussed above?[2] The people who moved into the Indian category in the first 10 years had to have substantially higher income than those already in the category in 1969. (The total increase in per capita incomes was 49 percent.) During the next 10 years, the additional people moving into the category had to have substantially lower incomes than those already in the category (low enough to cause a 7 percent decline in per capita income). In order for migration and self-identification to have affected observed income and poverty enough to explain the change between the decades, there would have to have been a sharp break in the pattern of migration or changes in self-identification across income classes between the two decades. Whatever influence might have caused this shift in pattern would have to have been one that affected the 23 reservations similarly over time.[3]

Causality could run in the opposite direction: during the 1970s, when reservation economies were becoming prosperous, members of the tribes may have been willing to return to them, whereas during the 1980s, as prosperity declined, fewer people may have been willing to return. More information is needed to determine the contribution of changes in the mix of Indians being counted on the 23 reservations to changes in income data. One cannot dismiss the possibility that there were effects, but to explain the pattern, there would have to be a similar change in the distribution of migration and in self-identification across reservations.

Possible Demographic Explanations

Two other trends that might be associated with changes in poverty and in per capita income are age and persons per family. Median ages increased on 21 reservations from 1970 to 1980 and on 22 reservations from 1980 to 1990. An increase in median age presumably means fewer

---

[2]Because per capita income is average income, one can use population data to calculate aggregate reservation income, add income over all reservations, and divide by total population to determine per capita income on all 23 reservations combined. This figure is $2,904 for 1969. It increased by 49 percent to $4,341 in 1979. Recall that the increase for the entire United States was 17 percent in that decade. Per capita income declined by 7 percent from 1979 to 1989 on these reservations combined, to a level of $4,020. (Because the Navajo-Hopi Joint Use Area is included in the 1969 data, the comparison is correct geographically for the full 20-year period.)

[3]Note that the five reservations that had an increase in per capita income in the second decade had patterns of change in the migration of people in their 20s and 30s that are very similar to the patterns of other reservations. See the last four columns of Table 8-6, for Flathead, Hopi, Northern Cheyenne, and Zuni. The Eastern Cherokee Reservation, however, looks very different in its percentage changes.

TABLE 8-5 Comparison of Cohort Sizes, 1970-1990

Cohort Age in 1990	Cohort Population Totals			Cohort Changes		Percentage Changes	
	1970	1980	1990	1980-1970	1990-1980	1980-1970	1990-1980
Male all ages	73,556	105,168	138,482	31,612	33,314	43	32
Under 5 years			19,015		19,015		15
5 to 9 years			18,275		18,275		2
10 to 14 years		14,291	16,381	14,291	2,090		15
15 to 19 years		13,684	13,937	13,684	253		2
20 to 24 years	10,627	13,739	10,512	3,112	(3,227)	29	-23
25 to 29 years	12,293	13,976	11,208	1,683	(2,768)	14	-20
30 to 34 years	11,011	9,475	10,040	(1,536)	565	-14	6
35 to 39 years	8,380	7,409	8,147	(971)	738	-12	10
40 to 44 years	4,717	6,603	6,941	1,886	338	40	5
45 to 49 years	3,763	4,978	5,252	1,215	274	32	6
50 to 54 years	3,908	4,177	4,777	269	600	7	14
55 to 59 years	3,367	3,486	3,560	119	74	4	2
60 to 64 years	2,872	3,213	3,392	341	179	12	6
65 to 69 years	2,528	2,662	2,567	134	(95)	5	-4
70 and above	10,090	7,475	4,478	(2,615)	(2,997)	-26	-40

	76,756	110,295	143,250	33,539	32,955	44	30
Female all ages	76,756	110,295	143,250	33,539	32,955	44	30
Under 5 years			18,599		18,599		
5 to 9 years			17,266		17,266		
10 to 14 years		14,545	15,742	14,545	1,197		8
15 to 19 years		14,098	13,216	14,098	(882)		-6
20 to 24 years	11,011	13,041	10,674	2,030	(2,367)	18	-18
25 to 29 years	12,334	13,854	11,743	1,520	(2,111)	12	-15
30 to 34 years	11,186	10,348	11,374	(838)	1,026	-7	10
35 to 39 years	8,909	8,424	9,047	(485)	623	-5	7
40 to 44 years	5,281	6,574	7,476	1,293	902	24	14
45 to 49 years	4,268	5,499	5,734	1,231	235	29	4
50 to 54 years	4,282	4,884	5,147	602	263	14	5
55 to 59 years	3,844	4,130	4,513	286	383	7	9
60 to 64 years	3,119	3,841	3,878	722	37	23	1
65 to 69 years	2,783	2,884	3,089	101	205	4	7
70 and above	9,739	8,173	5,752	(1,566)	(2,421)	-16	-30
Total population	150,312	215,463	281,732	65,151	66,269	43	31

SOURCES: U.S. Bureau of the Census (1973, 1983, 1993c), Stinson and Plantz (1986).

TABLE 8-6 Independent Variables for Selected Reservations, 1969-1989

Name of Reservation	Median Age			Persons per Family			20s Age Ratio		30s Age Ratio	
	1970	1980	1990	1970	1980	1990	1980	1990	1980	1990
Blackfeet Reservation	16.2	21.1	22.8	5.19	4.67	3.95	0.63	0.86	1.33	1.25
Cheyenne River Reservation	16.2	17.2	19.2	5.83	5.49	4.27	0.98	0.68	1.12	1.00
Crow Reservation	17.0	20.1	21.9	6.63	5.67	4.74	0.97	0.77	1.48	0.91
Eastern Cherokee Reservation	19.8	22.6	26.1	4.83	3.97	3.42	0.31	1.85	0.21	2.53
Flathead Reservation	20.0	20.6	24.2	4.76	4.75	3.44	0.82	0.80	1.41	1.57
Fort Apache Reservation	16.2	18.2	21.3	6.49	5.60	4.44	0.82	0.98	1.33	1.11
Fort Peck Reservation	17.4	19.9	22.3	5.98	4.61	3.82	1.00	0.91	1.22	1.11
Gila River Reservation	17.9	19.9	22.7	5.93	5.22	4.17	0.99	0.92	1.88	1.00
Hopi Reservation	18.3	23.1	25.9	6.39	4.87	4.46	0.89	0.61	1.18	1.12
Laguna Pueblo	22.5	22.9	29.5	4.96	4.56	4.08	1.36	0.69	1.08	0.88
Menominee Reservation	15.2	19.7	21.7	5.85	5.42	4.02	0.54	0.79	1.54	1.06
Navajo Reservation	16.4	18.8	22.0	5.82	5.30	4.52	1.14	0.83	1.62	1.11
Northern Cheyenne Reservation	17.6	17.8	19.9	5.13	4.87	4.10	0.78	0.67	1.00	0.97
Papago Reservation	21.9	21.6	24.2	5.98	5.13	3.99	1.11	0.71	1.26	1.07
Pine Ridge Reservation	16.7	17.9	18.9	5.62	5.92	4.89	0.91	0.55	1.25	0.67
Red Lake Reservation	14.8	17.9	21.3	6.24	5.08	4.06	0.50	0.68	1.04	1.22
Rosebud Reservation	16.5	17.9	18.4	5.53	5.07	4.27	0.64	0.82	1.13	1.03
San Carlos Reservation	16.3	19.6	21.4	6.46	5.33	4.49	0.88	0.74	1.41	0.94
Standing Rock Reservation	19.2	18.4	18.6	5.43	5.29	4.59	1.07	0.54	1.31	0.86
Turtle Mountain Reservation	16.4	19.5	18.4	5.55	4.66	3.95	0.56	1.01	1.20	1.68
Wind River Reservation	18.7	19.7	21.3	5.77	5.08	4.23	0.87	0.89	0.79	1.11
Yakima Reservation	16.7	20.1	21.9	5.43	4.78	4.01	1.08	0.72	2.10	1.18
Zuni Pueblo	15.4	18.8	24.1	7.95	5.93	4.91	0.85	0.85	1.24	1.00
Joint Use Area	16.2			6.24						

children per adult, and a movement into older age classes means a movement into relatively higher-wage-earning years. Thus, an increase in
median age should accompany an increase in income. This occurred in
1969 to 1979, but from 1979 to 1989, incomes decreased.

Persons per family also showed a steady trend, toward lower numbers. There were 22 reservations that had a decrease in persons per family from 1970 to 1980, and all reservations had a decrease from 1980 to
1990. A decrease in persons per family should accompany an increase in
per capita income and a decrease in poverty, given steady incomes for the
adults in a family. Thus, the increase in per capita income and the decrease in persons per family from 1969 to 1979 are understandable. But
from 1979 to 1989, there was a decrease in per capita income at the same
time that there was a further decrease in persons per family.

Possible Political Explanations

President Nixon initiated tribal self-determination in 1970, although
the law was not changed until Public Law 92-638 was adopted in 1975.
Cornell and Kalt (1992) propose that tribal self-determination causes economic development. Although we do not have quantitative measures of
tribal self-determination, it apparently increased during both decades.

Changes in Federal Expenditures

Federal spending priorities changed from preservation of the social
safety net during the 1970s to military spending and tax cuts during the
Reagan years after 1980. Figure 8-1 shows the trends in real budget
amounts for the total Indian budget and for components of the budget
from the mid-1970s to 1991. Expenditures of the Labor Department are
omitted from these trends. In real terms, expressed in 1990 dollars, federal expenditures for Indian programs peaked in 1979 at a total of
$4,446,000,000. By 1989, federal expenditures had fallen to $2,500,000,000.
A large component of the decline was expenditures for Indian housing.
Within the Bureau of Indian Affairs (BIA) budget, expenditures for economic development programs were $143.3 million in 1979 and $47.2 million in 1989 (U.S. Senate, 1992).[4]

---

[4]The identified Indian budget excludes some types of expenditure that are important on
reservations: general welfare assistance, such as Aid to Families with Dependant Children;
job programs supported by the Department of Labor and the Economic Development Administration; and nonhousing programs in the Department of Housing and Urban Development, such as Community Development Block Grants. The Select Committee did not
publish data on these expenditures, which are also in categories targeted by the Reagan-
Bush budget priorities.

1990 Dollars (millions)

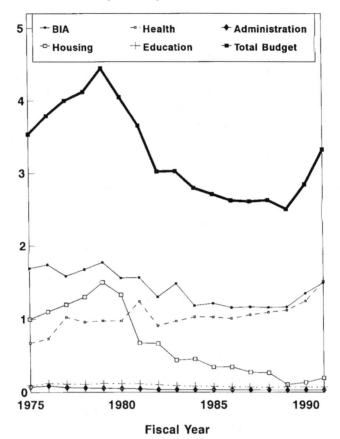

Fiscal Year

FIGURE 8-1 Budget data for elements of the Indian budget in 1990 dollars. NOTES: BIA, Bureau of Indian Affairs; Health, Indian Health Service; Administration, Administration for Native Americans; Housing, Indian Housing Program for U.S. Department of Housing and Urban Affairs; Education, Indian Education Office in U.S. Department of Education; Total Budget, overall Indian Budget. SOURCE: U.S. Senate (1992).

The public sector plays an important role on most reservations. Employment in federal agencies and in programs funded by federal agencies and administered by tribes are significant sources of money for reservation economies. Thus reductions in the public-sector role should have large effects on economic activity as measured by census income data.

In 1990, the population of the 23 reservations was 282,000; the enumerated population on all reservations was 730,000. Thus the 23 reservations accounted for 39 percent of the reservation population. The following comparison of magnitudes assumes that federal expenditures were proportional among reservation residents. In 1979, total federal expenditures on reservations expressed in 1990 dollars were $4.4 billion; of this sum, $1.7 billion would have been spent for the 23 reservations. In the next decade, the population on reservations increased by 31 percent, while the federal expenditures decreased by 57 percent. Measured in 1990 dollars, identified federal expenditures on reservations in 1989 were $2.5 billion; about $1.0 billion of this would have been spent on these 23 reservations. Federal expenditures per person on these 23 reservations would have been approximately $7,900 in 1979 and $3,500 in 1989.[5]

Increases in Wage Inequality

One other factor that might contribute to the turn-around in poverty levels on reservations is the general increase in inequality of the American economy. Table 8-4 provides information on the trends in wage inequality and total inequality over the 20 years under consideration. Harrison and Bluestone (1988) note that there has been a "great U-turn" in the patterns of inequality in the United States. Until the 1970s, inequality decreased. Subsequently, however, it increased. Nelson (1994) provides Gini coefficients based on median family income for 1969, 1979, and 1989, showing that inequality as measured by family income increased in both the 1970s and 1980s, with a greater increase in the 1980s. Trends in inequality in wage income are less easily observed at the overall level; however, Levy and Murnane (1992) review data showing that within groups of wage earners (men, women, men and women classed by educational attainment), inequality was fairly level in the 1970s, but grew rapidly in the 1980s. Thus while it would appear that increases in inequality occurred in both decades, a pattern that is not consistent with the large income increases on reservations in the 1970s, the fact that inequality growth *accelerated* in the 1980s may have contributed to the income declines observed on reservations.

Changes in Gambling and Casinos as a Possible Explanation

Because gaming has become important on reservations, two questions arise. First, was gaming important in 1989? Second, since federal

---

[5]Because some of the salaries and many other federal expenditures on reservations are paid to non-Indians, an exact match of federal expenditures and Indian income is of course not possible. In addition, some federal expenditures occur in the central and area offices of the BIA and the Indian Health Service.

budget expenditures are probably continuing to fall and will not increase, will increases in gaming income reverse the pattern of the 1980s? The answer to the first question is no; widespread gaming is a phenomenon of the 1990s. According to *International Gaming and Wagering Business*, the total amount wagered on Indian reservations was $0.3 billion in 1987, $0.4 billion in 1989, and $29.0 billion in 1993 (Christiansen, 1990, 1994). Bingo, however, was important on some reservations in the 1970s. Of the 23 reservations, three had significant bingo revenue in 1987: Eastern Cherokee, Menominee, and Red Lake (Cordiero, 1992). Of these three, only Eastern Cherokee departed from the overall pattern and had improvements in income and decreases in poverty.

Since 1990, gaming has become important on selected reservations; among the 23 examined here, 8 did not have gaming or a gaming compact as of 1995: Blackfeet, Cheyenne River, Flathead, Hopi, Navajo, Wind River, Yakima, and Zuni. All the others are probably developing gaming to some degree. By 1999, one would expect to see dispersion in income and poverty on Indian reservations: those with large successful gaming operations will do well, and those without will not. If the federal government uses gaming as an excuse for further across-the-board reductions in its reservation expenditures, tribes without gaming will be hard hit. Whether gaming will survive as an income source is also an open question since many state governments oppose Indian gaming, and the Supreme Court recently decided that a tribe could not sue a state in federal court to force the state to negotiate a gaming compact.

MULTIVARIATE ANALYSIS

Multivariate analysis can help sort out the influences of the various factors just discussed. Unfortunately, no data are available for federal expenditures by reservation for each of the years observed. Such data would directly test the influence of changes in the federal budget on income and poverty rates. While a more complete analysis could use such additional data, the results presented here are based on dummy variables for 1979 and 1989, median age, average family size, and two ratios that reflect migration and changes in self-identification.

The dummy variables for 1979 and 1989 should catch the effects of all omitted variables that correlate with national trends or are not adequately correlated with included variables. The dummy for 1979 should show an increase in income and a decrease in poverty. The dummy for 1989 should show a decrease in income and an increase in poverty. These patterns are consistent with the changes in the federal budget and in inequality. Increases in median age should increase per capita income and decrease poverty rates. Larger family sizes should result in lower per capita income and greater percentages of families in poverty.

Migration and changes in self-identification are measured by two age ratios that showed significant average changes across the reservations in the results reported in Table 8-4. The "20s age ratio" is the numbers of persons aged 20 to 29 divided by the number of persons aged 10 to 19 in the previous census. Because of the low earning ability of this age group, an increase in this ratio should be associated with a decrease in per capita income and an increase in poverty. The "30s age ratio" is the number of persons aged 30 to 39 divided by the number of persons aged 20 to 29 in the previous census. Because persons in this age group have higher wages, an increase in this ratio should lead to an increase in per capita income and a decrease in poverty. Because we do not have data by age for these reservations in 1960, we cannot construct these variables for the 1970 census. To test for the effects of migration and changes in self-identification, the database must be reduced to 1980 and 1990.

Table 8-7 presents three ordinary least-squares regressions with per capita income as the dependent variable. The independent variables are provided in Table 8-6. The first regression uses the 70 observations available for the three census years.[6] All variables have the expected signs. The dummy for 1989 does not have a large t-value. The regression explains 55 percent of the variation in per capita income. The second regression is just like the first, but for the smaller sample of 46 observations available for 1980 and 1990. The reference year for the constant term switches to 1979, and the coefficients change in size but not signs. The third regression adds the two age ratios to the second regression. The age ratios have the expected signs, but only the 30s age ratio has a large t-value. The effect of adding the variables is to reduce the size of the constant term and the dummy for 1989; the coefficients for median age and persons per family do not change much. After controlling for the demographic changes measured by these variables, there still is a significant negative impact on income in moving from 1979 to 1989.

Table 8-8 has the same structure as Table 8-7, with a change in dependent variable to the percentage of families in poverty. The signs of all variables are as expected. Neither the 20s nor 30s age ratios have high t-values. The increase in poverty from 1979 to 1989 remains significant after controlling for changes in age, persons per family, and age ratios.

---

[6]In the 1970 census, the Navajo-Hopi Joint Use Area was reported separately. The area was included in the Navajo and Hopi reservations in 1980 and 1990.

TABLE 8-7 Multivariate Analysis of Per Capitqa Income

	1969-1989			1979-1989					
	Coeff.	Stand. Error	t-value	Coeff.	Stand. Error	t-value	Coeff.	Stand. Error	t-value
Constant term	6482	1702	3.81	9592	2250	4.26	8700	2257	3.86
Dummy for 1979	812	269	3.02						
Dummy for 1989	-520	381	-1.36	-1781	339	-5.26	-1654	339	-4.88
Median age	79	49	1.63	88	57	1.53	86	57	1.50
Persons per family	-792	198	-4.01	-1275	301	-4.23	-1224	297	-4.13
Twenties age ratio							-303	641	-0.47
Thirties age ratio							730	431	1.69
Standard error of est.	787			789			774		
R squared	0.55			0.45			0.49		
No. of observations	70			46			46		
Degrees of freedom	65			42			40		

TABLE 8-8 Multivariate Analysis of Percent of Families in Poverty

	1969-1989			1979-1989					
	Coeff.	Stand. Error	t-value	Coeff.	Stand. Error	t-value	Coeff.	Stand. Error	t-value
Constant term	0.329	0.223	1.47	0.345	0.250	1.36	0.415	0.260	1.60
Dummy for 1979	-0.075	0.035	-2.12						
Dummy for 1989	0.127	0.050	2.55	0.217	0.038	5.69	0.208	0.039	5.33
Median Age	-0.011	0.006	-1.74	-0.016	0.006	-2.54	-0.017	0.007	-2.54
Persons per family	0.066	0.026	2.54	0.069	0.034	2.02	0.064	0.034	1.88
Twenties age ratio							0.052	0.074	0.71
Thirties age ratio							-0.068	0.050	-1.37
Standard error of est.	0.103			0.089			0.089		
R Squared	0.40			0.47			0.50		
No. of Observations	70			46			46		
Degrees of Freedom	65			42			40		

CONCLUSION

Because of the important role played by federal expenditures on Indian reservations, it is plausible that reductions in real federal budget expenditures on Indian programs and components of the social safety net contributed to the sharp increase in Indian poverty in the 1980s. Other trends may have contributed, particularly the general increase in inequality in the United States. Also, there may have been changes in the characteristics of people migrating to reservations or deciding to self-identify as Indian. The multivariate analysis in the preceding section controls for two demographic variables and two variables related to migration and changes in self-identification. Increases in age and decreases in family size, both of which worked to reduce poverty, did not have a large enough impact to counteract negative effects on American Indian income. A more complete analysis would draw on disaggregated data on federal expenditures—which would be difficult to assemble—and would control for variables such as education and occupation. These results suggest but do not unequivocally establish the role of federal expenditures in explaining changes in American Indian poverty.

REFERENCES

Bureau of Economic Analysis, U.S. Department of Commerce
  1992   *Business Statistics: 1963-91.* 27th Edition. Washington, D.C.: U.S. Government Printing Office.
Christiansen, E.M.
  1990   1989 gross annual wage. *International Gaming and Wagering Business* 11(7):29.
  1994   1993 gross annual wage. *International Gaming and Wagering Business* 15(7):16.
Cordiero, E.
  1992   The economics of bingo: Factors influencing the success of bingo operations on American Indian reservations. Pp. 205-238 in S. Cornell and J.P. Kalt, eds., *What Can Tribes Do? Strategies and Institutions in American Indian Economic Development.* Los Angeles, CA: American Indian Studies Center, UCLA.
Cornell, S., and M.C. Gil-Swedberg
  1995   Sociohistorical factors in institutional efficacy: Economic development in three American Indian cases. *Economic Development and Cultural Change* 43(2):239-268.
Cornell, S., and J.P. Kalt
  1992   Reloading the dice: Improving the chances for economic development on American Indian reservations. Pp. 1-59 in S. Cornell and J.P. Kalt, eds., *What Can Tribes Do? Strategies and Institutions in American Indian Economic Development.* Los Angeles, CA: American Indian Studies Center, UCLA.
Geisler, C.
  1995   Land and poverty in the United States. *Land Economics* 71(1):16-34.
Harrison, B., and B. Bluestone
  1988   *The Great U-Turn: Corporate Restructuring and the Polarizing of America.* New York: Basic Books.

Kalt, J.P., and S. Cornell
  1994   The redefinition of property rights in American Indian reservations: A compara-
         tive analysis of Native American economic development. Pp. 121-150 in L.H.
         Legters and F.J. Lyden, eds., *American Indian Policy: Self-Governance and Economic
         Development*. Westport, CT: Greenwood Press.
Levy, F., and R.J. Murnane
  1992   U.S. earnings levels and earnings inequality: A review of recent trends and pro-
         posed explanations. *Journal of Economic Literature* 30(3):1331-81.
McDonnell, J.A.
  1991   *The Dispossession of The American Indians:1887-1934*. Bloomington, IN: Indiana Uni-
         versity Press.
Nelson, C.T.
  1994   Levels of and changes in the distribution of U.S. income. Pp. 29-63 in J.H.
         Bergstand, ed., *The Changing Distribution of Income in an Open U.S. Economy*.
         Amsterdam: North-Holland.
Otis, D.S.
  1973   *The Dawes Act and the Allotment of Indian Land*. Norman, OK: University of Okla-
         homa Press.
Sacks, J.D., and F.B. Larrain
  1993   *Macroeconomics in the Global Economy*. Englewood Cliffs, NJ: Prentice Hall.
Snipp, C.M.
  1989   *American Indians: The First of This Land*. New York: Russell Sage Foundation.
Stinson, F.S., and M.C. Plantz.
  1986   *The American Indian/Alaska Native Data Base*. Available from National Technical
         Information Service, Tape PB87-152732, Documentation PB87-152724. Washing-
         ton, D.C.: CSR, Inc.
Sutton, I., ed.
  1985   *Irredeemable America*. Albuquerque, NM: University of New Mexico Press.
U.S. Bureau of the Census
  1972   *General Social and Economic Characteristics: United States Summary*. Subject Reports
         PC(1)-C1. Washington, D.C.: U.S. Government Printing Office.
  1973   *American Indians*. 1970 Census of Housing and Population, Subject Report PC(2)-
         1F. Washington, D.C.: U.S. Government Printing Office.
  1983   *General Social and Economic Characteristics*. 1980 Census of Housing and Population.
         Washington, D.C.: U.S. Government Printing Office.
  1993a *American Indian and Alaska Native Areas*. 1990 Census of Housing and Population.
         Washington, D.C.: U.S. Government Printing Office.
  1993b *Social and Economic Characteristics*. 1990 Census of Housing and Population. Wash-
         ington, D.C.: U.S. Government Printing Office.
  1993c *Summary Tape File 3 on CD ROM*. 1990 Census of Housing and Population.
         Suitland, MD: Data User Services.
U.S. Senate
  1992   *Budget Views and Estimates for Fiscal Year 1993*. Select Committee on Indian Affairs
         102d Congress, 2d Session (S. Prt. 102-91). Washington, D.C.: U.S. Government
         Printing Office.

9

The Demography of American Indian Families

Gary D. Sandefur and Carolyn A. Liebler

INTRODUCTION

This chapter describes some key features of contemporary American Indian families and changes in these features over time. A major theme of the discussion is that a growing proportion of American Indian children reside with only one parent. The prevalence of single-parent families is especially pronounced on some reservations. These family patterns, combined with depressed economic conditions, place many American Indian children at risk.

To examine American Indian families, we rely primarily on data from the U.S. Bureau of the Census. These data show that American Indian children are less likely to reside with two parents than are children in the total U.S. population. Also, American Indian women are less likely to ever marry and more likely to be divorced than women in general. The trends in these characteristics over time roughly follow trends in the overall U.S. opulation.

The extent of single parenthood, never marrying, and divorce is higher on some of the reservations than among other segments of the Indian population. These reservations also tend to have high unemployment and poverty rates, and some have unfavorable sex ratios for mar-

This research was supported by funds provided to the Graduate School at the University of Wisconsin-Madison by the Wisconsin Alumni Research Foundation. We appreciate the comments of Barney Cohen, Ronald Rindfuss, and two anonymous reviewers.

riage. The conditions on the ten largest reservations are such that American Indian women and children, as well as others, on these reservations are likely to need free medical assistance, along with other forms of public assistance, well into the future.

The next section looks at some of the limitations of census data for understanding American Indian families. This is followed by a review of the various groups within the American Indian population that are examined in the ensuing discussion of selected features of American Indian families. The chapter ends with a summary and conclusions.

LIMITATIONS OF CENSUS DATA FOR UNDERSTANDING AMERICAN INDIAN FAMILIES

Studying American Indian families with census data involves some difficulties. The two major problems are the lack of information on kinship and family relationships beyond the household and changes in self-identification that make it very difficult to interpret trends among American Indians. A true story illustrates these two problems.[1] The first author, a member of the Chickasaw Nation in Oklahoma, is one of the great great grandchildren of Ishtokenahe (male) and Simonteche (female). Ishtokenahe and Simonteche came to Oklahoma from Mississippi during the Chickasaw era of the "Trail of Tears," the forced removal of the Cherokee, Chickasaw, Choctaw, Creek, and other groups from the southeastern United States during the early to mid-1800s. Among their children was Gabriel Underwood, the great grandfather of the first author. During his adult years, Mr. Underwood, a full-blood, had three full-blood wives who maintained somewhat separate households. Mr. Underwood moved periodically from household to household during the late 1800s and early 1900s. Although polygamy had been officially outlawed by the Chickasaw Nation before that time, a number of Chickasaws continued to maintain such relationships.

Gabriel Underwood had several children, all full-bloods, some of whom married other Chickasaws, but most of whom married non-Chickasaws. Most of his grandchildren, both full- and half-blood, married non-Chickasaws. His great grandchildren, the first author's generation and the great great grandchildren of Ishtokenahe and Simonteche, are all at least one-quarter Chickasaw and could be members of the Chickasaw nation if they chose to be. But the records about the different people do not always reflect their Indian heritage. Some of their births were recorded as Indian births if the doctor decided that the race of one of the

---

[1]This account is based on tribal and census records and on family oral history. The spellings of Ishtokenahe and Simonteche are phonetic and vary across written records.

parents was Indian; some were recorded as white births. Yet some of the people who were considered Indian at birth have never identified themselves as Chickasaws in censuses or elsewhere, while some of those who were not recorded as Indian at birth have always identified themselves as Chickasaws. Others have changed their self-identification back and forth over the years in different censuses.

Further, census data on these individuals will reveal only some features of their family and kinship relationships. The data will show with whom they are currently living and some characteristics of their households and families. But the data will not reveal the relatively recent experience of polygamy in this family, the complexity of kinship networks beyond the nuclear family, or the extent of intermarriage in previous generations.

Many contemporary American Indians can tell similar and in many cases more complicated stories about their family histories and their current family situations. Clan systems, relationships with non-nuclear family members, and ritualistic adoptive relationships play very important roles in the family lives of many contemporary Native Americans. Many American Indians have ancestors who were members of two or more Native American groups and/or ancestors who were not Indian. For these reasons, many American Indians and students of American Indians see census data as inadequate for describing and understanding contemporary American Indian families, households, and kinship systems.

Nonetheless, we assert that one can learn a good deal about contemporary American Indian families by examining census data. In fact, census data provide information that is relevant to consideration of the implications of healthcare reform for Native Americans—the purpose of organizing the workshop at which this paper was originally presented. Information on household size and composition and trends in these over time provide useful background information for this purpose. The aims of this chapter are to examine the trends in these characteristics among American Indians over time, as they are currently, and across subgroups of the American Indian and Alaska Native populations. These subgroups include the national population of American Indians and those people living on reservations and trust lands (shortened here to "reservations"), in Alaska Native Village Statistical Areas (Alaska NVSAs), in Oklahoma Tribal Jurisdiction Statistical Areas (Oklahoma TJSAs), and on 1990's ten most populated reservations.

GROUPS WITHIN THE AMERICAN INDIAN POPULATION

Table 9-1 contains selected characteristics of the groups that are examined in this chapter. The purposes of this table and this section of the

TABLE 9-1 Selected Characteristics of the American Indian Population, 1990

Population	Population Size	Median Age	Sex Ratio 25-34	Family Size	Poverty Rate	Unemp. Rate	Female LFP Rate[a]
Total U.S.	248,710,000	33.0	100.1	3.2	13.1	6.3	56.8
U.S. Indian	1,959,234	26.9	103.4	3.6	31.0	14.4	55.1
Reservation	437,358	22.4	94.5	4.2	50.7	25.6	45.1
Oklahoma TJSA	200,789	26.4	94.7	3.4	29.8	12.4	51.9
Alaska NVSA	47,244	23.1	111.2	4.3	26.8	24.5	48.3
Navajo	123,944	22.0	92.6	4.6	56.5	29.9	38.5
Pine Ridge	10,455	18.9	103.5	4.9	66.0	32.6	42.7
Fort Apache	9,825	21.3	96.5	4.6	52.7	35.3	45.7
Gila River	9,116	22.7	87.7	4.1	64.4	30.6	35.5
Papago	8,480	24.2	97.1	4.0	65.7	23.4	32.7
San Carlos	7,110	21.4	92.7	4.6	62.5	31.0	29.4
Zuni Pueblo	7,073	24.1	100.1	5.0	52.5	13.8	65.2
Hopi	7,061	25.9	110.1	4.4	49.4	26.8	44.8
Blackfoot	7,025	22.8	89.1	4.0	50.1	31.1	53.2
Rosebud	6,883	18.6	98.1	4.4	56.6	27.3	44.6

[a]LFP = labor force participation.

SOURCES: U.S. Bureau of the Census (1992a:Tables 1, 3, 5, and 6; 1992b:Tables 16, 23, and 40; 1993a: Tables 4, 5, and 9; 1993b:Tables 2, 3, and 44).

chapter are to provide some contextual information about these different groups that can aid in interpreting differences in family patterns and to introduce evidence that might be related to these differences.

The U.S. Indian population includes all individuals who identified themselves or were identified by a respondent in their households as American Indians, Eskimo, or Aleuts on the "race" question in the census. The reservation Indian population includes all of the first category who resided on an American Indian reservation or trust land as defined by the federal or a state government. The Oklahoma TJSA population includes all American Indians who live in areas delineated by federally recognized tribes in Oklahoma without reservations (only the Osage in Oklahoma officially have a reservation), for which the Census Bureau tabulates data. The population of the Alaska NVSA includes American Indians, Eskimo, or Aleuts residing in tribes, bands, clans, groups, villages, communities, or associations in Alaska that are recognized pursuant to the Alaska Native Claims Settlement Act of 1972, Public Law 92-203.[2]

Each of these populations is diverse. The U.S. Indian population, for example, contains individuals who have lived on isolated reservations for their entire lives and those whose families left their traditional tribal areas two or more generations ago. The population residing on reservations includes individuals who live on reservations where most of the other residents are Indians and those who live on reservations where the majority of the population is non-Indian. The Oklahoma TJSAs include those of tribes, such as the Cherokee and Choctaw, that were removed to Oklahoma in the 1830s, along with those of tribes, such as the Comanche and Kiowa, that have been in parts of Oklahoma for hundreds of years. The Alaska NVSAs include Indian, Eskimo, and Aleut areas, containing several distinct cultural groups.

To examine some groups that are more homogeneous, we also look at the ten largest reservations in the United States. These range in size from the Navajo reservation, which contains over one-quarter of the total U.S. reservation population, to the Blackfoot reservation, with a population of 7,025.

As one can see from Table 9-1, the American Indian population differs substantially from the total U.S. population in many respects. The U.S. Indian population is younger, poorer, and more likely to be unemployed and has larger families on average than does the U.S. population in general. This is especially true of the reservation population, whose

---

[2]This information is based on descriptions of these populations in U.S. Bureau of the Census (1993a:A2-A3). Further discussion of specific reservations can be found in Hirschfelder and de Montano (1993).

median age is over 10 years younger than that of the general U.S. population, whose poverty and unemployment rates are close to four times higher, and whose average family size is one full person larger.

The lower median age among American Indians reflects their higher fertility and mortality rates, as discussed elsewhere in this volume. In addition, a population with a lower median age than that of another probably has a higher proportion of adult women in younger age groups, which may well affect differences in marital patterns across populations. Poverty and unemployment represent obvious disadvantages. In addition, larger families have more difficulty making ends meet, other things being equal (Blake, 1989; Sandefur and Sakamoto, 1988; Sweet and Bumpass, 1987).

Each of the ten largest reservations has its own set of distinctive characteristics. The Navajo reservation is located in three states—Arizona, New Mexico, and Utah—and the Zuni Pueblo is in both Arizona and New Mexico. Pine Ridge and Rosebud are Sioux reservations in South Dakota, and the Blackfoot reservation is in Montana. The other reservations are in Arizona. Fort Apache and San Carlos are Apache reservations; Gila River contains the Pima and Maricopa; the Papago have expressed an official preference to be known as the T'Ohono Odham. The populations of these reservations are characterized by their youthfulness, large families, and extraordinarily high poverty and unemployment rates.

Previous research suggests that the characteristics shown in Table 9-1 may very well be connected with the family patterns described below. The median age, poverty rate, and unemployment rate both reflect and affect fertility, marriage, and family patterns among the different segments of the American Indian population, including the reservations. Poor and unemployed individuals are less likely to marry and more likely to divorce (Cherlin, 1992). Consequently, variations in poverty and unemployment across different populations are generally associated with differences in family patterns.

In addition, the sex ratio and the rate of female labor force participation are likely associated with family patterns. The sex ratio—the ratio of men to women—for individuals aged 25-34 is higher for the U.S. Indian population and considerably higher for the Alaska NVSAs than it is for the U.S. population in general. But it is lower for the reservation Indian population and the Oklahoma TJSAs than for the U.S. population in general. Among the reservations, the sex ratio ranges from 87.7 on the Gila River reservation to 110.1 on the Hopi reservation. The sex ratio varies significantly across these reservations.

Table 9-1 displays differences in women's labor force participation across segments of the American Indian population. The female labor force participation rates are very similar for the general U.S. population and the U.S. Indian population, but considerably lower on the reservations. Among the reservations, the rate of labor force participation ranges from 29.4 percent on the San Carlos reservation to 65.2 percent in the Zuni Pueblo.

SELECTED FEATURES OF AMERICAN INDIAN FAMILIES

Children Living with Two Parents

The data from the U.S. census provide us with a "snapshot" of family life that allows us to determine whether children were living with two parents at the time the census was taken, although the data do not permit us to know how long the child has lived with these two parents.[3] But differences across population subgroups on this criterion are good indicators of differences in exposure to single parenthood during childhood.

Table 9-2 shows the percentage of children under 18 residing with two parents. This number has been declining for the U.S. Indian population over the past two decades in a pattern similar to the well-known pattern for the general U.S. population. In 1990, just over one-half of American Indian children under 18 lived with two parents, compared with 70 percent of all U.S. children. Fewer than one-half of children on reservations were residing with two parents, while the percentages of children living with two parents in the Oklahoma TJSAs and the Alaska NVSAs were higher than for the national Indian population.

The ten largest reservations in 1990 varied considerably in the percentage of children who resided with two parents. Among the Navajo, approximately 57 percent of children under 18 lived with two parents in 1990, while on the Pine Ridge reservation, just over 35 percent did so. Yet the proportion of children under 18 who lived with two parents was lower on all of the reservations than it was among the U.S. population, and was less than 50 percent on many of the reservations.

Should we be concerned about the prevalence of single-parent families among American Indians? Certainly, the functioning of a child's family is an important factor in the chances that child will have in later life. As Zill and Nord (1994:1) point out, "Among the functions families are expected to fulfill are providing for the basic physical needs of their members, including food, clothing, and shelter; teaching children right from wrong, to respect the rights of others, and to value other social

---

[3]The data also do not permit us to know whether the two parents are the biological parents. Further, those children living with two cohabiting biological parents who do not consider themselves to be married are reported as residing with a single parent.

TABLE 9-2 Percentage of Children
Under 18 Residing with Two Parents

Population	1970	1980	1990
Total U.S.	82.1	76.7	70.2
U.S. Indian	68.6	62.9	54.4
Reservation			48.8
Oklahoma TJSA			65.8
Alaska NVSA			60.8
Navajo			57.2
Pine Ridge			35.2
Fort Apache			55.1
Gila River			35.8
Papago			37.1
San Carlos			53.8
Zuni Pueblo			47.2
Hopi			42.6
Blackfoot			53.2
Rosebud			37.1

SOURCES: U.S. Bureau of the Census (1973a; 1973b:
Table 54; 1983b:Tables 100 and 141; 1992a:Table 6;
1992b:Tables 37 and 41).

institutions; and monitoring and supervising children in their daily activities to protect them from harm and to ensure that they behave according to the rules of society." Family structure affects the ability of families to fulfill these key functions and thus affects the well-being of children (Hernandez, 1993).

One aspect of family structure that is associated with how well families are able to do their jobs is whether the family has two parents. In examining the consequences of growing up in a single-parent family, McLanahan and Sandefur (1994) show that the benefits children receive from their families depend in part on whether one or both parents are present. When one parent is forced or voluntarily chooses to be a sole parent, children suffer.

Information from the census, the Current Population Surveys, and other data show clearly that one-parent families have considerably fewer *economic resources* than two-parent families. In 1993, approximately 35.6 percent of families headed by single mothers had incomes below the poverty line, as compared with 6.5 percent of families headed by two parents (U.S. Bureau of the Census, 1995). Not all of the difference in income is due to the consequences of divorce or a decision to bear a child out of wedlock. But our research and that of other social scientists has clearly shown that divorce and out-of-wedlock childbearing do substantially reduce the income of custodial parents relative to what it would be if they were married. A number of factors create this situation. Among them is that many noncustodial fathers do not pay adequate child support.

The absence of a parent also leads to lower access to *parental resources*. Fathers who live in separate households see their children less frequently. Interacting with a former spouse and maintaining a relationship with a child who lives in another household can be very difficult and painful. Many fathers respond by reducing the amount of time they spend with their children or disengaging completely (Wallerstein and Kelly, 1980). Family disruption also alters the mother-child relationship. Most single mothers are forced to fill multiple roles simultaneously, without adequate support. Some experience high levels of stress and become anxious and depressed (McLoyd and Wilson, 1991; McLeod and Shanahan, 1993; Hetherington et al., 1978). This can lead to inconsistent and ineffective parenting.

Finally, residing in a one-parent family can lower access to *community resources*. This occurs partially through income: families with more income can afford to live in communities with better facilities, such as daycare centers, schools, parks, and community centers. Another reason for the connection between family structure and community resources is the higher residential and geographical mobility of children with divorced and separated parents relative to those with two parents (McLanahan, 1983; Haveman et al., 1991; Speare and Goldscheider, 1987). When parents and children live in a community for a long time, they develop close ties that provide emotional support, as well as information about the broader community. When a family moves from town to town or from neighborhood to neighborhood, these ties are undermined and often destroyed.

In sum, then, research suggests that family structure affects the economic, parental, and community resources available to children. The availability of these resources in turn affects direct measures of child and later adult well-being, such as social and emotional adjustment, educational attainment, family formation, and labor force participation.

The data from the census do not allow us to examine in a careful manner the impact of residing in a single-parent family on the economic, parental, and community resources available to children. If, however, living with two parents is an advantage for children, then American Indians are less likely on average to have this advantage.

Possible Factors Associated with the
Prevalence of Single-Parent Families

Among the trends associated with the increasing proportion of children living with single parents are the increasing percentages of women who have never married and who are divorced. These increases, in turn, appear to be associated with the growing economic independence of women, due primarily to increased labor force participation, changes in attitudes and values about out-of-wedlock childbearing, and the declining economic situation of men (Cherlin, 1992; McLanahan and Sandefur, 1994). These trends that have affected the U.S. population in general have probably also affected the American Indian population.

No research has explored carefully the factors that might account for Indian and white differences in family patterns. Wilson and Neckerman (1986), Bennett et al. (1989), Mare and Winship (1991), and Cherlin (1992) explore some of the factors that might account for the differences in family patterns among blacks and whites. Among the factors that seem to be involved are a tighter marriage squeeze (ratio of men to women, taking into account the usual difference in the average ages of brides and grooms), the lower employment prospects for black men relative to white men, differences in the meaning of marriage as an institution among blacks and whites, and the continuation of historical patterns that date back at least to the turn of the century. As a group, these factors do not completely account for black/white differences or for changes in the black and white patterns over time. According to Cherlin (1992:112), "The evidence is inconclusive and has been read differently by people with different points of view." Moreover, the experiences of Indians are as different from those of blacks as from those of whites; for example, the rate of intermarriage for Indians is much higher than for either whites or blacks. Thus explorations of black and white differences in family patterns are not necessarily a good guide for the exploration of white and Indian differences.

A detailed examination of the factors associated with white/Indian differences in family patterns would require more work than is possible to summarize in this chapter. Moreover, such an examination would be complicated by the difficulty of examining trends over time among a population growing rapidly as a result of changes in self-identification; the lack of data on the marriage squeeze; and the lack of data on attitudes toward marriage, divorce, and childbearing among American Indians. Nonetheless, it is possible to describe some of the characteristics of the American Indian population that might be associated with the above-described patterns in percentage of children residing with two parents, including marriage and divorce.[4]

Women Who Have Never Married

Cherlin (1992) describes the trends in the percentage of U.S. men and women aged 20-24 who have never married for the period 1890 through 1990. These percentages changed very little between 1890 and 1940, declined from 1940 to 1960, and have increased since then. In 1990, however, they were at a level similar to that in 1890. If the increase continues during the 1990s, we will reach historic highs in the percentages of people aged 20-24 who have never married.

Most women eventually marry—historically, over 90 percent of women in each cohort. Projections for those born during the baby boom, however, suggest that under 90 percent of these women will ever marry (Cherlin, 1992; Schoen, 1987). Nonetheless, it is important to bear in mind that it is a delay in age at marriage more than a decline in the percentage who ever marry that primarily accounts for the increase in the percentage of never-married women at the early adult ages.

Figure 9-1 displays trends in the percentages of American Indian and all U.S. women aged 25-34 who have never married. This is an older age group than that used by Cherlin. The U.S. trend shows the familiar pattern of a decline in this percentage through 1960 and an increase since then, especially during the most recent two decades. The curve for the U.S. Indian population shows that in 1940, a smaller percentage of Indian women than of all U.S. women had never married, but that this relationship had reversed by 1960. (The percentage of American Indians aged 25-34 who had never married in 1950 is not available in census publications.) The increase in the percentage for American Indians was not as dramatic in the 1970s as it was for all women, but it was larger in the 1980s than for all women.

One must be very cautious about interpreting these trends because of changes in census enumeration procedures and self-identification over

---

[4]A thorough job of explaining variations in family patterns across the different Indian populations would require a careful exploration of nondemographic sources of these variations. Each reservation, for example, has its own history of traditional family patterns, traditional marriage norms, and traditional divorce norms. In addition, some reservations have been heavily influenced by Catholicism or other Christian religions, while others have retained more of their traditional religious practices. The available ethnographic research does not provide a clear picture of how these combinations of traditional cultural practices, traditional religious beliefs, and Western religious norms and values about marriage and divorce have influenced contemporary Indian attitudes toward marriage and divorce. We focus here on the demography of family patterns.

Percentage

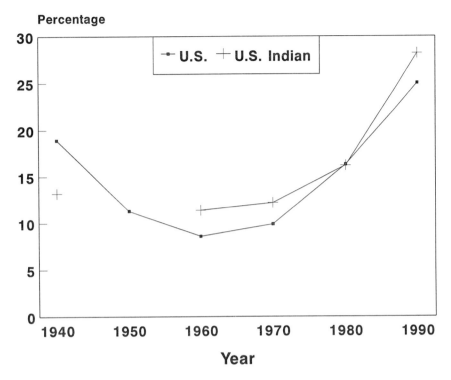

FIGURE 9-1 Percentage of women aged 25-34 who have never married. SOURCES: U.S. Bureau of the Census (1992b:Table 34; 1983b:Tables 100 and 121; U.S. 1973a:Tables 2 and 3; 1973b:Tables 89 and 203; 1963:Table 20; 1953:Table 102; 1943:Table 4).

time, but the fact that the percentage was lower for American Indian women than for white women in 1940, yet higher than for white women in 1960, does match the historical pattern for the nonwhite population in general (Cherlin, 1992).

Because of limitations in the published data, we shift from an age-specific rate to the general rate and look at women aged 15 and over to compare different segments of the Indian population. According to Table 9-3, a higher percentage of women on reservations and in the Alaska NVSAs have never married relative to those in the U.S. Indian population and all women. A smaller percentage of women in the Oklahoma TJSAs have never married relative to all women. A portion of these differences is undoubtedly due to the substantially lower median age on the reservations (22.4) and in the Alaska NVSAs (23.1) than among the other groups (e.g., 33.0 among U.S. women) (see Table 9-1).

TABLE 9-3 Percentage of Women
Aged 15+ Who Were Never
Married, 1990

Population	Percentage
United States	23.4
U.S. Indian	29.7
Reservation	37.1
Oklahoma TJSA	21.7
Alaska NVSA	35.6
Navajo	37.2
Pine Ridge	43.5
Fort Apache	35.2
Gila River	44.1
Papago	52.0
San Carlos	34.0
Zuni Pueblo	31.3
Hopi	35.0
Blackfoot	32.8
Rosebud	40.7

SOURCES: U.S. Bureau of the Census
(1992a:Table 6; 1992b:Table 34).

We also see that the percentage of women on the ten largest reservations aged 15 and over who had never married was higher than that for the U.S. population. The numbers range from a low of approximately 31 percent on the Zuni reservation to a high of 52 percent on the Papago reservation. All of these figures are above the percentage for all women in the United States (23.4). The median ages of the Zuni (24.1) and Papago (24.2) reservations are relatively the same, but the poverty and unemployment rates are higher on the Papago than on the Zuni reservation. In addition, the sex ratio is slightly more favorable in the Zuni Pueblo than among the Papago (see Table 9-1).

Unfortunately, we do not know very much about the historical patterns of marriage on these specific reservations, so it is not clear whether these figures represent new or continuing patterns of delayed marriage and/or permanent single status. Also, we do not have the appropriate data to examine what accounts for the variation across segments of the national Indian population or differences among the ten largest reservations. We can speculate on some possibilities. First, the marriage market may differ significantly across the reservations in ways that are only partially reflected in the descriptive data on the median age, sex ratio, and economic situations of young men and women. Second, the differences may be due to cultural norms and values regarding the institution of marriage, issues we do not explore here.

Divorce

Cherlin (1992:20-22) summarizes the changes in the divorce rate (proportion of marriages that end in divorce) that have taken place in the United States since 1860. The rate has been rising since the middle of the nineteenth century, with a smaller increase than expected from 1950 to 1960, but a sharp rise from the early 1960s to 1979. The divorce rate declined slightly in the 1980s, but nevertheless is currently higher than predicted by the long-term trend. Nationwide events show a clear effect on the divorce rate: it has increased temporarily after every major war and was lower during the depression of the 1930s.

It is impossible to compare trends in the proportion of marriages that end in divorce for whites and Indians because of the lack of racial identification in marriage and divorce records. What we can do is examine the percentage of women among the American Indian and U.S. populations who are divorced. To reiterate, this is not the same as the percentage of marriages that end in divorce. Such figures are sensitive not only to the proportion of marriages that end in divorce, but also to the marriage and remarriage rates. Figure 9-2 shows the percentage of women aged 14+ or 15+ who were divorced for the years 1940 through 1990. In 1940, a very small percentage of women by contemporary standards were divorced. This figure was slightly higher for American Indians than for the U.S. population in general. The percentage of women divorced has increased steadily since then, and the gap between American Indians and whites has widened since 1960. The combination of an increased proportion of women who have never married and a higher percentage of women who have been divorced helps explain why more American Indian children reside with a single parent.

Table 9-4 shows the percentages of women aged 15+ who were divorced as of 1990 for different segments of the American Indian population. The percentage divorced is the same for Indians on reservations as for the total population of women, and lower for those in Alaska NVSAs. On the other hand, the percentage is higher among Indian women in the Oklahoma TJSAs than among women in general.

The reservations with the highest percentages of divorced women (Pine Ridge and Rosebud) also have the third and fourth highest percentages of women never married (see Table 9-3), and this helps explain the low percentage of children residing with two parents on these reservations (see Table 9-2). In contrast, the Papago reservation has a low general divorce rate, but this is accompanied by the highest percentage of women

Percentage

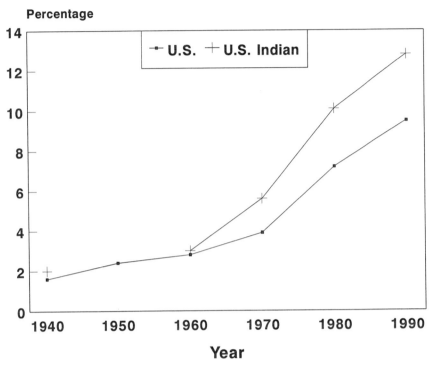

FIGURE 9-2   Percentage of women aged 14+ or 15+ who are divorced.
SOURCES: U.S. Bureau of the Census (1992b:Table 34; 1983a:Table 46; 1973b:
Table 203; 1973a: Table 5; 1964:Tables 49 and 177; 1963:Table 10; 1943:Table 4).

never married, which leads in turn to a low percentage of children residing with two parents. And the Navajo reservation has a low divorce rate,
is intermediate in the percentage never married, and has the highest percentage of children residing with two parents. In sum, several combinations of factors can result in lower percentages of children residing with
two parents.

Interracial Marriage

Intermarriage between whites and Indians in the United States has a
long history (Sandefur and McKinnell, 1986). Practical political and economic reasons have promoted marriages between whites and Indians.
Prior to the decision of the U.S. government in the early 1800s to "re-
move" most of the Indians who were east of the Mississippi to western
areas, intermarriage facilitated good relations between Indians and
whites. The French were reputed to have no aversion to marrying Indi-

TABLE 9-4 Percentage of Women
Aged 15+ Who Were Divorced,
1990

Population	Percentage
United States	9.5
U.S. Indian	12.8
Reservation	9.5
Oklahoma TJSA	12.4
Alaska NVSA	5.6
Navajo	5.6
Pine Ridge	12.4
Fort Apache	10.0
Gila River	8.7
Papago	5.8
San Carlos	9.0
Zuni Pueblo	6.8
Hopi	8.9
Blackfoot	9.5
Rosebud	14.5

SOURCES: U.S. Bureau of the Census
(1992a:Table 6; 1992b:Table 34).

ans (Lauber, 1913), and one celebrated intermarriage in the colony of New York involving a prominent white man and a wife from the Six Nations was said to have greatly facilitated cooperation between the New York colonial government and the government of the Six Nations (Maury, 1872). Soldiers on the frontier sometimes married Indians; trappers, traders, and agents often did so. There were, in fact, some legal attempts to promote marriages between whites and Indians. In 1784, a bill was presented to the Virginia legislature providing that "every white man who married an Indian woman should be paid ten pounds, and five for each child born of such a marriage; and that if any white woman married an Indian she should be entitled to ten pounds with which the county court should buy them livestock" (Beveridge, 1919:239-241). In 1824, William H. Crawford advocated similar legislation before the U.S. Congress. Neither measure became law (Beveridge, 1919).

Past federal government definitions of its Indian service population, which generally used one-quarter Indian blood as the minimum blood quantum, and contemporary tribal definitions of citizenship, which in some cases require demonstrated descent but no blood quantum, represent a response to this history of intermarriage. The proportion of the

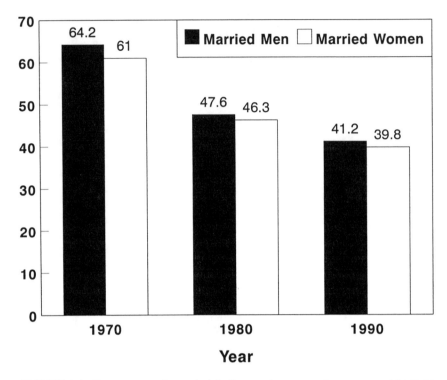

FIGURE 9-3 Percentage of married indians who are endogamous. SOURCE: Calculations with Public Use Microdata Samples from the 1970, 1980, and 1990 United States censuses.

American Indian population that is the product of intermarriages with non-Indians is quite high and continues to rise (Snipp, 1989).

Figure 9-3 shows that the percentage of both Indian men and women who were exogamous increased considerably over the 20 years from 1970 to 1990. Part of this increase was probably due to the fact that American Indians who changed their self-identification to Indian during the period were more likely to be married to a non-Indian than those who kept the same identity. Our analyses with data from the 1990 public-use microdata samples show as well that younger American Indian cohorts were much more likely to be exogamous than were older cohorts of both American Indian men and women. American Indian men were more likely than American Indian women to be endogamous, i.e., to marry other American Indians.

SUMMARY AND CONCLUSIONS

Our description of American Indian families has relied largely on published data from the decennial censuses, making it a mostly quantitative exploration. Yellow Bird and Snipp (1994) and John (1988) summarize some of the ethnographic and other qualitative work on American Indian families. Most of this work has focused on specific nations or tribes, and demonstrates that there is as much variation among families and households within the American Indian population as there is between American Indians and other groups in the U.S. population. Our analysis of published census data also illustrates the variations across broad segments of the American Indian population—Oklahoma TJSAs, Alaska NVSAs, and the ten largest reservations.

Nonetheless, the data also show that the trends in marriage, divorce, and living arrangements among the American Indian population have corresponded with these trends in the general population. Over time, the percentage of children living with two parents has decreased, and the percentages of women who have never married and who have divorced have increased, just as has been the case among the U.S. population in general. At the same time, American Indian children are less likely to live with two parents than all U.S. children, and American Indian women are less likely to ever marry and more likely to divorce than are all U.S. women.

The differences are more pronounced on some of the reservations. On the Pine Ridge reservation, for example, 35.2 percent of children lived with two parents, compared with 70.2 percent of all U.S. children; 43.5 percent of women aged 15+ had never married, compared with 23.4 percent of all U.S. women aged 15+; and 12.4 percent of women aged 15+ were divorced, compared with 9.5 percent of all U.S. women aged 15+. The bottom line is that American Indian women and children, especially those on reservations, are in more vulnerable social and economic situations than are all U.S. women and children.

The Oklahoma TJSA statistics for average household size and percentage of women over 15 who have never married are more similar to those for the general U.S. population in some respects than to those for the other Indian groups. But the unemployment rate for the Oklahoma TJSAs is almost twice that of the U.S. population as a whole, and the poverty rate is more than double.

The combination of statistics about the Alaska NVSAs paints an unusual picture. The sex ratio is 111.2 men per 100 women; on the other hand, a high percentage of women over 15 (36 percent) have never married. Part of this is probably due to the very low median age, 23.1, in the

Alaska NVSAs. Those who do marry stay married or remarry right away, putting the percentage of women currently divorced at a remarkably low 5.6 percent and the children living with two parents at 60.8 percent. Even though the people in the Alaska NVSAs are similar to those on reservations in their female labor force participation, large household size, and unemployment, the percentage of people in poverty in the Alaska NVSAs is about half that on reservations (26.8 compared with 50.7).

The reservation population consists of only 94.5 men per 100 women aged 25 to 34, and the median age is quite low. Men may leave the reservation to find work, but this means that 37.1 percent of women over age 15 have never married. This low incidence of marriage does not seem to hold down the average family size (4.2 people per family), but it does mean that fewer than half of children under 18 who live on reservations live with two parents. With the highest unemployment rate of any Indian group (25.6), only 45.1 percent of American Indian women on reservations bother to join the workforce. All of this is exacerbated by the overwhelmingly high poverty rates on reservations.

The variations in marriage and living arrangements for children across the segments of the Indian population and across the reservations are associated with different patterns in median age, sex ratios, female labor force participation, poverty, and unemployment. It is likely that poverty, unemployment, and unfavorable sex ratios on some reservations make marriages very difficult to begin and to maintain. Other differences in cultural norms and values regarding marriage, divorce, and childbearing across the different segments of the Indian population and among the reservations are probably also important factors in creating the differences observed in the data from the decennial censuses.

One implication for health policy of the conditions among American Indians, especially on the reservations, seems obvious. The availability of healthcare through the Indian Health Service, tribal health services, and Medicaid is likely to continue to be very important for American Indian mothers and children because they are in a particularly vulnerable social and economic situation. The levels of poverty and unemployment on some of the reservations make it virtually impossible for many of these women and children to obtain healthcare through employer-based health insurance.

This vulnerability also has implications for proposed changes in social welfare policy. The high percentage of American Indian children living with one parent, combined with high levels of poverty and unemployment, probably leads to greater reliance on Aid to Families with Dependent Children (AFDC), Food Stamps, and other forms of public assistance than is the case among the U.S. population of children. Some of the proposed changes in the AFDC program, such as caps on benefits, limits

on the amount of time a family can receive AFDC, and work requirements, are likely to be very damaging to American Indian mothers and
children on reservations, where there are few alternative ways to support
a family.

In the long run, improving the lives of American Indian families and
children will require substantial investments in the health and education
of American Indian people on and off the reservations. In addition, tribal
governments, working with private industry, state governments, and the
federal government, must continue their efforts to create employment
opportunities on the reservations and in traditional Indian areas in Alaska
and Oklahoma. Economic self-sufficiency for many Native Americans is
still an impossibility in many of the most economically depressed areas.

REFERENCES

Bennett, N.G., D.E. Bloom, and P.H. Craig
  1989   The divergence of black and white marriage patterns. *American Journal of Sociology*
         95:692-722.
Beveridge, A.
  1919   *The Life of John Marshall*. Vol. 1. New York: Houghton Mifflin.
Blake, J.
  1989   *Family Size and Achievement*. Berkeley: University of California Press.
Cherlin, A.J.
  1992   *Marriage, Divorce, and Remarriage*. Cambridge, MA: Harvard University Press.
Haveman, R., B. Wolfe, and J. Spaulding
  1991   Childhood events and circumstances influencing high school completion. *Demog-
         raphy* 23:133-158.
Hernandez, D.J.
  1993   *America's Children: Resources from Family, Government, and the Economy*. New York:
         Russell Sage Foundation.
Hetherington, M., M. Cox, and R. Cox
  1978   The aftermath of divorce. Pp. 148-176 in J.H. Stephens and Marilyn Matthews,
         eds., *Mother-Child, Father-Child Relations*. Washington, D.C.: National Association
         for the Education of Young Children Press.
Hirschfelder, A., and M.K. de Montano
  1993   *The Native American Almanac: A Portrait of Native America Today*. New York:
         Prentice Hall.
John, R.
  1988   The Native American Family. Pp. 325-363 in C.H. Mindel, R.W. Habenstein, and R.
         Wright, Jr., eds., *Ethnic Families in America: Patterns and Variations*. New York:
         Elsevier Science Publishing Co., Inc.
Lauber, A.W.
  1913   *Indian Slavery in Colonial Times, within the Present Limits of the United States*. New
         York: Columbia University Press.
Mare, R.D., and C. Winship
  1991   Socioeconomic change and the decline of marriage for blacks and whites. Pp. 175-
         202 in C. Jencks and P.E. Peterson, eds., *The Urban Underclass*. Washington, D.C.:
         The Brookings Institution.

Maury, A.
1872 *Memories of a Hugenot Family.* New York: Putnam.
McLanahan, S.
1983 Family structure and stress: A longitudinal comparison of male- and female-headed families. *Journal of Marriage and the Family* 45:347-357.
McLanahan, S., and G. Sandefur
1994 *Growing Up with A Single Parent: What Hurts? What Helps?* Cambridge, MA: Harvard University Press.
McLeod, J.D., and M.J. Shanahan
1993 Poverty, parenting, and children's mental health. *American Sociological Review* 58:351-366.
McLoyd, V.C., and L. Wilson
1993 The strain of living poor: Parenting, social support, and child mental health. Pp. 105-135 in A.C. Huston, ed., *Children in Poverty: Child Development and Public Policy.* New York: Cambridge University Press.
Sandefur, G.D., and T. McKinnell
1986 American Indian intermarriage. *Social Science Research* 15:347-371.
Sandefur, G.D., and A. Sakamoto
1988 American Indian household structure and income. *Demography* 25:71-80.
Schoen, R.
1987 The continuing retreat from marriage: Figures from 1983 U.S. marital status life tables. *Social Science Research* 71:108-109.
Snipp, C.M.
1989 *American Indians: The First of This Land.* New York: Russell Sage Foundation.
Speare, A.Jr., and F.K. Goldscheider
1987 Effects of marital status change on residential mobility. *Journal of Marriage and Family* 49:455-464.
Sweet, J., and L. Bumpass
1987 *American Families and Households.* New York: Russell Sage Foundation.
U.S. Bureau of the Census
1943 *Sixteenth Census of the United States: 1940, Population Characteristics of the Nonwhite Population by Race.* Washington, D.C.: U.S. Government Printing Office.
1953 *U.S. Census of Population: 1950, Vol. 2, Characteristics of the Population, Part 1, United States Summary.* Washington, D.C.: U.S. Government Printing Office.
1963 *1960 Census of Population, Subject Reports, Nonwhite Population by Race: Social and Economic Statistics for Negroes, Indians, Japanese, Chinese, and Filipinos,* PC(2)-1C. Washington, D.C.: U.S. Government Printing Office.
1964 *1960 Census of Population, Vol. 1, Characteristics of the Population, Part 1, United States Summary.* Washington, D.C.: U.S. Government Printing Office.
1973a *1970 Census of Population, Subject Report: American Indians,* PC(2)-1F. Washington, D.C.: U.S. Government Printing Office.
1973b *1970 Census of Population, Vol. 1, United States Summary, Part 1.* Washington, D.C.: U.S. Government Printing Office.
1983a *1980 Census of Population, Characteristics of the Population, General Population Characteristics, United States Summary,* PC80-1-B1. Washington, D.C.: U.S. Government Printing Office.
1983b *1980 Census of Population, Characteristics of the Population, General Social and Economic Characteristics, United States Summary,* PC80-1-C1. Washington, D.C.: U.S. Government Printing Office.
1992a *1990 Census of Population, General Population Characteristics, American Indian and Alaska Native Areas,* CP-1-1A. Washington, D.C.: U.S. Government Printing Office.

1992b *1990 Census of Population, General Population Characteristics, United States*, CP-1-1. Washington, D.C.: U.S. Government Printing Office.

1993a *1990 Census of Population, Social and Economic Characteristics, American Indian and Alaska Native Areas*, CP-2-1A. Washington, D.C.: U.S. Government Printing Office.

1993b *1990 Census of Population, Social and Economic Characteristics, United States*, 1990 CP-2-1. Washington, D.C.: U.S. Government Printing Office.

1995 *Current Population Reports, Series P60-188, Income, Poverty, and Valuation of Noncash Benefits, 1993*. Washington, D.C.: U.S. Government Printing Office.

Wallerstein, J.S., and J.B. Kelly

1980 *Surviving the Breakup: How Children and Parents Cope with Divorce*. New York: Basic Books.

Wilson, W.J., and K.M. Neckerman

1986 Poverty and family structure. Pp. 232-259 in S. Danziger and D. Weinberg, eds., *Fighting Poverty*. Cambridge, MA: Harvard University Press.

Yellow Bird, M., and C.M. Snipp

1994 American Indian families. Pp. 179-201 in R.L. Taylor, ed., *Minority Families in the United States: A Multicultural Perspective*. Englewood Cliffs, NJ: Prentice Hall, Inc.

Zill, N., and C.W. Nord

1994 *Running in Place: How American Families Are Faring in a Changing Economy and an Individualistic Society*. Washington, D.C.: Child Trends, Inc.

10

Demography of American Indian Elders: Social, Economic, and Health Status

Robert John

INTRODUCTION

Although age 65 has become the standard age at which individuals are considered elderly in American society, there is no such consensus among Indians.[1] The Older Americans Act permits individual tribes to determine the age at which elders are eligible to receive aging services provided by the tribe. In exercising their discretion on this issue, tribes differ in their designation of the chronological age at which a person is entitled to services. There is no dispute, however, that both the overall American Indian and American Indian elderly populations have grown substantially during the last decade. In 1980, American Indians aged 60 and over comprised approximately 8 percent of the total Indian population, compared with a figure of 16 percent for the general U.S. population. By 1990, these percentages had increased to 9 and 17 percent, respec-

This chapter is an abbreviated version of a paper prepared at a Workshop on the Demography of American Indian and Alaska Natives, held at the National Research Council in May 1995. The original version is available from the author. Partial support for this research was provided by the National Institute on Aging grant number R01-AG11294. I would like to acknowledge the assistance of Heather Goggans, Research Scientist in the University of North Texas Minority Aging Research Institute, and Patrice H. Blanchard, Executive Director of the Southwest Society on Aging.

[1]For the purpose of this study, the terms "Indian" and "American Indian" are used interchangeably and refer to American Indians and Alaska Natives (Eskimo and Aleuts).

tively. In absolute numbers, there were 108,800 American Indian elders out of a total Indian population of 1,423,043 in 1980 and 165,842 elders out of a total American Indian population of 1,959,234 in 1990, a 52 percent increase during the decade.

American Indian elders may be particularly vulnerable to a number of conditions experienced by elderly populations generally, including social isolation, economic hardship, and health problems. Yet for various reasons, accurate demographic information has been difficult to obtain for American Indians in general and for American Indian elders in particular. Only the decennial census conducted by the U.S. Bureau of the Census and vital events data compiled by the National Center for Health Statistics represent attempts to collect information about the entire American Indian population. However, the accuracy of census data has been an area of debate among demographers for some time (Passel, 1976; Passel and Berman, 1986; Snipp, 1989; Harris, 1994), and the accuracy of vital statistics is now under scrutiny (Sugarman et al., 1993; Indian Health Service, 1995a). The general lack of demographic data on the American Indian elderly population must inevitably confound the targeting of efforts aimed at identifying and addressing their needs.

The purpose of this chapter is to provide a description of the status and characteristics of American Indian elders in rural/reservation and urban environments. Using data primarily from the most recent census, the chapter presents a profile of the American Indian elderly population, focusing on marital status, household composition, economic status, and place of residence. This profile is followed by a review of mortality and disability patterns. The concluding section addresses the data limitations and the implications these limitations have for the well-being of American Indian elders.

MARITAL STATUS AND HOUSEHOLD COMPOSITION

Demographic information on social characteristics such as marital status and household composition is vital to understanding the needs of the American Indian elderly and to planning for the provision of appropriate healthcare and other services for this population. Overall, female American Indian elders aged 60 and over are far less likely than male Indian elders to be married (38 versus 66 percent) and nearly three times more likely to be widowed (45 versus 15 percent). Among American Indian elders aged 60 and over, 66 percent of males have a spouse, while 62 percent of females do not. In fact, the majority of male American Indian elders are married until advanced old age. In comparison, a majority of American Indian female elders aged 65 to 74 no longer have a husband. After age 85, when widowhood is extremely pervasive, only 9 percent of female elders still have a spouse. In contrast, even at advanced old age, a substantial proportion of American Indian male elders are still married (43 percent) and in a proportion roughly equivalent to widowers (44 percent).

In general, the sex-ratio imbalance among American Indian elders is not very different from that among the white elderly population, according to 1990 data. Approximately 57 percent of the American Indian population aged 60 years and over is female, compared with 58 percent of the white elderly population (U.S. Department of Commerce, 1993). However, the sex ratio differs substantially between urban and rural American Indian elderly populations. Females comprise 59 percent of the urban but only 53 percent of the rural American Indian elderly population.

These differences in the marital status of male and female elders are reflected in the composition of their households. According to 1990 census data (U.S. Department of Commerce, 1992), 28 percent of all American Indian elders aged 65 and over lived alone. However, consistent with differences in marital status, only 20 percent of American Indian male elders aged 65 and over lived alone, compared with 35 percent of their female counterparts.

Because of the lack of aging services, elderly American Indians often rely heavily upon family members for support and assistance with healthcare needs. However, as American Indian elders grow old, the likelihood of living alone increases, thus limiting their immediate access to care provided by family members. Twenty-four percent of American Indian elders aged 65-74, 35 percent of those aged 75-84, and 38 percent of those aged 85 and over lived alone in 1990. When gender and age are considered separately, women elders were far more likely to live alone than male elders: among those 65-74, 18 percent of males versus 29 percent of females; among those 75-84, 22 percent of males versus 43 percent of females; and among those over 85, 27 percent of males versus 45 percent of females.

ECONOMIC STATUS

The social characteristics discussed above have direct effects on economic status in later life. Two income measures are used to assess the economic status of American Indian elders: personal income or the individual income from all sources received by a particular American Indian elder, and family income, the sum of the incomes of all members of a family who are at least 15 years old.

Poverty

As defined by the federal government, the poverty line is meant to signify the minimum income required to provide the necessities of life.[2] Many researchers, however, believe that the official poverty line does not provide an adequate standard of living and prefer using 125 percent above the poverty line (also known as near poverty) as a more accurate gauge of economic deprivation (Chen, 1994). If near poverty is used as the standard for judging economic deprivation, then 39 percent of American Indian elders over age 60 experienced this hardship in 1989. If the official poverty line is used, then 29 percent of all American Indians aged 60 and older lived in poverty in 1989 (U.S. Department of Commerce, 1994). Table 10-1 reveals the extent of poverty among American Indian, black, and non-Hispanic white elders using different poverty standards. The overall similarity between black and American Indian elders on this measure of well-being is conspicuous.

Poverty among the general American Indian population increased during the 1980s. Regardless of age, poverty among American Indians is relatively common. Nearly 31 percent of all American Indians lived below the poverty line in 1989 (U.S. Department of Commerce, 1993:49). American Indian families also experience poverty. In 1979, there were 81,078 American Indian families (24 percent) with income below the poverty line. By 1989, this figure had risen to 125,432 (27 percent). Of these financially impoverished American Indian families, approximately 9 percent were headed by a householder 65 years of age or older.

Marital status and living arrangements influence the likelihood of living in poverty among American Indian elders. In 1989, among households headed by an American Indian aged 65 or over, only 20 percent of married-couple families, compared with 37 percent of female-headed families with no husband present, lived in poverty. Poverty among unrelated American Indian individuals[3] was even higher than among American Indian families in 1989: approximately 43 percent of unrelated American Indian individuals aged 65 and over were impoverished in 1989.

Poverty among American Indian elders is also influenced by rural or urban residence: it is substantially higher among the former than the

---

[2]The income level used to determine federal poverty status is lower for elders than for younger age groups. It is reasoned that elders do not need as much income since, for example, they do not incur commuting expenses or need to purchase clothes to participate in the labor force, and they no longer need to purchase a home.

[3]According to the U.S. census definition, an unrelated individual is someone who lives alone or with nonrelatives, is not related to the householder, or is a person living in group quarters who is not living in an institution.

TABLE 10-1 Poverty Status Among Persons 60 Years and Over by Race: 1990 (percent)

	Poverty Status			
Race	Below Poverty	Below 125% of Poverty	Below 150% of Poverty	Below 200% of Poverty
American Indian	28.5	38.5	46.4	58.5
Black	30.2	40.1	48.0	59.9
White, non-Hispanic	9.8	15.5	21.0	31.6

SOURCE: U.S. Department of Commerce (1994:Table 1)

latter, regardless of living arrangements. In fact, 63 percent of American Indian elders in poverty lived in a rural environment in 1989 (U.S. Department of Commerce, 1993).

Sources of Income

Figure 10-1 contrasts the sources of personal income among American Indian and non-Hispanic white elders. It shows that American Indian elders receive substantially more of their income from Social Security; public assistance, including Supplemental Security Income; and other sources (which include all forms of native craft production). In comparison, non-Hispanic whites have a distinct advantage in the proportion of their income received from accumulated assets such as interest, dividends, and net rental income.

These findings are consistent with previous research based on the 1980 census (John, 1995), which found that major differences in sources of income distinguished Indian elders who lived above the poverty line from their financially impoverished Indian counterparts who lived in the same type of family arrangement. Families headed by an American Indian elder with income above the poverty line had substantially more earnings (49 vs. 22 percent) and were far less dependent on Social Security (25 vs. 47 percent) and public assistance (5 vs. 25 percent) than financially impoverished families. Moreover, 7 percent of their income came from accumulated assets, compared with less than 1 percent among impoverished families.

Significant earnings also distinguished the families headed by a female elder who had income above the poverty line (59 vs. 24 percent). These families, too, were far less dependent on Social Security income (19

American Indians

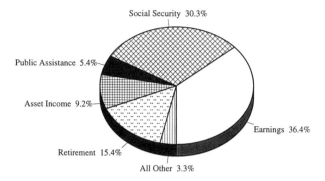

Non-Hispanic Whites

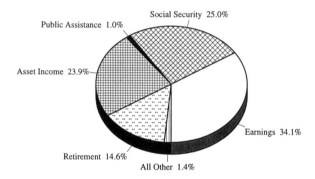

FIGURE 10-1 Source of income of persons aged 60 years and over: 1989. SOURCE: U.S. Department of Commerce (1994:Table 11b).

vs. 36 percent) and public assistance (8 vs. 32 percent) than impoverished female-headed families. Moreover, they received significantly more income from accumulated assets (6 vs. 1 percent). Among unrelated American Indian elders with income above the poverty line, income from earnings, assets, and other sources was substantially higher than among financially impoverished elders in the same living arrangement. Indeed, unrelated individual American Indian elders with income below the poverty line received 89 percent of their income from Social Security and public assistance, compared with only 48 percent among unrelated Indian elders with income above the poverty line.

Among U.S. elders aged 60 and over, regardless of race or ethnicity, Social Security is the foundation of old-age income security. Among the American Indian elderly population aged 60 and over, 52 percent depend on Social Security for half or more of their total income (U.S. Department of Commerce, 1994). Moveover, Social Security constitutes the only source of income for 30 percent of American Indian elders. What is surprising about this situation is the marginal difference among groups on this important measure of well-being. Even the most privileged group (non-Hispanic whites) is also highly dependent on Social Security: half of non-Hispanic whites receive half or more of their income from Social Security, and 26 percent rely on Social Security as their only source of income.

At the same time, as indicated by personal income figures, non-Hispanic whites receive higher income from Social Security, thus preserving income differences into old age. According to census data (U.S. Department of Commerce, 1994), non-Hispanic whites aged 60 and over had a median personal income of $11,581 in 1989, compared with $7,109 for their American Indian counterparts. In other words, the median income of non-Hispanic white elders was $373 per month more than that of American Indian elders. The income difference is even greater if one looks at average income: the average income of white elders ($19,070) was approximately 1.7 times that of American Indian elders ($11,368).

There is a similar income differential between the family incomes of American Indian and non-Hispanic white elderly householders (U.S. Department of Commerce, 1994). Whether one considers median or average family income, non-Hispanic white householders aged 60 and over have 1.6 times the income of their American Indian counterparts.

SPATIAL DISTRIBUTION

Access to healthcare and other services varies by place of residence, so it is important to consider the geographic location of American Indian elders in addition to other social and economic characteristics. U.S. Census data show that the American Indian elderly population is highly concentrated. As of 1990, two-thirds of all American Indian elders aged 60 and over lived in ten states, and approximately half lived in five states (U.S. Department of Commerce, 1991). Oklahoma had the largest number of American Indian elders, with approximately 18 percent of the nation's total. Another 13 percent of all Indian elders lived in California, followed by Arizona (9 percent), New Mexico (6 percent), and North Carolina (5 percent). Alaska, New York, Texas, Washington, and Michigan are the remaining states with large American Indian elderly populations.

Overall, 48 percent of the America Indian elderly population aged 60 years and over lived in a rural environment in 1990. Although there is a slight decrease after age 75, rural residence among the American Indian population tends to increase with age (John and Baldridge, 1996). This tendency contrasts with the non-Hispanic white and Hispanic populations, which both show a consistent negative association between advancing age and rural residence. Rural residence among aging blacks increases with age, although a much smaller percentage of the black population resides in a rural area.

A related issue with significant policy and programming implications for health and social service providers concerns the extent of and reasons for migration associated with aging among American Indians. It is commonly held that urban American Indians move to a reservation environment upon retirement, although a study of urban American Indian elders living in Los Angeles found that this is not the case (Kramer et al., 1990; Kramer, 1991; cf. Weibel-Orlando, 1988). It is possible that urban-to-rural migration occurs for reasons other than retirement. For example, one factor that could contribute to this pattern is the migration of aging urban American Indians back to rural or reservation environments because of worsening health, based on the assumption that their healthcare needs will be addressed through access to free Indian Health Service (IHS) medical care. This suggests that reverse migration may be associated with health status rather than work status or advancing chronological age.

MORTALITY AND DISABILITY

Life Expectancy at Birth

The last 50 years has seen a remarkable improvement in life expectancy at birth for American Indians. Based on calculations that exclude the IHS service areas with documented underreporting of Indian deaths, life expectancy at birth for American Indians increased by 19 years from 51 to 70 years during the 50-year period between 1940 and 1990-1992 (Indian Health Service, 1991, 1995a). This improvement is attributable largely to the efforts of IHS to eliminate infectious disease and meet the acute-care needs of the Indian population, including aggressive efforts to improve maternal and child health. Over the last 40 years since IHS assumed responsibility for American Indian healthcare, the shift in prevalence from acute and infectious diseases to chronic and degenerative diseases among American Indians has prompted several researchers to conclude that the American Indian population is undergoing an epidemiologic transition (Broudy and May, 1983; Kunitz, 1983; Manson and Callaway, 1990; Young, 1994; see also the chapters by Young and Snipp in this volume). Consistent with this interpretation, Johnson and Taylor (1991) documented the fact that chronic diseases are rising among the IHS American Indian service population. This change in morbidity is leading to a change in the mortality profile of American Indian elders.

Comparative Mortality Rates

Despite recognizable health improvements, life expectancy at birth among American Indians remains below that of whites. This difference in life expectancy is attributable to higher age-specific death rates among American Indians under the age of 65 years. Indeed, according to IHS figures, among American Indian elders aged 75 and over the mortality rate from all causes of death is lower than that for elders among the general U.S. population. In addition to the differences in overall mortality, there are substantial differences in cause-specific mortality rates among American Indian elders and the general elderly population. American Indian elders had lower mortality rates than the general elderly population for the four leading causes of death—heart disease, cancer, cerebrovascular diseases, and chronic obstructive pulmonary disease—but higher mortality for all other causes (John, 1995). In particular, American Indian elders had higher mortality from diabetes mellitus, accidents, and pneumonia and influenza.

Trends in Mortality: 1977-1988

Figure 10-2 shows changes in mortality for the six leading causes of death among American Indian elders between 1977 and 1988.[4] Cardiovascular disease showed little change during the period, while two causes of mortality—malignant neoplasms and diabetes mellitus—increased. Three of the leading causes of mortality—cerebrovascular diseases, pneumonia and influenza, and accidents—showed improvement.

Although mortality caused by cardiovascular disease appears to have decreased slightly from 1977 to 1983, the overall trend remained relatively constant if one considers the entire period. In contrast to the trend for cardiovascular disease, rates of death due to malignant neoplasms among Indian elders showed a steady increase of 19 percent during the period. Mortality rates from cerebrovascular disease decreased by approximately 26 percent.

Death rates attributable to pneumonia and influenza fell by approxi-

---

[4]This figure does not reflect the recent modifications introduced by IHS in the calculation of mortality rates. Therefore, it should be interpreted as showing relative rather than absolute changes in mortality trends.

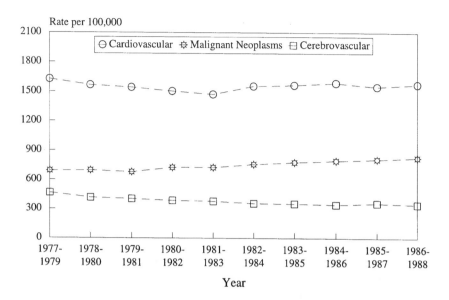

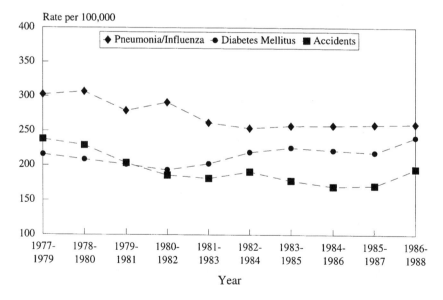

FIGURE 10-2 Leading causes of mortality among American Indians aged 65 and over (1977-1988). SOURCE: Indian Health Service, Division of Program Statistics.

mately 14 percent between 1977 and 1988. Diabetes appears to be a growing health problem among American Indian elders, and Figure 10-2 shows
that diabetes mellitus replaced accidents as the fifth leading cause of mortality during the period, with death rates attributable to diabetes increasing by approximately 11 percent. Death rates due to accidental injuries
decreased by approximately 18 percent between 1977 and 1988 among the
American Indian elderly population. This trend is encouraging and appears to be sustained in the latest mortality figures, which show that
death rates due to chronic obstructive pulmonary diseases among this
population are now higher than those due to accidental causes. Nevertheless, despite continued improvement in mortality, accidents remain
the seventh leading cause of death among American Indian elders, according to the most recent figures (Indian Health Service, 1995b).

Disability Status

In comparison with previous decennial census surveys, the 1990 census collected more data about a person's health or functional status. For
the first time, the census included questions about the existence of two
types of disability: a mobility and a self-care limitation. Each of these
conditions was defined as the result of the existence of a physical or
mental health condition that had lasted for 6 months or more. A mobility
limitation is a global measure of the ability to perform instrumental activities of daily living outside the home, such as shopping or going to the
doctor's office. A self-care limitation is a global measure of the ability to
perform personal activities of daily living inside the home, such as dress-
ing or bathing.

As seen in Figure 10-3, the data suggest that such limitations are more
common among female than male American Indian elders. This gender
difference is particularly pronounced for mobility limitations; overall, the
differences in the percentages of elders with self-care limitations are quite
small. In contrast, far fewer whites experience either type of disability.

Other data from the 1990 census (U.S. Department of Commerce,
1994:Table 6) indicate the level of work disability among the elderly U.S.
population aged 60 years and over. According to these data, American
Indian elders report the highest level of work disability among the five
racial groups. Among American Indian elders, 44 percent report a work
disability, compared to only 29 percent of non-Hispanic whites. Moreover, over one-third of American Indian elders (37 percent) report that
their condition prevents them from working, compared to only 23 percent
of their non-Hispanic white age peers.

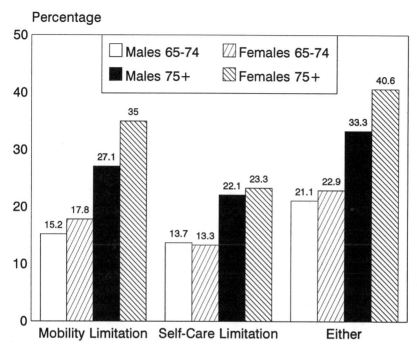

FIGURE 10-3 American Indian elders aged 65 years and over with a mobility or self-care limitation by age group and sex: 1990. SOURCE: U.S. Department of Commerce (1993:Table 40).

DISCUSSION

The above sections have provided a sketch of the demography of American Indian elders. The meagerness of available information reflects a number of limitations inherent in the current state of demographic knowledge about aging American Indians (John, 1994). Researchers who study American Indian aging issues are highly dependent upon the decennial census and annual vital statistics collection efforts. With few exceptions, what can be known about the entire American Indian population comes from these two sources. Persistent questions about data quality, gaps in the types of information collected, lack of funding to sustain special demographic studies or publications, delayed or exceptionally cumbersome access to data on American Indians, and other fundamental problems hamper our ability to construct a basic description of the American Indian elderly population so necessary for effective social planning.

The lack of comprehensive data and reliable research knowledge on the American Indian elderly population has obvious policy and programming implications. Even if resources are made available, it is possible that efforts to address the needs of this population will be poorly targeted. If the well-being of American Indian elders is to be improved, a sustained effort to determine the basic socioeconomic and health characteristics of rural and urban American Indian elders is imperative.

REFERENCES

Broudy, D.W., and P.A. May
   1983 Demographic and epidemiologic transition among the Navajo Indians. *Social Biology* 30(1):7-19.
Chen, Y.P.
   1994 Improving the economic security of minority persons as they enter old age. Pp. 22-31 in *Minority Elders: Longevity, Economics and Health.* Second Edition. Washington, D.C.: Gerontological Society of America.
Harris, D.
   1994 The 1990 Census count of American Indians: What do the numbers really mean? *Social Science Quarterly* 75:580-593.
Indian Health Service
   1991 *Trends in Indian Health—1991.* Rockville, MD: Indian Health Service.
   1995a *Regional Differences in Indian Health—1995.* Rockville, MD: Indian Health Service.
   1995b *Trends in Indian Health—1995.* Rockville, MD: Indian Health Service.
John, R.
   1994 The state of research on American Indian elders' health, income security, and social support networks. Pp. 46-58 in *Minority Elders: Longevity, Economics and Health.* Second Edition. Washington, D.C.: Gerontological Society of America.
   1995 *American Indian and Alaska Native Elders: An Assessment of Their Current Status and Provision of Services.* Rockville, MD: Indian Health Service.
John, R., and D. Baldridge
   1996 The NICOA Report: Health and Long-Term Care for American Indian Elders. A Report by the National Indian Council on Aging to the National Indian Policy Center. Washington, D.C.
Johnson, A., and A. Taylor
   1991 *Prevalence of Chronic Diseases: A Summary of Data from the Survey of American Indians and Alaska Natives.* AHCPR Pub. No. 91-0031. Rockville, MD: Public Health Service, Agency for Health Care Policy and Research.
Kramer, B.J.
   1991 Urban American Indian aging. *Journal of Cross-Cultural Gerontology* 6:205-217.
Kramer, B.J., D. Polisar, and J.C. Hyde
   1990 *Study of Urban American Indian Aging.* Final Report to the Administration on Aging. Grant No. 90AR0118. City of Industry, CA: The Public Health Foundation of Los Angeles County.
Kunitz, S.J.
   1983 *Disease Change and the Role of Medicine: The Navajo Experience.* Berkeley, CA: University of California Press.
Manson, S.M., and D.G. Callaway
   1990 Health and aging among American Indians: Issues and challenges for the biobehavioral sciences. Pp. 63-119 in M. Harper, ed., *Minority Aging: Essential Curricula Content for Selected Health and Allied Health Professions.* Washington, D.C.: U.S. Government Printing Office.

Passel, J.S.
   1976   Provisional evaluation of the 1970 census count of American Indians. *Demography*
           13:397-409.
Passel, J.S., and P.A. Berman
   1986   Quality of 1980 census data for American Indians. *Social Biology* 33:163-182.
Snipp, C.M.
   1989   *American Indians: The First of This Land.* New York: Russell Sage Foundation.
Sugarman, J.R., M. Holliday, K. Lopez, and D. Wilder
   1993   *Improving Health Statistics Among American Indians by Data Linkages with Tribal Envi-
           ronment Registries.* Washington, D.C.: National Center for Health Statistics.
U.S. Department of Commerce
   1991   *The Population 50 Years and Older, by Sex, Race, and Hispanic Origin for the United
           States, Regions and States: 1990.* Washington, D.C.: U.S. Government Printing
           Office.
   1992   *General Population Characteristics: United States.* Washington, D.C.: U.S. Govern-
           ment Printing Office.
   1993   *Social and Economic Characteristics: United States.* Washington, D.C.: U.S. Govern-
           ment Printing Office.
   1994   *Census of Population and Housing, 1990: Special Tabulation on Aging (STP 14).* Wash-
           ington, D.C.: U.S. Government Printing Office.
Weibel-Orlando, J.
   1988   Indians, ethnicity as a resource and aging: You can go home again. *Journal of
           Cross-Cultural Gerontology* 3:323-348.
Young, T.K.
   1994   *The Health of Native Americans: Towards a Biocultural Epidemiology.* Oxford: Oxford
           University Press.

IV

Health Issues and Health Care Access and Utilization

11
Overview of Alcohol Abuse Epidemiology for American Indian Populations

Philip A. May

The body of literature on drinking among American Indians[1] has been growing steadily over the past two decades. Since the publication of a comprehensive bibliography on the topic by Mail and McDonald in 1980, several hundred papers have been published in professional journals. Despite the publication of new epidemiological data, much of the life-cycle pattern of alcohol abuse among various Indian groups must be pieced together from a number of very different individual studies. The following discussion attempts to do just this by treating those individual studies as snapshots of a larger process. Thus, the objective is to describe a general pattern of drinking across the life cycle and its effects on the health of American Indians. Because different definitions and criteria were used in these studies, the data are rarely strictly comparable across sites or over time. Nevertheless the number of studies is now sufficiently

This paper was prepared with partial funding for clerical assistance provided by Grant No. T34-MH19101. Special thanks to Jan Gossage, Virginia Rood, Phyllis Trujillo and Thomas Welty for their assistance in its preparation. Also special thanks to Aaron Handler of the Office of Program Planning, Evaluation and Legislation of the Indian Health Service, Rockville, Maryland.

[1]"American Indian" is used in this paper as a general term for the approximately 2 million native peoples of North America in the United States and Canada, including Alaska Natives, Eskimo, and Indians. When possible, the exact tribal group being described is named.

large and their methodologies sufficiently similar that some broad trends can be established.

The next section briefly reviews some stereotypes associated with drinking among American Indians. This is followed by a discussion of the epidemiology of substance abuse among Indian youth. We then turn to a review of findings on alcohol abuse among adult American Indians, examining first survey data and then the results of two longitudinal studies. The discussion next focuses on current data on alcohol-involved mortality among American Indian populations. The problem of fetal alcohol syndrome is then briefly examined. The chapter ends with a discussion of potential preventive measures, followed by a summary of findings and areas for future research.

STEREOTYPES OF INDIAN DRINKING

There are a number of commonly held stereotypes with regard to alcohol use and abuse among American Indians (May 1994a, 1994b). One of the most pervasive of these is that Indians metabolize alcohol more slowly or differently than other ethnic groups. Approximately a dozen studies have now been published on the biophysiology of alcohol processing among American Indians (see, for example, Bennion and Li, 1976; Reed et al., 1976; Schaefer, 1981; Rex et al., 1985; Segal and Duffy, 1992). In general, the findings have shown that American Indians metabolize alcohol in a manner and at a speed similar to those of other ethnic groups in the United States (Bennion and Li, 1976); that there is a great deal of variation in alcohol processing within American Indian and Alaska Native ethnic groups (Reed et al., 1977; Segal and Duffy, 1992); that prior drinking experience and body weight are very influential in the metabolism process (Bennion and Li, 1976); and that overall liver structures among American Indians are not unique, and their liver phenotypes are similar to those of other, particularly European, ethnic groups (Rex et al., 1985). Thus, the findings of these studies are in keeping with those of studies conducted among ethnic groups throughout the world.

It is also said that American Indian drinking patterns and problems are uniquely Indian. However, review of the epidemiologic statistics of American Indians shows that high rates of alcohol problems among American Indians are influenced by many of the same factors or traits that influence drinking among other groups. Of particular importance are variables such as age, geography, social norms, and political and legal policies. Special combinations of these influences have created particular patterns of drinking and alcohol-involved injury, death, and arrest that are high to very high, and therefore perceived to be uniquely Indian when in fact they may not be (May, 1994a). Furthermore, the literature describes variation in alcohol consumption from one tribal culture to the next. There are some high-risk/rate groups, and there are also many low-risk/rate groups (see Levy and Kunitz, 1974; May et al., 1983; May, 1991; Kunitz and Levy, 1994; Young, 1994:Chapter 6). Studies show that the style of drinking also varies among American Indians, spanning the four commonly mentioned styles of abstinence, moderated social drinking, heavy recreational drinking, and anxiety or chronic alcohol-dependent drinking (see Ferguson, 1968; Levy and Kunitz, 1974; May, 1992).

Many studies support the commonly held belief that alcoholism and alcohol abuse are epidemic among some tribal populations (see, for example, Brod, 1975; Lamarine, 1988; Littman, 1970; Swanson et al., 1971; Stratton, 1973; Stewart, 1964). Yet the arrest and morbidity data used for these studies are frequently not descriptive of individual behavior; rather, they are aggregate data that reflect duplicate counts of arrests and problems generated by a select number of individuals. Thus the impression is given that many more individuals are involved in the deviant behavior than is actually the case (see, for example, Ferguson, 1968; May, 1988).

EPIDEMIOLOGY OF INDIAN YOUTH SUBSTANCE ABUSE FROM SURVEYS

There is a substantial body of literature on substance abuse among American Indian youth. Most of this literature is based on a large number (several hundred) of high school substance abuse surveys administered across the nation (see Oetting et al., 1988, 1989; Beauvais, 1992; Swaim et al., 1993).

In general, the survey literature indicates that, on average, rates of lifetime use and abuse of many drugs, including alcohol (and getting drunk), are higher among American Indian than non-Indian youth. Specifically, drug surveys among Indian youths reveal similar or slightly higher rates of current use of alcohol (particularly higher for getting drunk), cocaine, inhalants, stimulants, barbiturates (downers), and other drugs. At the same time, Indian youth are less prone to use some other drugs (heroin and PCP). Nonreservation Indians have the highest use rates of most drugs in high school surveys.[2]

Other studies corroborate the general points made above (Winfree and Griffiths, 1985; Winfree et al., 1989). Youthful drinking of alcohol, as well as some experimentation with other drugs among Indian youth peer

---

[2]It should be noted that while the above studies generally present averaged data for a variety of high schools in a variety of locales, there is substantial variation among high schools in different communities (Liban and Smart, 1982; May et al., unpublished data).

groups who drink, is described as predominantly recreational (Beauvais, 1992). Heavy binging may occur on weekends (at night) and during the summer when parents are not present, at parties, and on other special occasions. The pattern is similar to that among other youths in the United States, yet the settings (e.g., rural reservations and urban Indian neighborhoods) and norms of comportment are slightly to greatly different (Topper, 1980).

Various authors have provided consistent explanations of the etiology of substance abuse among American Indian youth. Most of these explanations are similar to those found in the mainstream literature. For example, Oetting and Beauvais (1989) have demonstrated that self-esteem and many isolated social/psychological variables do not differentiate between heavily substance abusing Indian youths and others. Rather, the authors point to association and identification with abusing peer clusters as the most influential factor in causing persistent and serious substance abuse and polysubstance abuse among Indian youths (see also Swaim et al., 1993). Other researchers make similar observations, attributing drinking and other substance abuse problems among Indian youth to differential association with subcultures of abuse and the social learning that occurs within them (Winfree et al., 1989; Sellers and Winfree, 1990). But rather than being fueled by a white youthful "hang loose" ethic, Indian peer groups may be more likely to interpret heavy drinking as an "Indian thing to do" (Winfree and Griffiths, 1985; Winfree et al., 1989; Lurie, 1971; Mohatt, 1972; Graves, 1971).

In addition to the above themes, the literature has identified other variables within some communities as influential in substance abuse among Indian youth (Winfree and Griffiths, 1985). Of particular importance is the influence of norms in the home as a predisposing factor to association with abusing peer groups (see Oetting and Beauvais, 1989; Beauvais, 1992).

ADULT ALCOHOL ABUSE SURVEYS

There have been eight major studies concerned with the prevalence and epidemiological features of drinking among adult Indian populations, as well as three survey samples of older adults recently completed as part of a cardiovascular disease study. Table 11-1 lists the prevalence rates for alcohol use among the populations sampled for these studies, along with the rate among the general U.S. population for comparison. It is important to note that different definitions and criteria were used in these studies, and that the data are not always comparable across sites or over time.

Overall, however, these studies support a number of generalizations:

TABLE 11-1 Prevalence of Alcohol Use Among Adults: Various Indian Tribes, Older Indian Adults, and U.S. General Population

Sample	Total	Male	Female	Source
	\% Current Users in Population			
U.S. General Population				
1983 (ages 18+)	61.0	72.0	50.0	NIAAA, 1993
1985 (ages 18+)	57.0	68.0	47.0	NIAAA, 1993
Standing Rock Sioux				
1960 (ages 15+)	69.0	82.0	55.0	Whittacker, 1962
1980 (ages 12+)	58.0	72.0	35.0	Whittacker, 1982
Cheyenne River Sioux				
1988 (ages 18+)	45.9	—	—	Welty, 1989
Navajo				
1969 (ages 18+)	30.0	52.0	13.0	Levy and Kunitz, 1974
1984 (ages 16+)	52.0	64.0	40.0	May and Smith, 1988
Ute				
1966 (no age specified)	80.0	—	—	Jessor et al., 1968
Ojibwa				
1978 (ages 18+)	84.0	—	—	Longclaws et al., 1980
Lumbee				
1978 urban (ages 21-64)	72.6	—	—	Beltrane and McQueen, 1979
1978 rural (ages 21-64)	45.7	—	—	Beltrane and McQueen, 1979
Cheyenne River, Devil's Lake, and Oglala Sioux				
1989-1992 (ages 45-74)	47.4	60.0	37.7	Welty et al., 1995
Central Arizona Pima, Maricopa, Papago				
1989-1992 (ages 45-74)	40.3	57.4	30.5	Welty et al., 1995
Southwestern Oklahoma, Apache, Caddo, Delaware, Comanche, Kiowa, and Wichita				
1989-1992 (ages 45-74)	36.8	49.0	27.9	Welty et al., 1995

• There is tremendous variation in the prevalence of drinking from one reservation to the next and also from one time period to the next.

• Every study shows that fewer Indian women than men drink.

• The more recent Indian studies show less drinking among Indians than among the general U.S. population; however, there is variation in the overall study results, with the older studies among the Ute and Canadian Ojibway indicating higher prevalence. Thus there may be some Indian populations in which a higher proportion drinks than in the U.S. general population, some in which the prevalence is similar to general U.S. levels, and some in which the prevalence is lower.

• Urban Indian populations generally have a higher prevalence of drinking than do many reservation populations, whereas reservation populations generally have a higher prevalence of abstention. For example, the Lumbee adult study, a study among the Navajo, and Indian youth studies clearly illustrate this pattern (Beltrame and McQueen, 1979; Levy and Kunitz, 1974; Beauvais, 1992).

The variations over time and by tribe are illustrated in studies of the Standing Rock Sioux (Whittacker, 1962, 1982) and the Navajo (Levy and Kunitz, 1974; May and Smith, 1988). Among the Standing Rock Sioux, study results in 1960 indicated a prevalence of drinking similar to that of the U.S. population (Whittaker, 1962), whereas by 1980, the prevalence of drinking had dropped below national averages; this decrease in drinking rates was particularly true for Sioux females (Whittaker, 1982). From a 1969 study of the Navajo, Levy and Kunitz (1974) report a vastly lower proportion of drinking among the tribal population than among the U.S. population; by 1984 however, the proportion of Navajo drinking had risen substantially (May and Smith, 1988). Yet even with this increase, the proportion of Navajo drinking in the 1980s was still less than that of the general U.S. population.

Patterns of Heavy Use

Generally, the studies listed in Table 11-1 reveal a number of indicators of problem drinking among these tribal groups, with the various heavy drinking measures being two to three times the magnitude found among the general U.S. population. Particularly evident in a number of the studies is a tendency toward heavy binge drinking (more than five to seven drinks per episode) and highly adverse results from drinking, such as delirium tremens and blackouts. For example, among the Cheyenne River Sioux (Welty et al., 1988), 37 percent of the respondents had consumed five or more drinks on at least one occasion in the previous month, whereas 29 percent of other South Dakotans had done so (Welty et al., 1988).[3] Furthermore, among the Navajo and Standing Rock Sioux, a large

---

[3]Both Indian and non-Indian groups in South Dakota are high on this measure and on driving after drinking as well; on the latter measure, the non-Indians exceed the Indians by 8.3 to 11.6 percent.

number of the male drinkers were classified as heavy or abusive drinkers by standard indicators of quantity, frequency, and variability of drinking. Similar measures were substantially less prevalent among the general U.S. population. Therefore, among those Indians who do drink, most surveys of adult drinking find that there is a very high percentage of heavy drinkers, particularly heavy binge drinkers.

The study among urban and rural Lumbee Indians (Beltrane and McQueen, 1979) makes several important points. First, urban Lumbees drink more than rural Lumbees and have higher rates of problem drinking. Second, traditional social norms among the rural North Carolina Lumbees result in more abstinence and a highly age-specific pattern similar to that found in other reservation Indian studies. Third, occupational considerations (prestige and satisfaction) are much more highly related to Indian drinking in the urban area (Baltimore) than among the rural sample. Finally, heavy drinking is most common among the lower social strata of the urban area residents. Such findings may be consistent with those for other Indians in urban areas, but this topic awaits further study.

Less-Problematic Patterns

The studies listed in Table 11-1 also show some less-problematic patterns of alcohol use among Indians:

• There is a substantial proportion of most tribal populations that practices total abstinence (nothing to drink in the previous year).
• There are many American Indian males in virtually every tribal community who have been problem or heavy drinkers in the past, but have quit in early or later middle age (e.g., early 30s to middle 40s), generally without the assistance of an alcohol treatment program.
• The abstention rate among Indian females is particularly high as compared with other U.S. females.
• There are some tribes in which drinking is confined to a relatively small proportion of the population.

These observations are underscored among the older adult samples (ages 45-74) examined by Welty et al. (1995). Generally, only 36-47 percent of this age group surveyed in 13 tribal sites was still drinking. The male drinkers still outnumbered the female by approximately two to one (Welty et al., 1995), but only half of the males were still drinking by their mid-50s. Thus Indian male-female differences in drinking prevalence appear to be substantial throughout the life span. Indicators of heavy use were also substantially lower among these older adult samples. There was less binge drinking reported at these later ages, although the indicators of binge drinking still existed, particularly among samples from the Dakotas and Arizona. Indeed, indicators from Welty et al.'s (1995) study suggest that binge drinking, not chronic use, is the most common pattern at these ages. For example, less than 20 percent of the male current drinkers and 10 percent of the female current drinkers had had more than 14 drinks in the previous week. Also, current drinkers in this age group averaged fewer than 11 drinks per week (males 8 to 10 and females 4 to 6).

In general, these studies among older adult Indians reinforce two important points. First, the recreational drinking pattern of sporadic binging persists among many Indian drinkers throughout the years during which they drink. Second, many Indian males reach a turning point in their 30s and 40s that influences them to quit drinking completely (see Levy and Kunitz, 1974; Kunitz and Levy, 1994; Leung et al., 1993).

More study of this phenomenon is needed for two reasons. First, it is important to understand why this phenomenon of "maturing out" occurs frequently among many Indian tribes (particularly among males). Second, such knowledge might enable professionals to apply some new insights and techniques to Indian alcohol rehabilitation and prevention programs, thus fostering sobriety and reducing harm from drinking at earlier ages (May, 1995).

The most complete examination to date of maturing out was conducted by Kunitz and Levy (1994). Among a sample of Navajo men who had stopped all drinking in their middle and later years, the following reasons were given: 42 percent said their health had been in jeopardy, 20 percent had joined the Native American church (which provides spiritual support and also prohibits drinking among its members), 18 percent said their responsibilities had dictated that they quit, 9 percent had found drinking unrewarding, and 4 percent had joined an established Protestant church. In general, Kunitz and Levy conclude that those who mature out leave life-styles/social groups/communities of friends who are supportive of drinking and find social and community support that reinforces abstinence behavior and values not related to drinking.

LONGITUDINAL FOLLOW-UP STUDIES OF ADULT INDIAN DRINKERS

Two longitudinal studies of adult Indian drinkers provide significant findings about drinking careers among the adult American Indian population.

A study by Leung et al. (1993) resurveyed respondents in a northwest coastal village 19 years after a baseline mental health epidemiology survey (Shore, 1974). A very high rate of cessation of drinking (60-63 percent) was found among adult drinkers over this time period. Men and women were found to drink very differently throughout the various ages. The present prevalence rates of alcoholism changed from 52 percent for men and 26 percent for women in 1970 to 36 and 7 percent, respectively, in the 1990s. The aging of the sample population had altered the prevalence of problem drinking. Women had a higher remission rate (82 versus 52 percent for males), but were also more likely to have been or to be alcohol abusers (rather than alcoholics) when drinking. Men were very likely (about 75 percent) to have been alcohol dependent at one time in their adult years and to have stopped after an average of 15 years of heavy drinking. The vast majority (83 percent) ceased drinking without the aid of treatment for alcohol misuse. Of the initial subjects who were found to have an alcohol problem, 22 percent had the same diagnosis in the second survey, 41 percent had stopped drinking, 17 percent had died of alcohol-related causes, and 20 percent had died of other causes (Leung et al., 1993).

Men and women participants in an extensive study of drinking conducted in 1969 (Levy and Kunitz, 1974) were located and followed up after 21 years (Kunitz and Levy, 1994). Most of the men were found to have stopped drinking at the time of follow-up or prior to their death. Male social drinkers were most likely (80 percent) to have stopped, while male solitary drinkers were less likely to have done so. Male solitary drinkers were also more likely to have died from alcohol-related causes, particularly those men who came from a wage work community (27 percent mortality) and from a group that had been hospitalized for problems in 1969 (38 percent mortality). Rural, culturally more traditional drinkers were found to have a lower prevalence of drinking and to have suffered fewer problems at follow-up. Both the differential drinking rates of Navajo males and females and the fact that many Navajos are able to stop drinking are cited by Kunitz and Levy as evidence that the majority of Navajo drinkers and the nature of their alcohol-related outcomes are shaped predominantly by culture (Kunitz and Levy, 1994).

CURRENT DATA ON ALCOHOL-INVOLVED MORTALITY

Mortality Rates

Table 11-2 presents current data (1987-1989) on alcohol-involved[4] mortality for U.S. Indians and Alaska Natives.[5] These 3-year averages for

---

[4] Three terms are used in this section to define mortality types and their link to alcohol. Alcohol-specific deaths are those that have a clear, highly unitary causal connection with heavy alcohol ingestion (e.g., cirrhosis with alcohol specified and alcohol dependence syndrome). Generally, these deaths are due to chronic diseases caused by alcohol consumption

Indians are compared with U.S. general population data[6] for 1988 by age, sex, rates per 100,000, and number of deaths. At the top of Table 11-2, the male age-specific death rates are presented for key categories. For the highly alcohol-related causes of death, such as motor vehicle crashes, other accidents, suicide, homicide, and alcoholism, Indian males have higher rates of death in every age and cause category, with the exception of suicide deaths for older ages. By age 55, Indian males have lower rates of suicide mortality, a pattern that continues into the later ages. But for all other causes of death, the mortality rates and ratios are substantially higher. For motor vehicle accidents, other accidents, and homicides, the rates are generally 1.4 to 3.9 times higher for Indian males than the U.S. averages. The ratios are even higher for the alcohol-specific category, alcoholism deaths. Alcoholism death rates among Indian males aged 15-24 are 13 times higher than U.S. averages, for ages 25-34 they are 8.8 times higher, and for ages 35-74 they are 3.3 to 5.4 times higher. Therefore, the data indicate that alcohol-related mortality is a substantially greater problem for Indian males than for males in the general U.S. population.

For female rates of death, Table 11-2 indicates somewhat similar results. Indian females die much less frequently than Indian males but more frequently than other U.S. females from all alcohol-related causes, with the sole exception of suicide rates above age 44. Similarly, the ratio of alcohol-related mortality for Indian females and U.S. females is even higher than the male ratio. Alcohol-related mortality is 1.2 to 3.5 times higher than U.S. averages. Individual alcohol-specific death rates (which

---

over many years, but not always (e.g., alcoholic psychosis or alcohol overdose). Alcohol-related deaths denote those causes, such as suicide, homicide, and vehicle crashes, in which alcohol is a highly necessary factor in the majority of deaths, but not a sufficient factor. In many cases, alcohol-related deaths are from injuries resulting from alcohol impairment, but not always (e.g., exposure). Alcohol-involved death is an all-inclusive term that includes both of the above categories.

[5]Data are for Indians identified as living in the 35 reservation states served by the Indian Health Service.

[6]Kunitz and Levy (e.g., Kunitz and Levy, 1994; Levy and Kunitz, 1987) caution against comparison of Indian mortality rates with those of the general U.S. population. They rightfully point out that some rural Indians, particularly in the southwestern United States, generally manifest patterns of mortality from suicide, homicide, and some other social pathologies that are similar to those of their non-Indian neighbors in the surrounding areas, and that patterns for both Indians and non-Indians in the West are different from overall U.S. patterns. However, as shown in some other studies, this observation does not always hold true for motor vehicle crashes (May, 1989b); suicides (Van Winkle and May, 1993); or other causes, such as alcoholism (New Mexico Department of Health, 1994). Furthermore, in this discussion, U.S. Indian averages (not averages for specific tribes) are presented, so U.S. averages provide more appropriate comparisons than specific tribal or regional studies.

are related primarily to cirrhosis and alcohol dependence syndrome) for Indian females ages 15-24 are 31 times higher than U.S. averages,[7] 13.3 times higher for ages 25-34, and 4.6 to 8.4 times higher for ages 35 and above. It therefore seems evident that alcoholism and alcohol-dependent mortality not only affect a disproportionate number of Indian women, but particularly affect the younger ages.

Male and Female Alcohol-Involved Deaths as a Percentage of All Deaths

The estimated numbers of deaths from alcohol-involved causes are given in the far right columns of Table 11-2. For U.S. Indian males in 1987-1989, there were 3,754 deaths from alcohol-involved causes. However, not all of these deaths were truly alcohol-involved. We estimate the magnitude of alcohol-involved causes by multiplying these deaths by an approximate proportion of alcohol involvement established from existing studies of these phenomena among American Indians (see May, 1989a, 1992).[8] On the basis of these calculations, it is estimated that 2,382 males and 783 females died from alcohol-involved causes during this 3-year time period. Deaths from alcohol-involved causes among males are estimated to be responsible for 13 percent of all Indian deaths and 22 percent of all male deaths during the period. Female alcohol-involved deaths are estimated to be responsible for 4.3 percent of all Indian deaths and 10.4 percent of all female Indian deaths. Overall then, 17.3 percent of all Indian deaths in 1987-1989 can conservatively[9] be estimated as having been alcohol-involved.

Age-Adjusted Rates

Table 11-3 shows the age-adjusted mortality for American Indians for more recent years, 1989-1991. The estimated alcohol involvement has been calculated for this table as well, and rates, numbers, and percentages of death are presented. The conclusion from this table with regard to all 12 Indian Health Service areas is that the age-adjusted alcohol-related death rate among American Indians is 2.4 times that of the general U.S.

---

[7]Small numbers in this age group invite caution in interpretation, however.

[8]These estimated proportions were developed from the published literature on American Indians and studies conducted by the author and his colleagues over the past two decades (see May, 1988, 1992).

[9]These estimates are likely to be conservative since alcohol-related heart disease, cerebrovascular disease, cancer, diabetes complications, and infectious diseases have not been considered.

TABLE 11-2 Estimated Alcohol-Involved Causes of Death for U.S. Indians and Alaska Natives (1987-1989) and the U.S. General Population (1988) by Age, Sex: Rates per 100,000 and Number

Rates

Cause of Death	Ages 15-24			Ages 25-34			Ages 35-44		
	Ind.	U.S.	Ratio	Ind.	U.S.	Ratio	Ind.	U.S.	Ratio
Male									
MV accident	134.2	56.6	2.4	117.9	36.2	3.3	85.8	25.8	3.3
Other accdt.	58.8	18.6	3.2	74.7	23.8	3.2	71.8	25.2	2.8
Suicide	64.0	21.9	2.9	61.1	25.0	2.4	26.5	22.9	1.2
Homicide	34.3	24.7	1.4	44.7	24.7	1.8	37.1	17.3	2.1
Alcoholism[a]	6.5	0.5	13.0	34.3	3.9	8.8	84.9	15.6	5.4
Female									
MV accident	44.1	20.1	2.2	40.3	11.6	3.5	30.2	9.3	3.2
Other accdt.	11.2	3.2	3.5	12.0	5.0	2.4	17.1	5.7	3.0
Suicide	11.5	4.2	2.7	6.8	5.7	1.2	7.7	6.9	1.1
Homicide	11.9	6.0	2.0	10.6	7.3	1.5	11.7	4.6	1.0
Alcoholism[a]	3.1	0.1	31.0	21.2	1.6	13.3	39.7	4.7	8.4

NOTE: Includes all Indians and Alaska Natives (population = 1,207,236) in all parts of the 35 reservation states served by the Indian Health Service (IHS) (total deaths in reservation states 1989-1991 = 19,084).

[a]Alcoholism deaths include the following causes: International Classification of Diseases (ICD)-9 death code groups of E291—alcoholic psychoses; E303—alcohol dependence syn-

Ages 45-54			Ages 55-64			Ages 65-74			Number		
									Total Deaths (all ages)	× Est. % Alcohol Involved	= Total Alcohol-Involved (all ages)
Ind.	U.S.	Ratio	Ind.	U.S.	Ratio	Ind.	U.S.	Ratio			
64.8	22.5	2.9	74.5	21.5	3.5	69.5	25.5	2.7	1212	(65%)	788
69.5	24.5	2.8	116.5	29.7	3.9	148.4	43.1	3.4	1007	(25%)	252
22.6	21.7	1.0	12.8	25.0	0.5	11.3	33.0	0.3	463	(75%)	347
20.3	11.4	1.8	14.0	8.2	1.7	18.8	5.9	3.2	383	(80%)	306
125.7	28.4	4.4	126.9	37.9	3.3	123.9	33.4	3.7	689	(100%)	689
		Total deaths for above causes							3754		2382
		% of all Indian deaths (N=18,336)							20.5%		13.0%
		% of all male Indian deaths (N=10,776)							34.8%		22.1%
27.9	9.5	2.9	19.2	10.5	1.8	22.4	14.1	1.6	461	(65%)	300
15.7	6.6	2.4	25.2	10.2	2.5	40.2	21.3	1.9	296	(25%)	74
2.9	7.9	0.4	6.1	7.2	0.8	3.0	6.8	0.4	101	(75%)	76
5.0	3.1	1.6	5.0	2.5	2.0	6.0	2.9	2.1	115	(80%)	92
68.0	8.7	7.8	11.7	11.2	6.4	38.8	8.4	4.6	317	(100%)	317
		Total deaths for above causes							1290		783
		% of all Indian deaths							7.0%		4.3%
		% of all female Indian deaths (N=7,560)							17.1%		10.4%

drome; E571.0-571.3—alcoholic liver disease; E305.0—alcohol overdose; E425.5—alcoholic cardiomyopathy; E535.3—alcoholic gastritis; E790.3—elevated blood-alcohol level; and E860.0, 860.1—accidental poisoning by alcohol, not elsewhere classified.

SOURCE: Computed from Indian Health Service (1993).

TABLE 11-3 Age-Adjusted Mortality (rates per 100,000) and Total Estimated Deaths from Alcoholism (Alcohol-Specific) and Alcohol-Related Causes for the U.S. General Population, 1990, and Indian Health Service Population, 1989-1991

Cause of death	Estimated % Alcohol-Involved	All IHS Areas (Rate)	All U.S. (Rate)	Ratio IHS/ U.S.	Total Indian Deaths (Number)
Alcohol-related					
Accidents					
Motor Vehicle	65	48.3	18.8	2.6	1642
Other	25	37.6	18.2	2.1	1283
Suicide	75	16.5	11.5	1.4	571
Homicide	80	15.3	10.2	1.5	529
Subtotal (Related Deaths)	—	(117.7)	(58.7)	(2.0)	(4025)
Alcoholism (Alcohol-Specific)	100	(37.6)	(7.1)	(5.3)	(1079)
Total (Related & Alcoholism)	—	155.3	65.8	2.4	5104
Summary of above Deaths as a percent of total deaths					
U.S. Total = 2,148,463	—	—	—	—	26.7%
IHS = 19,084					
Nine Areas IHS = 12,924					

NOTES: Estimated deaths are adjusted to the U.S. population in 1940. Includes deaths of Indians and Alaska Natives only in those counties within reservation states where IHS maintains services. This, however, is the vast majority of all Indian deaths in western states. Alcoholism deaths for both U.S. and IHS include the causes specified in note to Table 11-2.

[a]These nine areas are the ones IHS cites as not having major problems with underreporting of Indian deaths. They are Aberdeen (SD, ND, IA, NE), Alaska (AK), Albuquerque (NM,

Total Indian Alcohol-Involved Deaths (Number)	Total U.S. Deaths (Number)	Total U.S. Alcohol-Involved Deaths (Number)	Nine IHS[a] Areas (Rate)	Ratio Nine Areas/ U.S.	Total Deaths in Nine Areas (Number)	Total Alcohol Involved in Nine Areas (Number)
1067	46,814	30,429	64.9	3.5	1277	830
321	45,169	11,292	52.0	2.9	1015	254
428	30,906	23,179	21.3	1.9	432	324
423	24,932	19,946	18.4	1.8	369	295
(2239)	(147,821)	(84,846)	(156.6)	(2.7)	(3093)	(1703)
(1079)	(19,587)	(19,587)	(51.8)	(7.3)	(838)	(838)
3318	167,678	104,433	208.4	3.2	3931	2541
17.4%	7.8%	4.9%	—	—	32.7%	21.1%

CO), Bemidji (MN, WI, MI), Billings (MT, WY), Nashville (ME, MA, NY, CT, RI, PA, NC, MS, SC, FL, AL, TN, LA), Navajo (AZ, NM, UT), Phoenix (AZ, UT, NV), and Tucson (Southern AZ). Not included in the nine areas because of reporting problems are California (CA), Oklahoma (OK, KS), and Portland (WA, OR, ID).

SOURCES: Computed from Indian Health Service (1994a and 1994b).

population. However, Indian Health Service publications frequently rely more heavily on data from only 9 of the 12 Indian Health Service geographic areas, as a correction for assumed underreporting in 3 of the 12 areas. When only these 9 areas are considered, the age-adjusted alcohol-involved death rate among American Indians is 3.2 times that of the general U.S. population. The alcohol-involved factors that contribute most to this high ratio are alcoholism deaths and motor vehicle crashes.

Table 11-3 also shows estimates of alcohol-involved deaths for both sexes. Overall, in the 9 Indian Health Service areas where the data are most complete, the total number of alcohol-involved deaths for 1989-1991 is estimated to be 2,541, which represents 21 percent of all Indian deaths during this period. This is substantially higher than the estimated 4.9 percent of all U.S. deaths. Indeed, on the basis of this comparison, the Indian problem is four times greater than the U.S. average.

Alcohol-Related Versus Alcohol-Specific Mortality

In Table 11-3, the causes of death are separated into two categories: alcohol-related and alcohol-specific mortality. The alcohol-related causes of accidents, suicide, and homicide tend to be linked among American Indians with recreational, sporadic, binge drinking (see May, 1992). During the period covered by Table 11-3 (1989-1991), these causes were responsible for an estimated 2,239 of the 3,318 lives lost as a result of alcohol involvement in all 12 Indian Health Service areas. As noted earlier, alcohol-specific causes are those that typically result from chronic alcohol consumption, the pattern generally defined as alcoholic (alcohol dependence syndrome, cirrhosis of the liver from alcohol consumption, and others). These causes accounted for an estimated 1,079 of the total lives lost as a result of alcohol involvement. Therefore, alcohol-related causes accounted for 67.5 percent of the total alcohol-involved deaths, while alcohol-specific causes accounted for 32.5 percent. Thus focusing only on the alcohol-specific (alcoholism) deaths would address only one-third of the problem. Alcohol intervention/prevention programs for Indians must deal with more than alcohol dependence and must work to prevent alcohol misuse at other levels as well.

Comparison using only the 9 Indian areas with the best data shows a similar pattern. In these 9 areas, 33 percent of the alcohol-involved deaths were from alcohol-specific causes, while 67 percent were from alcohol-related causes. Similar comparisons for other time periods consistently exhibit a similar pattern (May, 1989a, 1992, 1994a, 1995). Between 25 and 33 percent of all alcohol-related mortality in any 1- or 3-year period over the past decade can be attributed to alcohol-specific causes, while 67 to 75 percent is attributable to alcohol-related causes. The significance of analyzing the data by separating alcohol-related and alcohol-specific causes is highlighted in the discussion of preventive measures in the next section.

Explanations of Tribal Variations in Rates

Explanations for the variations in alcohol-involved behavior among tribes have been proposed and tested for several decades in the Indian literature (see Levy and Kunitz, 1974, and May, 1977b and 1982, for reviews). The themes used are variations of Durkheim's (1957) Social Integration Theory, put forth to explain suicide. Social integration refers to the processes that make a society whole from a collection of individuals. It also refers to how the individual is attached symbolically and structurally to the larger social aggregates, such as the family and social, political, and religious groups (Jessor et al., 1968). Overall, American Indian tribes have levels of traditional social integration that have been classified by anthropologists as ranging from high to low (see Field, 1991, and Levy and Kunitz, 1974:Chapter 3, for specifics related to tribal alcohol patterns; see Davis, 1994, and Champagne, 1994, for general discussion). In low-integration societies, the individual is a member of fewer permanent groups, and the main reference groups are less likely to impose on the individual clear and strong mandates for conformity. Therefore, the individual has more freedom to define his or her own behavior. In high-integration societies, the opposite is true: the individual is expected to conform to clearer and more formal mandates of the social groups to which he or she belongs.

Tribes that have high traditional integration have lower rates of alcohol misuse and alcohol-involved problems than those with low integration (Field, 1991; Levy and Kunitz, 1974). However, when modernization, acculturation stress, and other social disorganizing forces are brought to bear on Indian social systems, rates of alcohol-related pathology rise (see Dozier, 1966). This is particularly true when family structure is affected (Jenson et al., 1977). Therefore, when a low-integration tribe is being affected by high rates of pressure from mainstream society, the highest average rates of alcohol-misuse problems result, whereas a high-integration tribal community under little pressure to modernize will generally have the lowest rates of alcohol abuse (for more detail see May, 1982). These concepts, it should be added, are equally important in understanding sociocultural influences in non-Indian societies (Jessor et al., 1968; Pittman and White, 1991). The rates of alcohol-related problems and alcohol-involved mortality from area to area and tribe to tribe generally conform to these patterns.

FETAL ALCOHOL SYNDROME

Fetal alcohol syndrome (FAS) and other alcohol-related birth defects vary greatly from one Indian community to the next (May et al., 1983). While no major study has been done on an urban Indian group, very complete surveys have been carried out in nine reservation areas in the United States and Canada (May, 1991). It was found that 15-year retrospective, population-based rates of FAS in the southwestern United States were lowest among the Navajo (1.6/1000 births), intermediate among the Pueblo (2.2), and highest among two southwestern plains culture tribes (10.3). The comparable U.S. estimate is 2.2. Overall, the rates vary quite predictably, given the level of social integration and drinking patterns among these tribes (May et al., 1983). A higher proportion of females in low-integration, plains culture groups drink (indulging particularly in heavy binging), and therefore the FAS rates among these groups are higher. In two studies of heavy-drinking Indian communities in Canada and Alaska, very high FAS rates were found where there were low integration and normative patterns of female drinking that allowed a high proportion of women to drink and to participate in frequent and very heavy binge drinking (Asante and Nelms-Matzke, 1985; Robinson et al., 1987).

A consistent finding is that FAS and most alcohol-related birth defects occur to a small number of women, 6.1/1000 women of childbearing age among seven Southwestern Indian communities (May et al., 1983). This finding reflects the drinking patterns in many tribes: a majority, or at least a very high percentage, of the women are abstainers, but among those who drink, there is generally a rather limited subset of women who are very heavy drinkers. In fact, many of these women are so severe in their alcohol involvement that they frequently have a number of alcohol-damaged children (1.3 to 1.6 per mother) before an almost inevitable, untimely alcohol-specific or alcohol-related death (see May et al., 1983; May, 1991). Therefore, these women pose a substantial challenge to intervention and prevention programs (Masis and May, 1991).

PREVENTION OF ALCOHOL PROBLEMS

Indian alcohol problems are influenced mainly by norms related to drinking and post-drinking behavior among the heavy-drinking sub-segment of the population (Dozier, 1966; Stewart, 1964; Levy and Kunitz, 1974; May, 1976; Kunitz and Levy, 1994; MacAndrew and Edgerton, 1969). Preventive efforts to alter attitudes, beliefs, and social structures offer the promise of reducing alcohol misuse and resultant problems (see Jessor et al., 1968; May, 1992, 1995).

An example of sociocultural change for the prevention of alcohol abuse problems, well portrayed in videos and frequently presented at workshops, is offered by Alkali Lake, a British Columbia Indian community. Over the course of a few years, this community achieved a striking reduction in problems with alcohol dependence and misuse—reportedly from 95 percent alcohol abusive or alcoholic to 95 percent alcohol free. This change was accomplished through community organization around principles of abstinence and group support taken from the traditions of Alcoholics Anonymous (Guillory et al., 1988). These values and traditions were advocated by selected leaders and eventually gained wide acceptance as specific means to promote and maintain abstinence from alcohol consumption. Tactics used included moral persuasion; social policies to control alcohol possession, sale, and consumption; and economic sanctions. In addition, traditional Indian spiritual and cultural activities were reintroduced to reinforce abstinence and to improve and maintain social functioning in a historical, cultural, and spiritual sense (see Guillory et al., 1988).

The patterns of alcohol-related problems highlighted here raise a number of public health issues. Before one begins prevention or intervention efforts in any Indian community, it is vital to have data that are locally specific. The motivation of a community to change must also be considered before any prevention initiative is undertaken (May et al., 1993).

The extant data warrant many public health approaches. These approaches are grouped below under the standard prevention terminology of primary, secondary, and tertiary levels (Bloom, 1981; May and Moran, 1995).

Primary Prevention

Primary prevention consists of measures taken to stop a problem in its developmental stages, or in other words to keep the problem from arising (Last, 1988). In general, a comprehensive, community-wide program of alcohol-misuse prevention should embrace two general approaches: motivating populations to change and changing the environment to make it more protective (May et al., 1993). The goal of these programs is to keep problematic and heavy alcohol use from causing premature morbidity and mortality so that individuals remain healthy and live long enough to mature out of youthful and young adult drinking patterns.

In many cases, public education has been undertaken as the major form of primary prevention. In one survey of the Navajo population (May and Smith, 1988), 63 percent of all Navajos agreed with the statement that "Indians have a biological weakness to alcohol that non-Indians do not have," even though this is an erroneous statement in light of scientific evidence. Such beliefs must be transcended before it becomes possible to motivate positive behaviors.

Alcohol policy has not received much attention as it affects alcohol-involved problems among Indians. For example, tribes have an almost absolute power to regulate the possession, sale, consumption, and taxing of beverages on reservation (May, 1977a). Yet few evaluations of such policies have been undertaken (May, 1976; Landen, 1993). New studies are warranted, for policy has been found to be very influential in many communities (Beauchamp, 1980; May, 1992), and some tribes are now involved in major policy-directed efforts (Van Norman, 1992). In one "natural experiment," the fetal alcohol syndrome rate in a small Indian community dropped from 14/1000 to zero for a 5-year period as the latent consequence of a change in economic policy that suspended monthly payments of gas and oil royalties to individual families (May, 1991). In other cases, alcohol-related arrests have been reduced by 30 to 60 percent because of policies related to alcohol availability (May, 1975, 1976). Also, alcohol-involved mortality has been found to be up to 20 percent lower over a 15-year period on reservations having policies of alcohol availability believed to encourage norms of more controlled drinking (May, 1976).

Secondary Prevention

Secondary prevention measures are those taken to recognize and arrest a problem in its earliest stages (Last, 1988). In few communities in the United States is early detection of problem drinkers undertaken or practiced by healthcare and social service providers for either males or females. Indian communities are not a major exception. Social detoxification centers that screen and assess drinking problems among individuals could be set up as extensions of, or diversions from, the criminal justice system. Early detection of problem drinkers in Indian communities could be instituted in routine health settings as well.

Also of great promise in the secondary arena is the institution of brief motivational therapeutic interventions for Indian populations. As practiced among other populations, such interventions might provide cost-efficient alcohol therapy for drinkers who have not yet developed severe dependency or other extreme levels of alcohol misuse (Miller and Rollnick, 1991). Brief motivational therapies could be used in lieu of expensive inpatient therapy, which is commonly used yet relatively unsuccessful among Indians today. Furthermore, brief therapies could be used to speed up or better prepare Indian males who are in the early stages of maturing out, which, as noted earlier, is now becoming recognized as a common pattern among Indians (see Arbogast, 1995, for case studies of this process).

Tertiary Prevention

At the tertiary level of prevention, the problem condition—alcoholism or severe alcohol misuse—is already present in an individual (see Last, 1988). Indian alcohol abuse treatment programs are available to deal with the problems at this level. However, those programs have been criticized in the literature as being understaffed and insufficient to meet the needs (see Shore and Von Fumetti, 1972; Wilson and Shore, 1975; Shore and Kofoed, 1984; May, 1986). Indian treatment programs might be substantially improved by upgrading services and redesigning them to take advantage of the maturing-out process. Furthermore, Indian programs seldom have special provisions for Indian females. This must be changed, as too many Indian females who do drink cause an unacceptably high level of alcohol-specific death. The literature (May, 1991) indicates a very strong need for tertiary care for women who produce children with fetal alcohol syndrome and other alcohol-related birth defects (Masis and May, 1991). Indian mothers (and mothers of other ethnic groups) who produce one such child frequently progress in their problem drinking to produce a second, third, or subsequent number of alcohol-affected children (May et al., 1983). In such cases, tertiary care delivered in sheltered environments (e.g., half-way houses) could prove to be very important, yet few such programs exist.

Social detoxification centers, mentioned above under secondary prevention, can also be an important tool for tertiary prevention. Individuals in advanced states of alcohol misuse could be identified in detox centers and aggressively referred to alcohol treatment and other therapeutic health and behavioral interventions.

SUMMARY OF FINDINGS AND
AREAS FOR FUTURE RESEARCH

There is a great deal of heavy and problematic drinking and therefore alcohol-involved mortality among American Indians, but there are a number of positive findings as well. While the rates of heavy drinking for youth and adults and rates of death from alcohol-involved causes are very high overall, a lower proportion of the adult population in many of these groups is drinking. Therefore, the problem of alcohol misuse is highly concentrated within most Indian communities. Furthermore, there is substantial variation from one community to the next in the overall prevalence of drinking. Yet the existence of subgroups of heavy drinkers within many tribal communities results in extremely high rates of death, arrest, and other alcohol-related social problems.

A number of research topics related to the epidemiology of alcohol problems among American Indians need to be pursued. First, the data presented here describe a pattern that is rather common across the life cycle in many Indian communities. That is, from a high prevalence of drinking (almost universal in the late teens) and experimentation with drugs in the teens and early 20s among most Indians, various drinking styles evolve in the late 20s through the mid-40s. These drinking styles range from abstinence to some isolated, very heavily alcohol-dependent patterns. The bulk of the alcohol-related problems surrounding heavy recreational and binge drinking occur from the late teens through the mid-30s, and alcohol dependency problems increase dramatically from ages 25 through the late years among a select minority of the Indian population. Confirmation of these life-cycle trends is needed. Furthermore, there is very little literature currently available on alcohol-specific causes of death among Indians. Epidemiologic or biomedical analyses of Indian deaths from liver cirrhosis or other alcohol-specific causes are badly needed.

As is the case among the population generally, there have been virtually no prevention trials examining what public health measures or prevention programs are effective in Indian communities. Therefore, research is needed to address the question, "Does prevention work?"

Studies of treatment for alcohol misuse and dependence are also lacking among Indian populations. Very few studies of treatment effectiveness have been undertaken among Indians, and they are severely needed. Furthermore, many Indian alcohol programs offer a narrow, and often unsophisticated, range of treatment modalities. A broader range of both new and old treatment modalities of proven effectiveness should be pursued and their results carefully studied. Evaluation of effectiveness would be particularly important for programs using traditional, culture-based therapies as well as mainstream therapies. As most Indian populations include a variety of individuals with a broad range of both traditional and modern traits, biculturalism and acculturation are important concepts for treatment and research in such programs and for evaluation of the effectiveness of various programs for individual clients.

REFERENCES

Arbogast, D.
  1995 *Wounded Warriors: A Time for Healing.* Omaha, NE: Little Turtle Publishers.
Asante, K.O., and J. Nelms-Matzke
  1985 *Report on the Survey of Children with Chronic Handicaps and FAS in the Yukon and Northwest British Columbia.* Terrace, B.C.: Mills Municipal Hospital.

Beauchamp, D.E.
  1980   *Beyond Alcoholism: Alcohol and Public Health Policy.* Philadelphia: Temple University Press.
Beauvais, F.
  1992   Indian adolescent drug and alcohol use: Recent patterns and consequences. *American Indian and Alaska Native Mental Health Research* 5(1):1-67.
Beltrame, T., and D.V. McQueen
  1979   Urban and rural Indian drinking patterns: The special case of the Lumbee. *The International Journal of the Addictions* 14(4):533-548.
Bennion, L., and T-K Li
  1976   Alcohol metabolism in American Indians and whites. *New England Journal of Medicine* 284:9-13.
Bloom, M.
  1981   *Primary Prevention: The Possible Science.* Englewood Cliffs, NJ: Prentice-Hall, Inc.
Brod, T.M.
  1975   Alcoholism as a mental health problem of Native Americans. *Archives of General Psychiatry* 32(11):1385-1391.
Champagne, D., ed.
  1994   *The Native North American Almanac.* Detroit, MI: Gale Research, Inc.
Davis, M.B., ed.
  1994   *Native America in the Twentieth Century: An Encyclopedia.* New York: Garland Publishing, Inc.
Dozier, E.P.
  1966   Problem drinking among American Indians: The role of sociocultural deprivation. *Quarterly Journal of Studies on Alcohol* 27:72-84.
Durkheim, E.
  1957   *Suicide.* New York: The Free Press.
Ferguson, F.N.
  1968   Navajo drinking: Some tentative hypotheses. *Human Organization* 27:159-167.
Field, P.B.
  1991   A new cross-cultural study of drunkenness. Pp. 48-74 in D.J. Pittman and C.R. Snyder, eds., *Society, Culture and Drinking Patterns.* New York: Wiley.
Graves, T.D.
  1971   Drinking and drunkenness among urban Indians. Pp. 275-311 in J. Waddell and O.M. Watson, eds., *The American Indian in Urban Society.* New York: Little, Brown and Company.
Guillory, B., E. Willie, and E. Duran
  1988   Analysis of a community organizing case study: Alkali Lake. *Journal of Rural Community Psychology* 9(1):27-35.
Indian Health Service
  1993   *Trends in Indian Health 1993.* Rockville, MD: U.S. Department of Health and Human Services.
  1994a *Trends in Indian Health 1994.* Rockville, MD: U.S. Department of Health and Human Services.
  1994b *Regional Differences in Indian Health.* Rockville, MD: U.S. Department of Health and Human Services.
Jenson, G., J. Stauss, and V. Harris
  1977   Crime, delinquency, and the American Indian. *Human Organization* 36(3):252-257.
Jessor, R., T.D. Graves, R.C. Hanson, and S.L. Jessor
  1968   *Society, Personality and Deviant Behavior: A Study of Tri-Ethnic Community.* New York: Holt, Rinehart, and Winston.

Kunitz, S.J., and J.E. Levy
    1994   *Drinking Careers: A Twenty-five Year Study of Three Navajo Populations.* New Haven: Yale University Press.
Lamarine, R.J.
    1988   Alcohol abuse among Native Americans. *Journal of Community Health* 13(3):143-155.
Landen, M.G.
    1993   Alcohol-related Mortality and Tribal Alcohol Legislation. Master's Thesis. University of North Carolina.
Last, J.M., ed.
    1988   *A Dictionary of Epidemiology, 2nd edition.* New York: Oxford University Press.
Leung, P.K., J.D. Kinzie, J.K. Boehnlein, and J.H. Shore
    1993   A prospective study of the natural course of alcoholism in a Native American village. *Journal of Studies on Alcoholism* 54:733-738.
Levy, J.E., and S.J. Kunitz
    1974   *Indian Drinking.* New York: Wiley Interscience.
    1987   A suicide prevention program for Hopi youth. *Social Science and Medicine* 25(8):931-940.
Levy, J.E., S.J. Kunitz, and M. Everett
    1969   Navajo criminal homicide. *Southwestern Journal of Anthropology* 25(2):124-152.
Libran, C.B., and R.G. Smart
    1982   Drinking and drug use among Ontario Indian students. *Drug and Alcohol Dependence* 9:161-171.
Littman, G.
    1970   Alcoholism, illness, and social pathology among American Indians in transition. *American Journal of Public Health* 60(9):1769-1787.
Longclaws, L., G. Barnes, L. Grieve, and R. Dumoff
    1980   Alcohol and drug use among the Brokenhead Ojibwa. *Journal of Studies on Alcohol* 41(1):21-36.
Lurie, N.O.
    1971   The world's oldest ongoing protest demonstration: North American Indian drinking patterns. *Pacific History Review* 40(3):311-322.
MacAndrew, C., and R.B. Edgerton
    1969   *Drunken Comportment: A Sociological Explanation.* Chicago: Aldine.
Masis, K.M., and P.A. May
    1991   A comprehensive local program for the prevention of FAS. *Public Health Reports* 106(5):484-489.
May, P.A.
    1975   Arrests, alcohol, and alcohol legalization among an American Indian Tribe. *Plains Anthropologist* 20(68):129-134.
    1976   *Alcohol Legalization and Native Americans: A Sociological Inquiry.* Ph.D. Dissertation. University of Montana.
    1977a   Alcohol beverage control: A survey of tribal alcohol statutes. *American Indian Law Review* 5:217-228.
    1977b   Explanations of Native American drinking. *Plains Anthropologist* 22(77):223-232.
    1982   Substance abuse and American Indians: Prevalence and susceptibility. *International Journal on the Addictions* 17:1185-1209.
    1986   Alcohol and drug misuse prevention programs for American Indians: Needs and opportunities. *Journal of Studies on Alcohol* 47(3):187-195.

1988 Mental health and alcohol abuse indicators in the Albuquerque area of the Indian Health Service: An exploratory chart review. *American Indian and Alaska Native Mental Health Research* 2(1):31-44.

1989a Alcohol abuse and alcoholism among American Indians: An overview. Pp. 95-119 in T.D. Watts and R. Wright, eds., *Alcoholism in Minority Populations*. Springfield, IL: Charles C Thomas.

1989b Motor vehicle crashes and alcohol among American Indians and Alaska Natives. Pp. 207-223 in *The Surgeon General's Workshop on Drunk Driving: Background Papers*. Washington, D.C.: U.S. Department of Health and Human Services.

1991 Fetal alcohol effects among North American Indians: Evidence and implications for society. *Alcohol, Health and Research World* 15(3): 239-248.

1992 Alcohol policy considerations for Indian reservations and bordertown communities. *American Indian and Alaska Native Mental Health Research* 4(3):5-59.

1994a The epidemiology of alcohol abuse among American Indians: Mythical and real properties. *American Indian Culture and Research Journal* 18(2):121-143.

1994b Alcohol abuse. Pp. 23-27 in Mary B. Davis, ed., *Native America in the Twentieth Century: An Encyclopedia*. New York: Garland Press.

1995 The prevention of alcohol and other substance abuse among American Indians: A review and analysis of the literature. In P. Langton, ed., *The Challenge for Participating Research in the Prevention of Alcohol-related Problems in Ethnic Communities*. Washington, D.C.: National Institute on Alcohol Abuse and Alcoholism and Center for Substance Abuse Prevention.

May, P.A., K.J. Hymbaugh, J.M. Aase, and J.M. Samet
1983 Epidemiology of Fetal Alcohol Syndrome among American Indians of the southwest. *Social Biology* 30:374-387.

May, P.A., J.H. Miller, and N. Wallerstein
1993 Motivation and community prevention of substance abuse. *Experimental and Clinical Psychopharmacology* 1(1-4):68-79.

May, P.A., and J.R. Moran
1995 Prevention of alcohol misuse: A review of health promotion efforts among American Indians. *American Journal of Health Promotion* 9(4):288-299.

May, P.A., and M.B. Smith
1988 Some Navajo Indian opinions about alcohol abuse and prohibition: A survey and recommendations for policy. *Journal of Studies on Alcohol* 49:324-334.

Miller, W.H., and S. Rollnick
1991 *Motivational Interviewing: Preparing People to Change Addictive Behavior*. New York: The Guilford Press.

Mohatt, G.
1972 The sacred water: The quest for personal power through drinking among the Teton Sioux. Pp. 261-275 in McClelland et al., eds., *The Drinking Man*. New York: The Free Press.

National Institute on Alcohol Abuse and Alcoholism (NIAAA)
1993 *Alcohol and Health: Eight Special Report to the U.S. Congress*. Washington, D.C.: U.S. Department of Health and Human Services.

New Mexico Department of Health
1994 *Selected Health Statistics, Annual Report, 1992*. Sante Fe: Bureau of Vital Records and Health Statistics.

Oetting, E.R., and F. Beauvais
1989 Epidemiology and correlates of alcohol use among Indian adolescents living on reservations. Pp. 239-267 in *Alcohol Use Among U.S. Ethnic Minorities*. NIAAA Research Monograph No. 18, Rockville, MD: U.S. Public Health Service.

Oetting, E.R., F. Beauvais, and R.W. Edwards
  1988 Alcohol and Indian youth: Social and psychological correlates and prevention. *Journal on Drug Issues* 18:87-101.
Oetting, E.R., R.C. Swain, R.W. Edwards, and F. Beauvais
  1989 Indian and Anglo adolescent alcohol use and emotional distress: Path models. *American Journal of Drug and Alcohol Abuse* 15(2):153-172.
Pittman, D.J., and H.R. White
  1991 *Society, Culture and Drinking Patterns Reexamined.* New Brunswick, NJ: Rutgers Center on Alcohol Studies.
Reed, T.E., H. Kalant, R.J. Griffins, B.M. Kapur, and J.G. Rankin
  1976 Alcohol and acetaldehyde metabolism in Caucasians, Chinese and Americans. *Canadian Medical Association Journal* 115:851-855.
Rex, D.K., W.F. Bosion, J.E. Smialek, and T-K Li
  1985 Alcohol and aldehyde dehydrogenase isoenzymes in North American Indians. *Alcoholism: Clinical and Experimental Research* 9(2):147-152.
Robinson, G.C., J.L Coury, and R.F.Coury
  1987 Clinical people and prevalence of FAS in an isolated community of British Columbia. *Canadian Medical Association Journal* 137:203-207.
Schaefer, J.M.
  1981 Firewater myths revisited. *Journal of Studies on Alcohol* 9:99-117.
Segal, B., and L.K. Duffy
  1992 Ethanol elimination among different racial groups. *Alcohol* 9:213-217.
Sellers, C.S., and L.T. Winfree
  1990 Differential associations and definitions: A panel study of youthful drinking behavior. *International Journal on the Addictions* 25(7):755-771.
Shore, J.H.
  1974 Psychiatric epidemiology among American Indians. *Psychiatric Annals* 4(11):56-66.
Shore, J.H., and L. Kofoed
  1984 Community intervention in the treatment of alcoholism. *Alcoholism: Clinical and Experimental Research* 8(2):151-159.
Shore, J.H., and B. Von Fumetti
  1972 Three alcohol programs for American Indians. *American Journal of Psychiatry* 128(11):1450-1454.
Stewart, O.C.
  1964 Questions regarding American Indian criminality. *Human Organization* 23(1):64-76.
Stratton, J.
  1973 Cops and drunks: Police attitude and actions in dealing with Indian drunks. *International Journal of the Addictions* 8(4):613-621.
Swaim, R.C., E.R. Oetting, P.J. Thurman, F. Beauvais, and R.W. Edwards
  1993 American Indian Adolescent Drug Use and Socialization Characteristics: A Cross Cultural Comparison. *Journal of Cross Cultural Psychology* 24(1):53-71.
Swanson, D.W., A.P. Beatrude, and E.M. Brown
  1971 Alcohol abuse in a population of Indian children. *Diseases of the Nervous System* 12:835-842.
Topper, M.
  1980 Drinking as an expression of status: Navajo male adolescents. Pp. 103-147 in J.O. Waddel and M.W. Everett, eds., *Drinking Behavior among South-western Indians.* Tucson, AZ: The University of Arizona Press.
Van Norman, M.C.
  1992 Alcohol beverage control policy: Implementation on a Northern Plains Indian reservation. *American Indian and Alaska Native Mental Health Research* 4(3):120-125.

Van Winkle, N.W., and P.A. May
  1993 An update on American Indian suicide in New Mexico, 1980-1987. *Human Organization* 52(3):304-315.
Welty, T.K.
  1988 *Planned Approach to Community Health.* Rapid City, SD: U.S. Indian Health Service.
Welty, T.K., E.T. Lee, J. Yeh, L.D. Cowan, O. Go, R.R. Fabsitz, N.A. Le, A.J. Oopik, D.C. Robbins, and B.V. Howard
  1995 Cardiovascular disease risk factors among American Indians: The Strong Heart Study. *American Journal of Epidemiology* 142(3):269-287.
Whittaker, J.O.
  1962 Alcohol and the Standing Rock Sioux Tribe. *Quarterly Journal of Studies on Alcohol* 23:468-479.
  1982 Alcohol and the Standing Rock Sioux Tribe: A twenty-year follow-up study. *Journal of Studies on Alcohol* 43:191-200.
Wilson, L.G., and J.H. Shore
  1975 Evaluation of a regional Indian alcohol program. *American Journal of Psychiatry* 132:255-258.
Winfree, L.T., and C.T. Griffiths
  1985 Trends in drug orientations and behavior: Changes in a rural community, 1975-1982. *International Journal on the Addictions* 20(10):1495-1508.
Winfree, L.T., C.T. Griffiths, and C.S. Sellers
  1989 Social learning theory, drug use, and American Indian youths: A cross-cultural test. *Justice Quarterly* 6(3):395-417.
Young, T.K.
  1994 *The Health of Native Americans: Toward a Bio-cultural Epidemiology.* New York: Oxford University Press.

12
Diabetes Mellitus in Native Americans: The Problem and Its Implications

K.M. Venkat Narayan

INTRODUCTION

Diabetes mellitus is a group of metabolic disorders characterized by abnormally high levels of blood glucose secondary to inefficient insulin action and/or secretion. The disease often leads to significant disability, including renal failure, blindness, and limb amputation, and to premature death.

Diabetes was apparently rare among Native Americans until the middle part of the twentieth century (Joslin, 1940; West, 1974; Sievers and Fisher, 1985). However, since World War II, it has become one of the most common serious diseases among many Native American tribes (Sievers and Fisher, 1985); in 1987, there were at least 72,000 Native Americans in the United States with diagnosed diabetes (Newman et al., 1990). Diabetes occurring in Native Americans is almost exclusively the type referred to as NIDDM or non-insulin-dependent diabetes mellitus (Sievers and Fisher, 1985). The Pima Indians have the highest recorded prevalence and incidence of NIDDM in the world (Knowler et al., 1978; King and Rewers, 1991). High rates have also been observed among other Native American tribes (Sievers and Fisher, 1985; Gohdes, 1986; Young and Shah,

I wish to thank my colleagues, Drs. Maximilian de Courten, Richard Fernandes, Robert Hanson, Bill Knowler, Robert Nelson, and David Pettitt, for their help and advice. I am also grateful to the members of the Gila River Indian Community for their enormous contribution to the understanding of diabetes.

1987), as well as in many diverse societies worldwide that have recently adapted to western culture (Prior and Tasman-Jones, 1981; Cameron et al., 1986; Zimmet et al., 1990).

It is not entirely clear why the frequency has increased among Native Americans during this century, and the question is the subject of considerable research attention. While it is reasonable to conjecture a genetic predisposition to NIDDM, the role of environmental factors is of undoubted importance in explaining the dramatic increase in rates of NIDDM among many populations. Many of the known environmental determinants are potentially modifiable and offer immediate prospects for preventing or postponing NIDDM (Knowler and Narayan, 1994; Knowler et al., 1995). The complications of diabetes, which account for the increased mortality and morbidity among diabetic subjects, may also be prevented or delayed by systematic application of current knowledge (The DCCT Research Group, 1993; Weir et al., 1994). With a view to informing and influencing health policy, this paper:

- reviews the magnitude of the problem of NIDDM among Native American populations;
  - summarizes current knowledge about the determinants of NIDDM;
  - describes the major complications of NIDDM;
  - assesses the potential for preventing or delaying NIDDM and its main complications; and
  - suggests research directions that can facilitate the prevention of NIDDM and its complications in Native Americans.

PIMA INDIAN STUDY

Pima Indians, living in a geographically defined part of the Gila River Indian Community of Arizona, have participated in a longitudinal study of diabetes and its complications since 1965 (Bennett et al., 1971), from which much of our current understanding of diabetes among Native Americans has been obtained. As this paper repeatedly refers to data from the Pimas, a brief description of this study and of the Pimas is presented.

Approximately every 2 years, each resident of the study area who is at least 5 years old is invited for an examination that includes a medical history; a physical examination; an oral glucose tolerance test; and measurements of height and weight, serum lipids, serum insulin, and urinary proteins. The same standardized methods are used for subjects of all ages, and DNA samples are also collected for genetic studies (Knowler et al., 1990).

The Pimas originated from a much larger group of Native Americans who lived in an area that is now in northwestern Mexico and southern Arizona, and have lived for over 2000 years in the valleys of the Gila and Salt rivers in what is now Arizona. It is believed that the Pimas derived from the Paleoindians, those Native Americans descended from the first of the three migrations across the Bering Land Bridge from Asia to America (Williams et al., 1985). Originally a desert people who subsisted on riverine agriculture supplemented by hunting and gathering, they expanded their farming system after contact with early European missionaries (Castetter and Bell, 1942). Subsequent development of the region by European settlers resulted in diversion of the Pimas' water supply and curtailment of their farming activities (Lippincott, 1980). Today much of the Pima land is leased to non-Indian farmers, and the Pimas work in sedentary government jobs or as wage laborers on or off the reservation (Pablo, 1983).

MAGNITUDE OF THE PROBLEM OF
NIDDM IN NATIVE AMERICANS

Prevalence

Some idea of the prevalence (the proportion of the population that is affected by the disease at a given point in time) of diabetes among Native Americans can be obtained from case registries held at Indian Health Service (IHS) facilities. The prevalence rates of diagnosed diabetes among Native Americans vary across tribes and are generally higher than in the U.S. population as a whole (Carter et al., 1989; Freeman et al., 1989; Acton et al., 1993b; Valway et al., 1993). In one study, the age-adjusted rate of diagnosed diabetes among all IHS patients was 6.9 percent—2.8 times the U.S. all-races rate. Of the 11 IHS areas examined in this study, all except the Alaska Area had a significantly higher prevalence rate of diagnosed diabetes than the U.S. rate (Valway et al., 1993); however, there are indications that the rates of diagnosed diabetes among Alaska Natives may also be increasing (Schraer et al., 1993).

Because nearly 50 percent of diabetes may remain undiagnosed (Harris et al., 1987), population-based studies may provide more accurate estimates of true diabetes prevalence. Data on prevalence of NIDDM from population-based studies (Hall et al., 1992; Sugarman et al., 1992; Rith-Najarian et al., 1993; Lee et al., 1995) are available for only a few Native American tribes (see Table 12-1). These data reveal that the prevalence of diabetes among Native Americans is higher for women than for men and that the rates vary among tribes. However, not all these surveys used the World Health Organization (WHO) definition of diabetes (World Health Organization, 1981), and this is likely to have led to an underestimation of

TABLE 12-1   Age-Adjusted Prevalence of Diabetes Among Native
Americans from Population-based Studies

Author	Study Population	Prevalence[a] (%)		
		Male	Female	Total
Lee et al. (1995)	Men and women aged 45-74:			
	Pima/Maricopa/Papago, Arizona	65	72	70
	Apache, Caddo, Comanche, Delaware, Fort Sill Apache, Kiowa, Wichita, Oklahoma	38	42	40
	Oglala, Sioux, Cheyenne River Sioux, Devils Lake Sioux, Dakota	33	46	40
Rith-Najarian et al. (1993)[b]	Men and women of all ages, Red Lake Chippewa Indians	13	16	15
Sugarman et al. (1992)[b]	Men and women aged 20-74, Navajo Indians, Shiprock	14	18	17
Hall et al. (1992)[b]	Men and women aged ≥20 years, Navajo Indians, Many Farms- Rough Rock	11	14	12

[a]Prevalence rates are standardized to the U.S. general population for the relevant ages.
[b]These studies did not use the WHO criteria for NIDDM (World Health Organization, 1985), and therefore the prevalence rates are likely to be underestimates.

prevalence in some studies (Hall et al., 1992; Sugarman et al., 1992; Rith-Najarian et al., 1993). Overall, the prevalence of diabetes among Native Americans is higher than the rate of 6.6 percent for the U.S. population at large (Harris et al., 1987). Evidence for a higher prevalence of diabetes among Native Americans is also available from an epidemiological study that compared the Pima Indians with a predominantly white population of Rochester, Minnesota (Knowler et al., 1978). This study found that the Pimas had an age-sex standardized diabetes prevalence rate 12.7 times that of Caucasians and that, in contrast to the picture among the Pimas, diabetes prevalence in Rochester was higher for men than for women.

Diabetes among the Pimas is remarkably frequent at younger ages, and it is especially striking that about 50 percent of Pima adults over 35 years of age have NIDDM (Knowler et al., 1981). The prevalence of diabetes among the Pimas, defined by the oral glucose tolerance test (World Health Organization, 1985), has increased over three successive decades (Figure 12-1). Overall, the prevalence increased by 29 percent in men during 1965-1974 (17.62 percent) and 1985-1994 (22.69 percent) and by 35 percent in women during the same period (1965-1974: 23.10 percent, 1985-1994: 31.24 percent).

Why is the prevalence of diabetes increasing among Native Ameri-

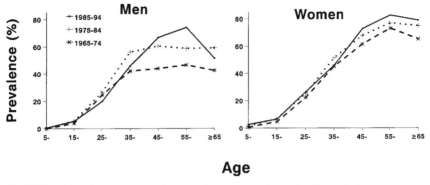

Age

FIGURE 12-1   Age-sex specific prevalence of diabetes in Pima Indians in three time periods. Prevalence rates were estimated from data for all subjects examined in each of the 10-year periods 1965-1974, 1975-1984, and 1985-1994. SOURCE: Updated from Knowler et al. (1990).

cans? Prevalence can increase for two reasons: improvement in survival and/or increase in the rate of development of new cases. The length of survival following the onset of diabetes may have increased over a period of time, probably as a result of better treatment or a change in the natural history of the disease. However, diabetes contributes little to mortality rates among people under the age of 55 (Pettitt et al., 1982), and an improvement in survival is thus an unlikely explanation for the increase in prevalence among younger Native Americans. This suggests that at least part of the increase in prevalence among Native Americans may be due to an increase in the incidence (the rate at which new cases develop) of the disease.

Incidence

The Pimas have the highest reported incidence of diabetes in the world—19 times the rate of diagnosed diabetes among the predominantly white population of Rochester, Minnesota (Knowler et al., 1978), and a high incidence of the disease has also been reported among other Native American tribes (Rith-Najarian et al., 1993). Figure 12-2 shows the age-sex specific incidence of diabetes among Pima Indians during three successive decades. As reported earlier (Knowler et al., 1990), the incidence rates vary by age, peaking between 35 and 44 years in men in 1965-1974 and between 45 and 54 years in men in more recent years. In women, the incidence rates peak between 45 and 54 years in 1965-1974 and 1985-1994 and between 55 and 64 years in 1975-1984. The incidence of diabetes has also increased over three successive decades at most ages and in both men

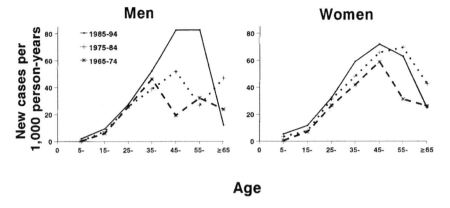

FIGURE 12-2 Age-sex specific incidence rates of diabetes among Pima Indians during three decades. Incidence rates are expressed as new cases of diabetes per 1000 person-years (PYR) of observation of nondiabetic subjects. Cases and PYRs are divided into three time periods: 1965-1974, 1975-1984, and 1985-1994. SOURCE: Updated from Knowler et al. (1990).

and women. Overall, in men, controlled for age, the incidence increased by 102 percent, from 11.79/1000 person-years (PYR) in 1965-1974 to 23.82/1000 PYR in 1985-1994. During this period, the incidence in women, controlled for age, increased by 87 percent, from 15.19/1000 PYR in 1965-1974 to 28.41/1000 PYR in 1985-1994.

Why is the incidence of diabetes increasing among Native Americans? While it is likely that there is an underlying genetic susceptibility to diabetes, the dramatic increase in incidence over a relatively short period of time emphasizes the overriding importance of environmental determinants. The discussion now turns to the determinants of diabetes, both genetic and environmental.

DETERMINANTS OF NIDDM

Genetic Factors

The risk of diabetes is associated with the degree of Indian heritage (Drevets, 1965; Brousseau et al., 1979; Knowler et al., 1986). Diabetes aggregates in Native American families (Lee et al., 1985; Knowler et al., 1990), and the risk of diabetes occurring at an early age is strongly transmitted from parent to offspring, but diabetes occurring at an older age in parents has less effect on the risk of diabetes in offspring (Knowler et al., 1990). Diabetes among Pima Indians is associated with the HLA-A2 phenotype (Williams et al., 1981), and genetic markers on chromosome 4q and 7q have been linked to insulin resistance (the underlying abnormality in NIDDM) among this population (Prochazka et al., 1993, 1995). However, knowledge concerning the genetics of NIDDM is still rudimentary, and it may be hoped that research will lead to a better understanding of the pathogenesis of the disease.

Environmental Factors

A number of potentially modifiable factors, including obesity, dietary composition, and physical inactivity, are thought to contribute to the progression from genetic susceptibility to NIDDM (Saad et al., 1988; Tuomilehto et al., 1992; Knowler et al., 1995).

Obesity

Obesity is a powerful and well-established risk factor for the development of NIDDM (Knowler et al., 1981). As shown in Figure 12-3, the age-sex adjusted incidence of diabetes among Pima Indians increases with body mass index (BMI), a measure of obesity. Compared with those with a BMI <20 kg/m^2, Pima Indians with a BMI of 20-25 have a 13.6-fold higher incidence of NIDDM, and those with a BMI of 25-30 have a 21.6-fold higher incidence (Knowler et al., 1981). Furthermore, the incidence of diabetes increases with the duration of obesity (BMI ≥30 kg/m^2); compared with Pima Indians with less than 5 years of obesity, those with 5-10 years of obesity have 1.4 times the incidence of NIDDM, while those with at least 10 years of obesity have 2.4 times the incidence (Everhart et al., 1992). The distribution of body fat may also be important, with central obesity having been found to be related to the risk of the disease (Knowler et al., 1991; Hall et al., 1991; Warne et al., 1995).

The prevalence of obesity among Native Americans is higher than among the U.S. general population in both males and females and at all ages (Broussard et al., 1991). The reasons for higher obesity among Native Americans are not entirely clear. Broussard et al. (1991) estimated that the overall prevalence of obesity[1] among Native Americans was 13.7 percent for men and 16.5 percent for women, higher than the U.S. rates of 9.1 percent and 8.2 percent, respectively. Data from the Pimas are consistent with this finding. Furthermore, the mean BMI among Pima adults has increased over time (Figure 12-4), and a secular increase in the preva-

---

[1]BMI ≥95th percentile of the National Health and Nutrition Examination Survey (NHANES) II reference: BMI(kg/m^2 ≥31.1 for men, ≥32.3 for women).

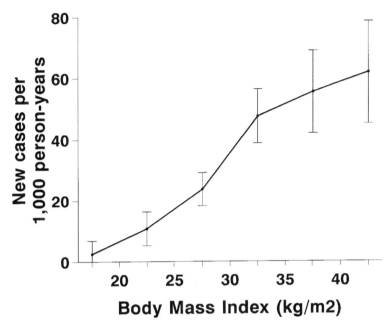

FIGURE 12-3 Age-sex adjusted incidence of diabetes by body mass index (BMI), with 95 percent confidence intervals. SOURCE: Knowler et al. (1990).

lence of overweight has been reported among the Navajo Indians (Hall et al., 1992). Pima children have also, on average, become heavier during this century and continue to do so (Knowler et al., 1991).

Diet

Diet has been linked with the development of diabetes for over 2,500 years (Gulabkunverba, 1949). The precise role of dietary factors, which has been reviewed elsewhere (Knowler et al., 1993), remains ambiguous. However, evidence suggests that a high-fat diet may be related to the development of the disease (Eriksson and Lingärde, 1991; Marshall et al., 1994). Few data are available for Native Americans linking dietary factors with the development of NIDDM, except for one study of the Pima Indians that found a possible association with a high-calorie diet (Bennett et al., 1984). The traditional Pima diet, derived from local agricultural produce, is believed to have been high in fiber and low in fat (Knowler et al., 1990), but this diet appears to have changed during this century and is now more or less similar to the diet in the rest of the United States (Smith et al., 1996). Similar secular changes in the diet of other Native American

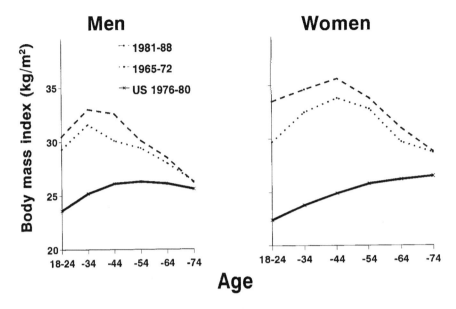

FIGURE 12-4 Mean body mass index (BMI) among Pimas for two periods and among the U.S. white population. The Pima data from each period were used for all subjects examined in each of the 8-year periods 1965-1972 and 1981-1988. The U.S. data are from the National Health and Nutrition Examination Survey (NHANES) II. SOURCE: Modified from Knowler et al. (1991).

populations are believed to have occurred; in particular, the fat content of Indian diets has increased dramatically—from 17 percent of total calories in the pre-European contact diet, to 28 percent in the reservation diet, to 38 percent in the current diet (Jackson, 1994).

Physical Activity

There is evidence that increased physical activity may have a protective effect on the development of NIDDM (Frisch et al., 1986; Schranz et al., 1991; Manson et al., 1991, 1992; Helmrich et al., 1991). As shown in Figure 12-5, the age-adjusted prevalence of NIDDM among Pima Indians aged 15-36 was lower with higher amounts of leisure physical activity in the preceding year. Among those aged 37-57, those with the lowest levels of physical activity had the highest prevalence of the disease (Kriska et al., 1993). When the exercise habits of 49 Zuni Indians of New Mexico presenting with NIDDM were compared with those of 99 nondiabetic controls (Benjamin et al., 1993), subjects with diabetes were found to be less likely to exercise frequently than those without. The hypothesis that high

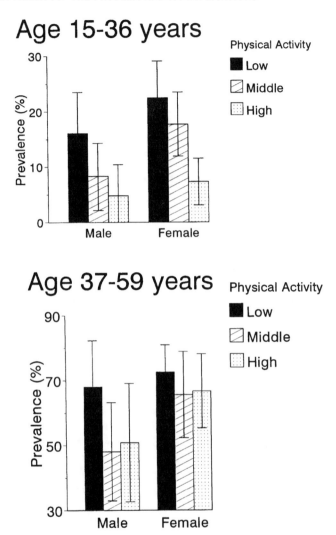

FIGURE 12-5 Age-adjusted prevalence and 95 percent confidence interval of NIDDM by tertile groups of past-year leisure physical activity among subjects aged 15-36 (upper panel) and 37-59 (lower panel). SOURCE: Modified from Kriska et al. (1993).

levels of physical activity may be protective against NIDDM is consistent with the observation that diabetes was apparently rare among Native Americans in the past, when they were a physically active agricultural and hunter-gatherer society.

COMPLICATIONS OF NIDDM

NIDDM is associated with premature mortality and significant morbidity, including renal failure, limb amputation, blindness, ischemic heart disease, adverse outcomes of pregnancy, gum disease, neuropathy, acute glycemic complications, lipid abnormalities, and psychosocial problems. The discussion here is limited to mortality, end-stage renal disease (ESRD), and lower-extremity amputation (LEA).

Mortality

Overall, Native Americans have higher death rates than the U.S. general population (Program Statistics Branch, 1986; U.S. Department of Health and Human Services, 1985), a fact confirmed by detailed investigations in Canada (Mao et al., 1986) and among specific U.S. Native American populations (Mahoney et al., 1989; Sievers et al., 1990). The patterns of death among members of the Seneca Nation of Indians in New York State between 1955 and 1984 were compared with those of the general New York State population (Mahoney et al., 1989). As seen in Figure 12-6, compared with the New York State population, a greater-than-expected number of both male and female members of the Seneca Nation died from all causes, from infectious diseases, from diabetes, from liver cirrhosis, from accidents and injuries, and from suicides, while a lower-than-expected number died from cancers and cardiovascular diseases. A similar pattern of deaths was found among the Pima Indians (Sievers et al., 1990), and the age- and sex-adjusted average annual death rate in the Gila River Indian Community (1639/100,000) was 1.9 times the 1980 rate for the United States, all races (878/100,000). Death rates were higher among Pima men than women, and Pima men had an age-adjusted death rate 2.3 times that of U.S. men, all races. Furthermore, young Pima men aged 25-34 had 6.6 times the mortality rate of men of the same age in the U.S. general population. The age-sex adjusted death rate among the Pimas was 11.9 times the rate of the United States, all races, for diabetes, 5.9 times the rate for accidents, 6.5 times the rate for cirrhosis, and 4.3 times the rate for suicide.

Pima Indian men and women with diabetes have higher death rates than those without, and the age-sex adjusted death rate among diabetic subjects was found to be 1.7 times that among nondiabetic subjects (Sievers et al., 1992). The major cause of this higher risk of death among diabetic subjects is increased deaths from kidney disease, ischemic heart disease, and infections. A study among Oklahoma Indians (Lee et al., 1993a) also confirmed higher death rates among diabetic than nondiabetic subjects and demonstrated that on average, Oklahoma Indians develop-

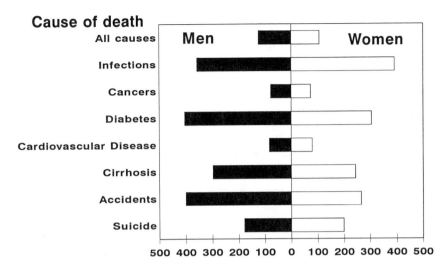

FIGURE 12-6 Standardized mortality ratios (SMR) among 1,572 male and 1,690 female members of the Seneca Nation of Indians in New York State, by cause of death, 1955-1984. Cause of death codes are from ICD-9, International Classification of Diseases, 9th Revision: all causes (001-999), infectious diseases (001-139), cancers (140-208), diabetes (250), cardiovascular disease (390-459), cirrhosis (571), accidents and injuries (800-949, 970-999), and suicides (950-959). SMR is the ratio (expressed as a percentage) of the number of deaths observed among male and female members of the Seneca Nation to the number that would be expected if this population had the same age-specific death rates as the New York State population. Expected number of deaths was calculated on the basis of New York State mortality rates, exclusive of New York City, for 1960, 1970, and 1980. SOURCE: Adapted from Mahoney et al. (1989).

ing diabetes before the age of 40 lived 16.5 years less than the general population of Oklahoma.

There is considerable variation among Native American tribes in diabetes mortality rates. The IHS area-specific diabetes mortality rates for 1984-1986, without accounting for underreporting of diabetes and Native American heritage in vital statistics, ranged from 10 to 93/100,000, compared with 15/100,000 for the U.S. general population. When underreporting of diabetes and Native American heritage were accounted for, the age-adjusted mortality rate for diabetes as the underlying cause of death for Native Americans (96/100,000) was 4.3 times that for whites and twice that for blacks (Newman et al., 1993a).

Data suggest that there has been a dramatic increase in diabetes mor-

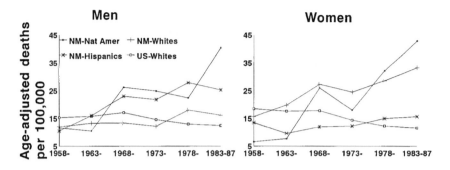

Time

FIGURE 12-7 Age-adjusted diabetic mortality rates for men and women by six 5-year time periods, 1958-1962, 1963-1967, 1968-1972, 1973-1977, 1978-1982, and 1983-1987, comparing three ethnic groups in New Mexico: Native Americans (NM-Nat Amer), Non-Hispanic whites (NM-Whites), and Hispanic whites (NM-Hispanics). U.S. white age-adjusted rates for the same period are also presented. SOURCE: Adapted from Carter et al. (1993).

tality rates among Native Americans (Carter et al., 1993). Figure 12-7 shows the age-adjusted sex-specific diabetes mortality rates over six 5-year time periods during 1958-1987 for three racial groups in New Mexico, along with rates for U.S. whites for comparison. Among both men and women, Native Americans had the highest diabetes mortality rates in New Mexico starting around the beginning of the 1980s. Furthermore, age-adjusted mortality rates for Native American women, which were the lowest for any group in 1958, increased by 5.5 times over the 30-year period; during the same period, rates for Native American men increased by 2.5 times. In contrast to the increasing diabetes mortality rates among minority groups in New Mexico, the rates among both white men and women in the United States have decreased over time (Carter et al., 1993).

End-Stage Renal Disease (ESRD)

ESRD is an important public health problem for Native Americans, and nearly 60 percent of these cases occur in people with diabetes (Newman et al., 1990; Muneta et al., 1993). Between 1983 and 1987, the number of Native Americans with diabetes referred to the Medicare ESRD treatment program in the United States increased by 61 percent, and the annual incidence of diabetic ESRD increased by 47 percent, from 80.6/ million to 118.2/million (Muneta et al., 1993). In 1987, the age-adjusted incidence rate of diabetic ESRD for Native Americans was 6.8 times that for whites and 1.8 times that for blacks (Muneta et al., 1993).

A population-based study among the Pima Indians found that the age-adjusted incidence of ESRD in subjects with diabetes was 62 times the rate in those without, and that 95 percent of ESRD among the Pimas occurred in diabetic subjects (Nelson et al., 1988a). Among diabetic subjects, the incidence of ESRD was related to duration of diabetes, and at 20 years' duration, 15 percent of subjects had developed ESRD. Furthermore, the incidence rates of ESRD among diabetic Pimas were 14 times as high as the estimates for the U.S. diabetic population for those aged 45-64 and 10 times as high for those aged 65 and older.

Navajo Indians had an age-adjusted incidence of diabetic ERSD 9.6 times that among U.S. whites. The incidence of ESRD in this population increased almost 10-fold from 18 per million in 1971 to 176 per million in 1985, and much of this increase was due to diabetic kidney disease (Megill et al., 1988). During the same 15-year period, the prevalence of ESRD among the Navajos increased 26-fold, from 27 per million in 1971 to 700 per million in 1985.

Zuni Indians had an average annual incidence of ESRD of 722 per million and a prevalence of 2902 per million in 1983. However, a large proportion of ESRD among Zunis was due to other diseases, and diabetes was responsible for only 24 percent of the prevalent cases (Pasinski and Pasinski, 1987).

High rates of ESRD have also been reported among several other Native American tribes. It was found that 88 percent of ESRD among the Cherokee Indians was attributable to diabetes, and the incidence of ESRD caused by diabetes was 2.5 times the rate reported among the U.S. Native American population (Quiggins and Farrell, 1993) and 6 times the rate among the U.S. white population (Farrell et al., 1993). The age-adjusted incidence rates of ESRD among Sioux Indians were 13.5 times the rates among U.S. whites (Stahn et al., 1993). Even among Alaska Natives, who have relatively low rates of diabetes, the incidence of ESRD is higher than that in the U.S. general population (Schraer et al., 1993).

ESRD is associated with considerable morbidity and substantial loss in quality of life. The average life expectancy for ESRD patients at age 49 and 59 years is 75 to 80 percent lower than that of the U.S. general population. Furthermore, treatment of ESRD is costly. The cost was estimated at an average of $44,800 per Medicare patient per year in 1990, which did not include a number of medical and nonmedical direct cost items, such as patient travel, almost all outpatient drugs, and lost labor production in and out of home (U.S. Department of Health and Human Services, 1993).

Lower-Extremity Amputation (LEA)

There have been a number of studies of amputations using IHS hospital statistics. Subjects with diabetes are at increased risk of amputation, and over 85 percent of IHS hospitalizations for LEA occur among diabetic patients. The risk of LEA varies by age. Compared with nondiabetic subjects of a similar age, the incidence of LEA among diabetic Native Americans is 160-fold higher in subjects aged 15-44, 52-fold higher in those aged 45-64, and 19-fold higher in those over age 65. During 1982-1987, the average annual age-adjusted incidence rates of all LEAs among diabetic subjects in the Tucson (240.8/10,000), Phoenix (203.1/10,000), Oklahoma (87.3/10,000), and Navajo (74.0/10,000) IHS areas were higher than the U.S. rate (73.1/10,000) (Valway et al., 1993). A study of 10 selected Indian reservations in the Pacific Northwest in 1989 found a prevalence of LEA of 4 percent among diabetic subjects (Freeman and Hosey, 1993), but in another study, 10.3 percent of known diabetic individuals had a history of LEA (Wirth et al., 1993). In one IHS area, diabetic subjects with amputations (32.5 visits/patient/year) visited the hospital 6 times more often than patients without diabetes (5.4 visits/patient/year) and 2.3 times more often than diabetic subjects without amputation (14.1 visits/patient/year) (Wirth et al., 1993). Among Cherokee Indians, diabetic patients had a 3 times higher rate of LEA than the rate for the United States (Farrell et al., 1993), and the Sioux Indians had a 1.5 times higher rate (Stahn et al., 1993).

A population-based 12-year follow-up study among the Pima Indians found that the incidence of LEA among diabetic subjects (10.4 per 1000 PYR) was over 100 times that among nondiabetic subjects (0.1 per 1000 PYR) (Nelson et al., 1988b). LEA rates were higher among men and increased with age and duration of diabetes. Diabetic subjects with amputation had an age-adjusted death rate 1.6 times higher than the rate among nonamputees; on average, 61 percent of diabetic subjects survived 5 years after their first LEA. Furthermore, the age-sex adjusted rate of LEA among diabetic Pima Indians was 3.7 times that found in a study by the Centers for Disease Control in six U.S. states (Nelson et al., 1988b).

Diabetic Oklahoma Indians had an LEA incidence of 18.0/1000 PYR, which was higher than the rate found among the Pima Indians (Lee et al., 1993b). Similar to the findings for the Pimas, the LEA incidence among diabetic Oklahoma subjects was higher in men and increased with age and duration of diabetes. The 5-year survival rate after the first LEA was only 40.4 percent among diabetic Oklahoma Indians; the main causes of death among amputees were diabetes, cardiovascular disease, and renal disease.

POTENTIAL FOR PREVENTION

Prevention of NIDDM

There are two broad approaches available for preventing any disease: a "high-risk strategy," which seeks to identify high-risk susceptible individuals and offer them some individual protection, and a "population strategy," which seeks to control the determinants of incidence among the population as a whole (Rose, 1985).

High-Risk Strategy

Given our current understanding of the pathogenesis of NIDDM, it is possible to identify individuals who are at high risk of developing the disease within 5 or 10 years. People with impaired glucose tolerance, defined as hyperglycemia during an oral glucose tolerance test, but not of sufficient degree for a diagnosis of NIDDM (World Health Organization, 1985), comprise an easily recognizable group at very high risk of developing NIDDM. Behavioral approaches aimed at modifying diet and exercise habits and a number of drug interventions offer potential means of delaying or preventing the progression from impaired glucose tolerance to NIDDM (see Knowler and Narayan, 1994; Knowler et al., 1995). These interventions merit testing, and a national, multicenter, randomized NIDDM prevention clinical trial in the United States is currently under way. This trial is expected to recruit about 4000 subjects from over 20 centers across the United States, and will include about 500 Native Americans with impaired glucose tolerance.

Population Strategy

For a disease such as NIDDM that is influenced by major life-style, cultural, and societal factors, a population strategy may be the most effective way of delivering prevention, particularly in communities like those of many Native Americans, where the incidence and prevalence of the disease is very high, and the risk is spread broadly across most of the community. A population strategy requires active community involvement and coordinated action by a number of agencies and thus can be organizationally demanding. Evaluation of such a strategy may also present special challenges because of the difficulty involved in performing controlled experiments. However, given the magnitude of NIDDM among Native American populations and the nature of the major risk factors involved, it would be well worthwhile to test carefully planned population-based life-style interventions in selected communities along the lines of some of the successful coronary heart disease prevention studies (World Health Organization, 1981; Farquhar et al., 1983; Farquhar, 1984; Lefebrve et al., 1987). Such action would be a further step forward from some preliminary efforts already evident in a few communities (Leonard et al., 1986; Heath et al., 1987; Heath et al., 1991).

Potential Benefit from Prevention

The impact of NIDDM on various adverse outcomes can be quantified by calculation of attributable risk fraction (AF) and population attributable risk fraction (PARF) (Miettinen, 1974). Suitable data for the Pima Indians were used to assess the potential impact of diabetes prevention on mortality, ESRD, and LEA, with the results shown in Table 12-2. AF and PARF were estimated as suggested by Levin (1953); the details of the computation are shown in the footnotes to Table 12-2. Among the Pimas, diabetes is associated with an excess incidence of 14.3 percent of all deaths, 92.1 percent of ischemic heart disease deaths, 94.4 percent of ESRD, and 96.6 percent of LEA.

The potential for decreasing the incidence of mortality, ESRD, and LEA by reducing the current prevalence of diabetes (27.6 percent) among

TABLE 12-2 Potential for Reduction of NIDDM Complications by Preventing Diabetes in Pima Indians

Complication	RR[a]	AF[b](%)	PARF[c](%)
Mortality (Sievers et al., 1992)			
All causes	1.6	37.5	14.3
All natural causes	1.7	41.2	16.2
Ischemic heart disease	43.4	97.7	92.1
Stroke	1.3	23.1	7.7
Infectious diseases	1.3	23.1	7.7
End-stage renal disease (Nelson et al., 1988a)	62.0	98.4	94.4
Lower-extremity amputation (Nelson et al., 1988b)	104.0	99.0	96.6

[a]RR = Risk ratio (ratio of incidence of complication in diabetic subjects relative to nondiabetic subjects).

[b]AF = Attributable or etiologic fraction (the proportion of the complication that can be attributable to diabetes): RR-1/RR.

[c]PARF = Population attributable risk fraction or prevented fraction (the proportion of incidence of the complication in the population associated with diabetes): P(RR − 1)/1 + P(RR − 1), where P is the prevalence of diabetes, which was 27.6 percent during 1984-1994.

TABLE 12-3 Estimated Percentage Reductions in the Incidence of Various Diabetes Complications If Current Prevalence of Diabetes Were Reduced to Five New Target Levels.

| Complication | $PARF_1{}^a$(%) | Expected % reduction in incidence[b] if diabetes prevalence were reduced to: | | | | |
		25%	20%	15%	10%	5%
All-causes mortality	14.3	1.5	4.0	6.5	9.1	11.7
Natural-causes mortality	16.2	1.5	4.5	7.4	10.4	13.3
IHD mortality	92.1	8.1	24.8	41.9	58.6	75.4
Stroke mortality	7.7	0.8	2.1	3.6	4.9	6.3
Infectious disease mortality	7.7	0.8	2.1	3.6	4.9	6.3
End-stage renal disease	94.4	9.7	26.3	43.4	60.3	77.3
Lower-extremity amputation	96.6	8.1	27.7	44.3	61.4	79.1

[a]$PARF_1$ = Population attributable risk fraction under the current diabetes prevalence of 27.6 percent.
[b]Expected (%) reduction in incidence = {1 - ($PARF_1/1$ - $PARF_2$)}*100, where $PARF_2$ is PARF at reduced prevalence of diabetes.

the Pimas to five target levels of 25, 20, 15, 10, and 5 percent was estimated as shown in the footnotes for Table 12-3 (Ruta et al., 1993). These estimates assume that diabetes and other potential risk factors bear a constant relationship with mortality, ESRD, and LEA at all levels of diabetes prevalence. As shown in Table 12-3, even small decreases in the prevalence of diabetes can result in considerable reduction in diabetes complications, particularly ESRD and LEA. Furthermore, if the prevalence of diabetes among the Pimas could be reduced to 6.6 percent, the rate among the U.S. general population, the following reduction in the incidence of diabetes complications could result: 10.9 percent of deaths from all causes, 74.7 percent of deaths from ischemic heart disease, 71.9 percent of ESRD, and 73.9 percent of LEA.

Prevention of diabetes is therefore worth considering. However, as in most real-life healthcare situations, the question may not be simply whether diabetes is worth preventing, but rather how much diabetes is worth preventing, given resource constraints? The kind of information presented in Table 12-3 allows the estimation of marginal benefits (for example, the extra benefit from reduction in the incidence of complications if the prevalence of diabetes were reduced by an extra 5 percent). Such estimation can support policy decisions, especially if it can be combined with data on estimated costs of achieving a given reduction in the prevalence of diabetes.

Prevention of Complications

In addition to the potential reduction in complications that could result from preventing NIDDM, a number of other measures could prevent or delay the onset of complications in subjects with diabetes.

Early Detection of NIDDM

A large proportion of subjects with NIDDM remain undiagnosed (Harris et al., 1987) and might benefit from early detection and treatment. However, there are a number of questions concerning which people would benefit from such early-detection activities. As noted earlier, being a Native American is a major risk factor for developing NIDDM. According to the American Diabetes Association (1989), all individuals with at least one risk factor for NIDDM should be identified through community screening programs (defined as screening not performed under the direct and close supervision of a physician), and individuals indicating symptoms should be referred for medical evaluation.

Blood Glucose Control

Complications of NIDDM in Native Americans are related to the concentration of blood glucose (Dorf et al., 1976; Pettitt et al., 1980; Nelson et al., 1989; Lee et al., 1992). It has been shown that tight control of blood glucose can prevent or delay the onset of complications, but this evidence is based on subjects with insulin-dependent diabetes mellitus (IDDM) (The Diabetes Control and Complications Trial Research Group, 1993). However, it is believed that the beneficial effect of glucose control in forestalling complications of IDDM may also apply to NIDDM (Weir et al., 1994). What is not clear is the means of achieving blood glucose control and their relative benefits and risks.

Early Detection and Management of Complications

Structured approaches aimed at early detection and management of hypertension, dyslipidemia, retinopathy, lower extremity problems, and nephropathy are also known to be of benefit in limiting the complications of diabetes (Weir et al., 1994). Essential features of many of these activities are good coordination, active patient involvement, a multidisciplinary team approach, acceptance of standards of care, and regular evaluation. A number of such programs have been implemented successfully within IHS facilities (Acton et al., 1993a; Newman et al., 1993b).

RESEARCH TO FACILITATE PREVENTION OF NIDDM AND ITS COMPLICATIONS

Understanding of the genetics of NIDDM among Native Americans is important and may lead to better identification of high-risk subjects and possibly to the development of newer treatments. Similarly, a well-designed clinical trial evaluating the efficacy and effectiveness of interventions aimed at preventing or delaying the progression from impaired glucose tolerance to NIDDM in Native Americans is also a priority. In addition to these topics, which are already receiving substantial attention, three key research areas can be emphasized.

Population-based Primary Prevention

Given the high prevalence of diabetes in Native American communities and the nature of the risk factors involved, much can be gained from implementing and evaluating a well-designed population-based life-style intervention study in selected communities. Such approaches are likely to complement clinical trials among high-risk individuals.

Blood Glucose Control

Multicenter studies in Native American communities aimed at understanding optimal ways of achieving blood glucose control in NIDDM subjects would facilitate the prevention of diabetic complications.

Economic Appraisal

Economic appraisal can assist in the optimal allocation of resources aimed at improving health. The total economic and social costs of diabetes and its complications among Native Americans should be estimated, and detailed assessments of the marginal costs and marginal benefits of various interventions should be undertaken.

REFERENCES

Acton, K., S. Valway, S. Helgerson, J.D. Huy, K. Smith. V. Chapman, and D. Gohdes
1993a Improved diabetes care for American Indians. *Diabetes Care* 16 (suppl. 1):372-375.
Acton, K., B. Rogers, G. Campbell, C. Johnson, and D. Gohdes
1993b Prevalence of diagnosed diabetes and selected related conditions six reservations in Montana and Wyoming. *Diabetes Care* 16 (suppl. 1):263-266.
American Diabetes Association
1989 Screening for diabetes: Position statement. *Diabetes Care* 12(8):588-590.

Benjamin, E., J. Mayfield, and D. Gohdes
1993   Exercise and incidence of NIDDM among Zuni Indians (abstract). *Diabetes* 42 (suppl. 1):203A.
Bennett, P.H., T.A. Burch, and M. Miller
1971   Diabetes mellitus in American (Pima) Indians. *Lancet* ii:125-128.
Bennett, P.H., W.C. Knowler, H.R. Baird, W.J. Butler, D.J. Pettitt, and J.M. Reid
1984   Diet and development of non-insulin-dependent diabetes mellitus: an epidemiological perspective. Pp. 109-119 in G. Pozza, P. Micossi, A.L. Catapano, and R. Paoletti, eds., *Diet, Diabetes and Atherosclerosis*. New York: Raven Press.
Broussard, B.A., A. Johnson, J.H. Hines, M. Story, R. Fichtner, F. Hanck, K. Bachman-Carter, J. Hayes, K. Frohlich, N. Gray, S. Valway, and D. Gohdes
1991   Prevalence of obesity in American Indians and Alaska Natives. *American Journal of Clinical Nutrition* 53:1535-42S.
Brousseau, J.D., R.C. Eelkema, A.C. Crawford, and T.A. Abe
1979   Diabetes among three affiliated tribes: Correlation with degree of Indian inheritance. *American Journal of Public Health* 69:1277-1278.
Cameron, W.I., P. Moffit, and D.R.R. Williams
1986   Diabetes mellitus in the Australian Aborigines of Bourke, New South Wales. *Diabetes Research and Clinical Practice* 2:307-314.
Carter, J., R. Horowitz, and R. Wilson
1989   Tribal differences in diabetes: Prevalence among American Indians in New Mexico. *Public Health Reports* 104:665-669.
Carter, J.S., C.L. Wiggins, T.M. Becker, C.R. Key, and J.M. Samet
1993   Diabetes mortality among New Mexico's American Indian, Hispanic, and non-Hispanic White populations, 1958-1987. *Diabetes Care* 16 (suppl. 1):306-309.
Castetter, E.F., and W.H. Bell
1942   *Pima and Papago Indian Agriculture*. Albuquerque, NM: University of New Mexico Press. Reprinted 1980.
The Diabetes Control and Complications Trial Research Group
1993   The effect of intensive treatment of diabetes on the development and progression of long-term complications in insulin-dependent diabetes mellitus. *The New England Journal of Medicine* 329(14):977-986.
Dorf, A., E.J. Ballintine, P.H. Bennett, and M. Miller
1976   Retinopathy in Pima Indians: Relationship to glucose level, duration of diabetes, and age at examination in a population with a high prevalence of diabetes mellitus. *Diabetes* 25(7):554-560.
Drevets, C.C.
1965   Diabetes mellitus in Choctaw Indians. *Journal of Oklahoma State Medical Association* 58:322-329.
Eriksson, K.F., and F. Lindgärde
1991   Prevention of type 2 (non-insulin-dependent) diabetes mellitus by diet and physical exercise: The 6-year Malmö feasibility study. *Diabetologia* 34:891-898.
Everhart, J.E., D.J. Pettitt, P.H. Bennett, and W.C. Knowler
1992   Duration of obesity increases the incidence of NIDDM. *Diabetes* 41:235-240.
Farrell, M.A., P.A. Quiggins, J.D. Eller, P.A. Owle, K.M. Miner, and E.S. Walkingtick
1993   Prevalence of diabetes and its complications in the Eastern band of Cherokee Indians. *Diabetes Care* 16 (suppl. 1):253-256.
Farquhar, J.W., S.P. Fortmann, P.D. Wood, and W.L. Haskell
1993   Community studies of cardiovascular disease prevention. Pp. 170-181 in N.M. Kaplan, ed., *Prevention of Coronary Heart Disease: Practical Management of Risk Factors*. Philadelphia: W.B. Saunders.

Farquhar, J.W.
  1984 The Stanford Five City Project: An overview. Pp. 1154-1164 in J.D. Matarazzo, ed., *Behavioral Health: A Handbook of Health Enhancement and Disease Prevention.* New York: John Wiley.
Freeman, W.L., G.M.H. Hosey, P. Diehr, and D. Gohdes
  1989 Diabetes in American Indians of Washington, Oregon, and Idaho. *Diabetes Care* 12(4):282-669.
Freeman, W.L., and G.M. Hosey
  1993 Diabetic complications among American Indians of Washington, Oregon, and Idaho. *Diabetes Care* 16(suppl. 1):357-360.
Frisch, R.E., G. Wyshak, T.E. Albright, N.L. Albright, and I. Schiff
  1986 Lower prevalence of diabetes in female former athletes compared with nonathletes. *Diabetes* 35:1101-1105.
Gohdes, D.M.
  1986 Diabetes in American Indians: A growing problem. *Diabetes Care* 9(6):609-6130.
Gulabkunverba, ed.
  1949 *Charaka Samhita (600 B.C.).* Jamnagar, India: Ayurvedic Society.
Hall, T.R., M.E. Hickey, and T.B. Young
  1991 The relationship of body fact distribution to non-insulin-dependent diabetes in a Navajo Community. *American Journal of Human Biology* 3:119-126.
  1992 Evidence for recent increases in obesity and non-insulin-dependent diabetes mellitus in a Navajo Community. *American Journal of Human Biology* 4:547-553.
Harris, M.I., W.C. Hadden, W.C. Knowler, and P.H. Bennett
  1987 Prevalence of diabetes and impaired glucose tolerance and plasma glucose level in U.S. population aged 20-74 yr. *Diabetes* 36:523-534.
Heath, G.W., B.E. Leonard, R.H. Wilson, J.S. Kendrick, and K.E. Powell
  1987 Community-based exercise intervention: Zuni diabetes project. *Diabetes Care* 10:579-583.
Heath, G.W., R.H. Wilson, J. Smith, and B.E. Leonard
  1991 Community-based exercise and weight control: Diabetes risk reduction and glycemic control in Zuni Indians. *American Journal of Clinical Nutrition* (suppl. 1):1642S-1646S.
Helmrich, S.P., D.R. Ragland, R.W. Leung, and F.S. Paffenbarder
  1991 Physical activity and reduced occurrence of non-insulin-dependent diabetes mellitus. *New England Journal of Medicine* 325:147-152.
Jackson, M.Y.
  1994 Diet, culture, and diabetes. Pp. 381-406 in J.R. Joe and R.S. Young, eds. *Diabetes As a Disease of Civilization: The Impact of Culture Change on Indigenous Peoples.* New York: Mouton de Gruyter.
Joslin, E.P.
  1940 The university of diabetes. *Journal of the American Medical Association* 115:2033-2038.
King, H., and M. Rewers
  1991 Diabetes in adults is now a Third World problem. *Bulletin of the World Health Organization* 69(6):643-648.
Knowler, W.C., P.H. Bennett, R.F. Hammam, and M. Miller
  1978 Diabetes incidence and prevalence in Pima Indians: a 19-fold greater incidence than in Rochester, Minn. *American Journal of Epidemiology* 108:497-504.
Knowler, W.C., D.J. Pettitt, P.J. Savage, and P.H. Bennett
  1981 Diabetes incidence in Pima Indians. Contributions of obesity and parental diabetes. *American Journal of Epidemiology* 113:144-156.

Knowler, W.C., R.C. Williams, D.J. Pettitt, A.G. Steinberg
1986 GM$^{3;5,13,14}$ and type 2 diabetes mellitus: An association in American Indians with genetic admixture. *American Journal of Human Genetics* 39:409-413.

Knowler, W.C., D.J. Pettitt, M.F. Saad, and P.H. Bennett
1990 Diabetes mellitus in the Pima Indians: Incidence, risk factors and pathogenesis. *Diabetes/Metabolism Reviews* 6(1):1-27.

Knowler, W.C., D.J. Pettitt, M.F. Saad, M.A. Charles, R.G. Nelson, B.V. Howard, C. Bogardus, and P.H. Bennett
1991 Obesity in the Pima Indians: Its magnitude and relationship with diabetes. *American Journal of Clinical Nutrition* 53:1543-51S.

Knowler, W.C., D.R. McCance, D.K. Nagi, and D.J. Pettitt
1993 Epidemiologic studies of the causes of non-insulin-dependent diabetes mellitus. Pp. 187-218 in R.D.G. Leslie, ed., *Causes of Diabetes*. Sussex, England: John Wiley and Sons.

Knowler, W.C., and K.M.V. Narayan
1994 Prevention of non-insulin-dependent diabetes mellitus. *Preventive Medicine* 23(5):701-703.

Knowler, W.C., K.M.V. Narayan, R.L. Hanson, R.G. Nelson, P.H. Bennett, J. Tuomilheto, B. Scherstèn, and D.J. Pettitt
1995 Preventing non-insulin-dependent diabetes mellitus. *Diabetes* 44:483-488.

Kriska, A.M., R.E. LaPorte, D.J. Pettitt, M.A. Charles, R.G. Nelson, L.H. Kuller, P.H. Bennett, and W.C. Knowler
1993 The association of physical activity with obesity, fat distribution and glucose intolerance in Pima Indians. *Diabetologia* 36:863-869.

Lee, E.T., P.S. Anderson, J. Bryan, C. Bahr, T. Coniglione, and M. Cleves
1985 Diabetes, parental diabetes, and obesity in Oklahoma Indians. *Diabetes Care* 8:107-113.

Lee, E.T., V.S. Lee, R.M. Kingsley, M. Lu, D. Russell, N.R. Asal, C.P. Wilkinson, and R.H. Bradford
1992 Diabetic retinopathy in Oklahoma Indians with NIDDM: Incidence and risk factors. *Diabetes Care* 15(11):1620-1627.

Lee, E.T., D. Russell, N. Jorge, S. Kenny, and M. Yu
1993a A follow-up study of diabetic Oklahoma Indians: Mortality and causes of death. *Diabetes Care* 16(suppl. 1):300-305.

Lee, J.S., M. Lu, V.S. Lee, D. Russell, C. Bahr, and E.T. Lee
1993b Lower-extremity amputation: Incidence, risk factors, and mortality in the Oklahoma Indian diabetes study. *Diabetes* 42:876-882.

Lee, E.T., B.V. Howard, P.J. Savage, L.D. Cowan, R.R. Fabsitz, A.J. Oopik, J. Yeh, O. Go, D.C. Robbins, and T.K. Welty
1995 Diabetes and impaired glucose tolerance in three American Indian Populations aged 45-74 years: The Strong Heart Study. *Diabetes Care* 18(5):599-609.

Lefebvre, R.C., R.M. Lasater, R.A. Carleton, and G. Paterson
1987 Theory and delivery of health programming in the community. *Preventive Medicine* 16:80-95.

Leonard, B.E., C. Leonard, and R.H. Wilson
1986 Zuni diabetes project. *Public Health Reports* 101:282-288.

Levin, M.L.
1953 The occurrence of lung cancer in man. *Acta Unio Internationalis Contra Cancrum* 9:531-541.

Lippincott, J.B.
1980 *Storage of Water on Gila River, Arizona*. Water Supply Paper No. 33. Washington, DC: U.S. Geological Survey.

Mahoney, M.C., A.M. Michalek, K.M. Cummings, P.C. Nasca, and L.J. Emrich
  1989 Mortality in a Northeastern Native American Cohort, 1955-1984. *American Journal of Epidemiology* 129(4):816-825.
Manson, J.E., E.B. Rimm, M.J. Stampfer, G.A. Colditz, W.C. Willett, A.S. Krolewski, B. Rosner, C.H. Hennekens, and F.E. Speizer
  1991 Physical activity and incidence of non-insulin-dependent diabetes mellitus in women. *Lancet* 338:774-778.
Manson, J.E., D.M. Nathan, A.S. Krolewski, M.J. Stampler, W.C. Willet, and C.H. Hennekens
  1992 A prospective study of exercise and incidence of diabetes among U.S. male physicians. *Journal of the American Medical Association* 268:63-67.
Mao, Y., H. Morrison, R. Semenciw, and D. Wigle
  1986 Mortality on Canadian Indian Reserves, 1977-1982. *Canadian Journal of Public Health* 77:263-268.
Marshall, J.A., S. Hoag, S. Shetterly, and R.F. Hamman
  1994 Dietary fat predicts conversion from impaired glucose tolerance to NIDDM. *Diabetes Care* 17:50-56.
Megill, d.M., W.E. Hoy, and S.D. Woodruff
  1988 Rates and causes of end-stage renal disease in Navajo Indians, 1971-1985. *Western Journal of Medicine* 149:178-182.
Miettinen, O.S.
  1974 Proportion of disease caused or prevented by a given exposure, trait or intervention. *American Journal of Epidemiology* 99:325-332.
Muneta, B., J. Newman, J. Stevenson, and P. Eggers
  1993 Diabetic end-stage renal disease among Native Americans. *Diabetes Care* 16 (suppl. 1):346-348.
Nelson, R.G., J.M. Newman, W.C. Knowler, M.L. Sievers, C.L. Kunzelman, D.J. Pettitt, and C.D. Moffett
  1988a Incidence of end-stage renal disease in Type 2 (non-insulin-dependent) diabetes mellitus in the Pima Indians. *Diabetologia* 31:730-736.
Nelson, R.G., D.M. Gohdes, J.E. Everhart, J.A. Hartner, F.L. Zwemer, D.J. Pettitt, and W.C. Knowler
  1988b Lower-extremity amputations in NIDDM: 12-year follow-up study in Pima Indians. *Diabetes Care* 11(1):8-16.
Nelson, R.G., J.A. Wolfe, M.B. Horton, D.J. Pettitt, P.H. Bennett, and W.C. Knowler
  1989 Proliferative retinopathy in NIDDM: Incidence and risk factors in Pima Indians. *Diabetes* 38:435-440
Newman, J.M., A.A. Marfin, P.W. Eggers, and S.D. Helgerson
  1990 End State Renal Disease among Native Americans, 1983-86. *American Journal of Public Health* 80(3):318-319.
Newman, J.M., F. DeStefano, S.E. Valway, R.R. German, and B. Muneta
  1993a Diabetes-associated mortality in Native Americans. *Diabetes Care* 16 (suppl. 1):297-299.
Newman, W.P., J.J. Hollevoet, and K.L. Frohlich
  1993b The diabetes project at Fort Totten, North Dakota, 1984-1988. *Diabetes Care* 16 (suppl. 1):361-363.
Pablo, S.G.
  1983 Contemporary Pima. Pp. 212-216 in A. Ortiz, ed., *Handbook of North American Indians*. Vol 10. Washington, D.C.: Smithsonian Institute.
Pasinski, R., and M. Pasinski
  1987 End-stage renal disease among Zuni Indians: 1973-1983. *Archives of Internal Medicine* 147:1093-1096.

Pettitt, D.J., J.R. Lisse, W.C. Knowler, and P.H. Bennett
    1980 Development of retinopathy and proteinuria in relation to plasma-glucose concen-
          trations in Pima Indians. *Lancet* ii:1050-1052.
    1982 Mortality as a function of obesity and diabetes mellitus. *American Journal of Epide-
          miology* 115:359-366.
Prior, I.A.M., and Tasman-Jones
    1981 New Zealand Maori and Pacific Polynesians. Pp. 227-267 in H.C. Trowell, and
          D.D. Bunkitt, eds., *Western Diseases: Their Emergence and Prevention.* London:
          Edward Arnold Publishers.
Prochazka, M., S. Lillioja, J.F. Tait, W.C. Knowler, D.M. Mott, M. Spraul, P.H. Bennett, and
C. Bogardus
    1993 Linkage of chromosomal markers on 4q with a putative gene determining maximal
          insulin action in Pima Indians. *Diabetes* 42:514-519.
Prochazka, M., B. Thompson, S. Scherer, L. Tsui, W. Knowler, P. Bennett, and C. Bogardus.
    1995 Linkage and association of markers at $7_q21.3-_q22.1$ with insulin resistance and
          NIDDM in the Pima Indians (abstract). *Diabetes* 44 (suppl. 1):42A
Program Statistics Branch
    1986 *Indian Health Service Chart Series Book.* Rockville, MD: DHHS, PHS, Indian Health
          Service.
Quiggins, P.A., and M.A. Farrell
    1993 Renal disease among the Eastern band of Cherokee Indians. *Diabetes Care* 16 (suppl.
          1):342-345.
Rith-Najarian, S.J., S.E. Valway, and D.M. Gohdes
    1993 Diabetes in a Northern Minnesota Chippewa tribe. *Diabetes Care* 16 (suppl. 1):266-
          270.
Rose, G.
    1985 Sick individuals and sick populations. *International Journal of Epidemiology* 14:32-38.
Ruta, D., T. Beattie, and V. Narayan
    1993 A prospective study of non-fatal childhood road traffic accidents: What can seat
          restraint achieve? *Journal of Public Health Medicine* 15 (l):88-92.
Saad, M.F., W.C. Knowler, D.J. Pettitt, R.G. Nelson, D.M. Mott, and P.H. Bennett
    1988 The natural history of impaired glucose tolerance in the Pima Indians. *New En-
          gland Journal of Medicine* 319:1500-06.
Schraer, C.D., L.R. Bulkow, N.J. Murphy, and A.P. Lanier
    1993 Diabetes prevalence, incidence and complications among Alaska Natives, 1987.
          Diabetes Care 16 (suppl. 1):257-259.
Schranz, A., J. Tuomilehto, B. Marti, R.J. Jarrett, V. Grabanskas, and A. Vassallo
    1991 Low physical activity and worsening of glucose tolerance: Results from a 2-year
          follow-up of a population sample in Malta. *Diabetes Research and Clinical Practice*
          11:127-136.
Sievers, M.L., and J.R. Fisher
    1985 Diabetes in North American Indians. Pp. XI. 1-20 in *Diabetes in America.* NIH
          Publication No. 85-1468. Bethesda, MD: U.S. Department of Health and Human
          Services.
Sievers, M.L., R.G. Nelson, and P.H. Bennett
    1990 Adverse mortality experience of a Southwestern American Indian Community:
          Overall death rates and underlying causes of death in Pima Indians. *Journal of
          Clinical Epidemiology* 43(11):1231-1242.
Sievers, M.L., R.G. Nelson, W.C. Knowler, and P.H. Bennett
    1992 Impact of NIDDM on mortality and causes of death in Pima Indians. *Diabetes Care*
          15(11):1541-1549.

Smith, C.J., R.G. Nelson, S.A. Hardy, E.A. Manahan, P.H. Bennett, and W.C. Knowler
   1996   A survey of the dietary intake of the Pima Indians. *Journal of American Dietetic Association* (In Press)
Stahn, R.M., D. Gohdes, and S.E. Valway
   1993   Diabetes and its complications among selected tribes in North Dakota, South Dakota, and Nebraska. *Diabetes Care* 16 (suppl. 1):244-247.
Sugarman, J.R., T.J. Gilbert, and N.S. Weiss
   1992   Prevalence of diabetes and impaired glucose tolerance among Navajo Indians. *Diabetes Care* 15(1):114-120.
Tuomilehto, J., W.C. Knowler, and P. Zimmet
   1992   Primary prevention of non-insulin-dependent diabetes mellitus. *Diabetes/Metabolism Reviews* 8:339-353.
U.S. Department of Health and Human Services
   1985   *Report of the Secretary's Task Force on Black and Minority Health, Volumes I-VII.* Washington, D.C.: U.S. Government Printing Office. 1985: Vols I, II:1986:Vols III-VII.
   1993   Prevalence and cost of ESRD therapy. *United States Renal Data System: 1993 Annual Data Report.* Bethesda, MD: The National Institutes of Health, NIDDK.
Valway, S., W. Freeman, and S. Kaufman
   1993   Prevalence of diagnosed diabetes among American Indians and Alaska Natives, 1987. *Diabetes Care* 16 (suppl. 1):271-276
Valway, S.E., R.W. Linkins, and D.M. Gohdes
   1993   Epidemiology of lower-extremity amputations in the Indian Health Service, 1982-1987. *Diabetes Care* 16 (suppl. 1):349-353.
Warne, D.K., M.A. Charles, R.L. Hanson, L.T.H. Jacobson, D.R. McCance, W.C. Knowler, and D.J. Pettitt
   1995   Comparison of body size measurements as predictors of NIDDM in Pima Indians. *Diabetes Care* 18(4):435-439.
Weir, G.C., D.M. Nathan, and D.E. Singer
   1994   Standards of care. *Diabetes Care* 17(12):1514-1522.
West, K.M.
   1974   Diabetes in American Indians and other native populations of the New World. *Diabetes* 23:841-55.
Williams, R.C., W.C. Knowler, W.J. Butler, D.J. Pettitt, J.R. Lisse, P.H. Bennett, D.L. Mann, A.H. Johnson, P.I. Terasaki
   1981   HLA-A2 and type 2 diabetes mellitus in Pima Indians: An association of allele frequency with age. *Diabetologia* 21:460-463.
Williams, R.C., A.G. Steinberg, H. Gershowitz, P.H. Bennett, W.C. Knowler, D.J. Pettitt, W. Butler, R. Baird, L. Dowda-Rea, and T.A. Burch
   1985   GM allotypes in Native Americans: Evidence for three distinct migrations across the Bering Land bridge. *American Journal of Physical Anthropology* 66:1-19.
Wirth, R.B., A.A. Marfin, D.W. Grau, and S.D. Helgerson
   1993   Prevalence and risk factors for diabetes and diabetes-related amputations in American Indians in Southern Arizona. *Diabetes Care* 16 (suppl. 1):354-356.
World Health Organization
   1981   *Community Control of Cardiovascular Diseases: The North Karelia Project.* Copenhagen, Denmark: World Health Organization.
   1985   Diabetes Mellitus: Report of a WHO study group. *WHO Tech Rep Ser 727.* Geneva, Switzerland: World Health Organization.

Young, T.K., and C. Shah
   1987   Extent and magnitude of the problem. Pp. 11-25 in T.K. Young, ed. *Diabetes in the Canadian Native Population: Bicultural Perspectives.* Toronto: Canadian Diabetes Association.
Zimmet, P., G. Dowse, C. Finch, S. Serjeantson, and H. King.
   1990   The epidemiology and natural history of NIDDM: Lessons from the South Pacific. *Diabetes/Metabolism Reviews* 6(2):91-124.

13

Healthcare Utilization, Expenditures, and Insurance Coverage for American Indians and Alaska Natives Eligible for the Indian Health Service

Peter J. Cunningham

INTRODUCTION

The Indian Health Service (IHS) was established in 1955 to raise the health status of American Indians and Alaska Natives who are members or descendants of federally recognized tribes and reside on or near federal reservations and other American Indian and Alaska Native communities. The Indian Health program became a primary responsibility of the federal government as a result of the Transfer Act of 1954 (P.L. 83-568). The establishment of federal Indian health services is consistent with the authority Congress has exercised to regulate commerce with American Indian nations as provided for in the Constitution. IHS operates a network of inpatient and ambulatory care facilities across the continental United States and Alaska, many of which are now managed by American Indian tribes and Alaska Native organizations. In addition, IHS directly subsidizes healthcare services through contracts with private providers, particularly for specialized services and other services not available in IHS direct care facilities (known as Contract Health Services).

The Center for Studying Health System Change is supported in full by the Robert Wood Johnson Foundation. This study was conducted while the author was a researcher at the Agency for Health Care Policy and Research. The views expressed in this paper are those of the author, and no official endorsement by the U.S. Department of Health and Human Services, the Agency for Health Care Policy and Research, or the Indian Health Service is intended or should be inferred.

289

Persons eligible for IHS have several advantages with respect to healthcare that are generally unavailable to the U.S. population as a whole. Unlike most persons who have some form of private health insurance, IHS "beneficiaries" do not pay premiums for IHS coverage, and there are no deductibles or copayments involved in receiving IHS-sponsored services, regardless of personal or family income level. Because IHS services are essentially free of charge to eligible persons, one might expect not to see significant differences in access to care by socioeconomic status, as is the case for the general U.S. population (Freeman et al., 1987; Rowland and Lyons, 1989).

Also, while many in the general U.S. population live in medically underserved rural or inner-city areas where few private medical providers are available (Lee, 1991; Berk et al., 1983), IHS facilities and resources are targeted specifically in areas where IHS eligibles generally live, including many rural and sparsely populated areas. Thus, IHS resources ideally can be distributed to areas where need is highest, without regard to other factors that affect the location decisions of private physicians.

Despite these advantages, access to care may still be limited for some IHS eligibles. First, many of the areas inhabited by IHS eligibles are among the most sparsely populated areas in the United States, and residential areas are frequently spread across vast distances. Thus, although many IHS facilities are located directly in these areas, it is difficult for IHS providers to reach all eligible persons. Transportation problems and long distances to medical providers are still a major barrier to care for many persons.

Second, limitations in IHS-sponsored services often result in problems that affect access to care for some IHS beneficiaries. Unlike the Medicare and Medicaid programs, IHS is not an entitlement program, and its funds are obtained through an annual appropriation by the U.S. Congress. No additional funds are available for the year if additional resources for health services are needed. Also, IHS resources are not distributed evenly across all IHS service areas, since the previous method of distributing those resources was based on historical funding patterns, rather than need (U.S. General Accounting Office, 1991).[1] Access to care for IHS eligibles may be inhibited to the extent that resource limitations in some IHS service areas result in staff and facility shortages. The result could be difficulties in obtaining health services in a timely manner even when IHS facilities are located in the area.

Moreover, access may be particularly limited for Contract Health Services—including expensive diagnostic and treatment services. These ser-

---

[1]A needs-based formula was recently included in the resource allocation models to achieve greater parity in funding across IHS service areas.

vices may be delayed or denied to patients if funds are unavailable. At times, such services have been restricted to emergency cases because of budget constraints (Office of Technology Assessment, 1986).

Given these resource limitations, some IHS eligibles may be compelled to obtain additional healthcare services from private providers. In fact, by law IHS is required to be only a "residual" provider of health services (i.e., it provides only those services not available through other sources), even though it often serves as the primary or sole source of care for much of the eligible population. As with the general U.S. population, one would expect that access to other sources of care would be enhanced for persons having higher socioeconomic status, having other private or public health coverage, and living in closer proximity to medical providers (e.g., metropolitan areas) (Spillman, 1992; Davis and Rowland, 1983; Freeman et al., 1987; Rowland and Lyons, 1989). However, given the high proportion of IHS eligibles who are poor and low-income, lack other sources of healthcare coverage, and live in rural or "frontier" areas, access to non-IHS services is no doubt severely constrained for many individuals.

As a result of resource constraints, it is likely that IHS will depend increasingly on more effective use of and coordination with other sources of healthcare, at least in areas where these other sources exist. Such measures might include contracting with private healthcare organizations, such as health maintenance organizations (HMOs), to provide all health services to IHS eligibles in a given area. In other words, IHS would provide the financing for the health services, but would not be directly involved in service delivery. However, given the substantial variations in geographic location and socioeconomic characteristics of the IHS population, it is doubtful whether complete privatization of IHS services could be implemented uniformly across all IHS service areas. While private providers could be used more effectively in some areas, it is likely that IHS direct care facilities would continue to be the sole or primary source of care for persons living in some of the most remote and sparsely populated areas in the United States, even were they to obtain other private or public health coverage.

The present discussion uses data from the 1987 Survey of American Indians and Alaska Natives (SAIAN) to examine various aspects of healthcare access, utilization, and expenditures for persons eligible for IHS services. The SAIAN is unique in that data on healthcare use and expenditures were collected for all sources of care—IHS and otherwise—so that the analyses of healthcare use and expenditures are comprehensive. The focus here is specifically on key policy variables that affect health service utilization, and in particular the decision to use IHS or non-IHS care. These factors include healthcare coverage (e.g., private insurance, Medicaid, Medicare), socioeconomic status, place of residence, and availability of IHS facilities. It is recognized that other factors are also important in explaining patterns of healthcare utilization, particularly cultural differences among tribes in interpreting and acting upon symptoms of illness, the value placed on seeking professional care, and trust in the efficacy of prescribed treatments (Susser et al., 1985). The effects of culture on health services are not a major focus of this discussion, and cultural measures (e.g., attitudes regarding health, healthcare seeking, and health services) are quite limited in the SAIAN data. However, there is some assessment of how involvement with native culture—including use of native language and involvement in tribal activities—affects the decision to use IHS or non-IHS healthcare.

DATA AND METHODS

Sources of Data

The SAIAN is part of the 1987 National Medical Expenditure Survey and was sponsored in part by IHS. It comprises a representative sample of American Indian and Alaska Native households in which at least one person was eligible to receive medical care from IHS. A multistage area probability design was used to select the sample (Harper et al., 1991). The sampling frame initially consisted of 482 U.S. counties served by IHS.[2] A total of 274 primary sampling units—consisting of counties or groups of counties—were created out of the initial frame, and 20 primary sampling units were selected for the initial sample. Segments were identified and sampled within each primary sampling unit, and households were sampled within each segment.[3] Altogether, about 2000 households and 7600 persons were included in the sample. About 6500 sampled persons were eligible for IHS services and are included in the present analysis (persons not eligible for IHS services are excluded).

Field operations for the entire SAIAN component consisted of three core interviews conducted at 5- to 6-month intervals (for more detailed discussion of the questionnaires and data collection methods used, see Edwards and Berlin, 1989). In each round of data collection, detailed

---

[2]For reasons of cost-efficiency, the frame was truncated to exclude counties with fewer than 400 American Indians or Alaska Natives. The truncated frame included 97.2 percent of the population of interest.

[3]Segments were defined as 1980 census enumeration districts or individual blocks or block combinations. For cost-efficiency, the sample frame was further restricted by excluding segments with less than 0.5 percent population representation of American Indians and Alaska Natives.

information was collected on each individual's health insurance coverage, health status, and healthcare utilization and expenditures, as well as sociodemographic and socioeconomic characteristics. Each round of data collection also included supplemental questions on specific topics, including more detailed treatment of health status and access to care. The combined response rate for all three rounds of data collection was 86 percent. A Medical Provider Survey was also conducted to obtain expenditure information from non-IHS medical providers used by sample households during 1987. This information was used to verify and supplement incomplete or missing information on expenditures obtained from the household respondents (Tourangeau and Ward, 1992).

Definition of Key Variables

In this discussion, a distinction is made between the use of "IHS" and "non-IHS" services. IHS services include all those obtained at IHS-owned and -operated hospitals, clinics, and health stations, including those managed by American Indian tribes or Alaska Native organizations (distinctions between IHS-operated and tribally managed facilities could not be made, however). Non-IHS services include all other health services, including those obtained from contract care providers and those with no affiliation with IHS.[4]

By definition, all persons included in the analysis have IHS coverage (i.e., there are no "uninsured" persons as such). Thus, the healthcare coverage variable was constructed to reflect persons having (1) only IHS coverage all year; (2) only IHS coverage for part of the year (i.e., other health coverage for part of the year); (3) other coverage all year, including some private insurance; and (4) other coverage all year, with only public coverage (i.e., Medicare, Medicaid, other state or local programs). The key comparisons are made between persons with only IHS coverage all year and those with other private or public healthcare coverage all year.

Additional data on the characteristics of each sample person's county of residence were also obtained and are used in this analysis. Urban vs. rural residence was determined based on whether the county of residence was part of a metropolitan statistical area or a nonmetropolitan area. The

---

[4]Other analyses by the author have included IHS contract care providers along with IHS direct care providers (Cunningham and Altman, 1993; Cunningham, 1993; Cunningham and Cornelius, 1995). These studies were concerned primarily with the use of care outside of the IHS "system." However, since the focus here is on highlighting the use of private resources, regardless of whether these providers are reimbursed by IHS for services provided to eligible persons, contract care providers are included along with other private providers.

population density of nonmetro counties was also used to distinguish very sparsely populated nonmetro areas from other areas. Thus nonmetro areas were divided into those counties with 10 or more persons per square mile and those with fewer than 10 persons per square mile. Variables that indicate the availability of IHS or tribal healthcare facilities in the county of residence were also included. For the descriptive analyses, the classification included counties with (1) any IHS hospital, (2) IHS clinics or health stations but no hospitals, and (3) no IHS facilities.

Data Limitations

It should be noted that the SAIAN population is a subset of the total U.S. population of American Indians and Alaska Natives. The SAIAN sample was selected to be representative of American Indians and Alaska Natives who were members or descendants of federally recognized tribes and eligible to receive IHS services. Thus, the findings are not necessarily representative for all persons who identify themselves as American Indians or Alaska Natives, especially those who are not eligible for IHS services either because they reside outside of IHS service areas or because they are not members or descendants of federally recognized tribes. To avoid misinterpreting the results as being generalizable to all American Indians and Alaska Natives, findings from the SAIAN are discussed in terms of the "SAIAN population" or the "IHS eligible population."

A second limitation with the SAIAN is that the effects of cultural factors on health service utilization cannot be thoroughly assessed because, as noted above, few direct measures of culture (e.g., health practices, attitudes regarding health and healthcare, use of traditional medicine) were included in the survey. In addition, resource constraints precluded sufficient subsampling within individual tribes or communities to allow assessment of differences among American Indian tribes or communities (which could be due to cultural differences). While cultural factors are not a focus here, it is possible that the effects of key variables of interest (e.g., health insurance coverage) on health service utilization are confounded by cultural factors. There is some control for cultural differences in the multivariate analysis through inclusion of the individual's primary language (i.e., English vs. a native tribal language) and participation in tribal activities. Although these measures probably do not capture all relevant dimensions of culture, they have significant effects on the use of healthcare services (as discussed in greater detail below). To the extent that other cultural factors not included here are correlated with socio-demographic characteristics and other control variables included in the analysis, the confounding effects of culture on key policy variables are minimized, although to what extent cannot be directly assessed.

Some estimates for the SAIAN population are compared with estimates for the general U.S. population. The latter estimates were derived from the National Medical Expenditure Survey's Household Survey (also conducted in 1987), which was designed to produce representative estimates of the civilian noninstitutionalized population. Field operations for this survey consisted of four core interviews conducted at 3- to 4-month intervals. Other than differences in the number of rounds of data collection, instruments and data collection procedures used in this survey and in the SAIAN were virtually identical, which facilitates making direct comparisons between the two populations.

All estimates for the SAIAN and U.S. populations were weighted. Population weights were designed to yield representative estimates for the IHS eligible and general U.S. populations for 1987. Standard errors for the estimates were adjusted to account for the complex design of the SAIAN and the Household Survey. While standard errors are not included in the tables, differences between specific estimates are discussed only if they are statistically significant at the 0.05 level, unless stated otherwise.

FINDINGS

Characteristics and Healthcare Coverage of the SAIAN Population

Socioeconomic and geographic differences between the SAIAN population and the general U.S. population are striking (Table 13-1). Almost two-thirds of the SAIAN population resided in nonmetropolitan areas, and 30.9 percent resided in nonmetro areas with very low population density (i.e., fewer than 10 persons per square mile). By contrast, three-fourths of the general U.S. population resided in metropolitan areas, and less than 3 percent in areas with very low population density.

Adults in the SAIAN population were less likely to be employed full-time and all year as compared with the general U.S. population (27 versus 43.9 percent) and more likely not to have been employed at all in 1987 (39 versus 29.7 percent). The SAIAN population had considerably higher rates of poverty and low income than the general U.S. population: 37.4 percent of the SAIAN population had incomes below the federal poverty line (compared with 13.5 percent for the general U.S. population), and more than two-thirds had family incomes below 200 percent of the poverty line (compared with about one-third for the general population).

Since employment and income are highly correlated with having private insurance or public healthcare coverage, it is not surprising that only 24.9 percent of the SAIAN population had private insurance coverage, compared with 70.7 percent of the general U.S. population. The SAIAN

TABLE 13-1 Characteristics of the Total U.S. and SAIAN Populations, 1987

Characteristic	Percentage Distribution	
	Total U.S. Population (239,393,000)	SAIAN Population (906,000)
Age		
0-5	9.2	14.6
6-17	17.6	27.0
18-44	42.7	38.8
45-64	18.8	13.2
65 and over	11.7	6.5
Sex		
Male	48.5	49.3
Female	51.5	50.7
Educational attainment		
Less than high school	26.1	40.1
Completed high school	36.3	34.6
Some college	36.3	20.9
Employment[a]		
All year, full-time	43.9	27.0
Part of year or part-time	26.4	34.0
Not employed	29.7	39.0
Family income[b]		
Poor	13.5	37.4
Low-income	18.5	30.6
Middle-income	34.9	23.1
High-income	33.1	8.9
Healthcare coverage[c]		
Not covered all year (other than IHS)	10.3	42.5

population had somewhat higher rates of other public coverage all year (16 versus 9.2 percent), largely because of the disproportionately high number of poor and low-income persons eligible for Medicaid coverage. Almost 60 percent of the SAIAN population relied exclusively on IHS coverage for at least part of the year.

Table 13-2 shows considerable variation in healthcare coverage by employment status, socioeconomic status, and place of residence. Of adults employed full-time and all year, 51.6 percent had private insurance coverage for all of 1987, compared with 21.9 percent of adults employed part-time or part of the year and about 15.2 percent of adults not employed. Those employed part-time or part of the year were more likely to rely exclusively on IHS coverage than were those not employed, largely because of greater availability of other public coverage for persons not

TABLE 13-1 Continued

| | Percentage Distribution | |
Characteristic	Total U.S. Population (239,393,000)	SAIAN Population (906,000)
Not covered part of year (other than IHS)	9.8	16.5
Covered all year		
Any private	70.7	24.9
Public only	9.2	16.0
Place of residence		
Metropolitan statistical area	75.7	37.0
Nonmetro area		
At least 10 persons per square mile	21.6	32.1
Fewer than 10 persons per square mile	2.7	30.9

[a]Employed full-time includes those working at least 35 hours per week. Employed all year includes those employed at least 45 weeks during 1987.

[b]Poor refers to individuals in families with incomes below the poverty line; low-income to those with incomes between the poverty line and 200 percent of the poverty line; middle-income to those with incomes over 200 to 400 percent of the poverty line; and high-income to those with incomes over 400 percent of the poverty line.

[c]Private and public coverage is in addition to IHS coverage for persons in SAIAN. Public coverage includes Medicare, Medicaid, Civilian Health and Medical Programs of the Uniformed Services (CHAMPUS), Civilian Health and Medical Programs of the Veterans Adminstration (CHAMPVA), and other state or local public assistance.

SOURCE: Agency for Health Care Policy and Research. National Medical Expenditure Survey—Survey of American Indians and Alaska Natives and Household Survey.

employed (i.e., Medicare for elderly persons and Medicaid for unemployed nonelderly persons). All-year private insurance coverage increased sharply with income level: 44.8 percent of middle-income persons and almost 72.1 percent of high-income persons had private coverage all year, compared with only 6.9 percent of those with incomes below the poverty level. Of the SAIAN population living in poverty, 60 percent relied exclusively on IHS coverage for all of 1987, compared with 30 percent of middle-income persons and 12.9 percent of high-income persons.

Scarce employment opportunities and high levels of poverty were prevalent for the majority of the SAIAN population living in nonmetro areas. Many of these areas have very low population densities and are far

TABLE 13-2 Healthcare Coverage of the SAIAN Population, 1987

Characteristic	IHS Coverage Only		Other Coverage All Year	
	All year (%)	Part of year (%)	Any private(%)	Public only(%)
All persons	42.5	16.5	24.9	16.0
Age				
0-17	43.3	18.1	22.1	16.6
18-64	46.2	16.3	27.0	10.5
65 years and older	8.1	7.9	27.3	56.7
Sex				
Male	44.7	16.7	24.5	14.3
Female	40.7	16.3	25.4	17.7
Employment[a]				
Full-time, all year	32.8	14.7	51.6	0.9[b]
Part-time or part of year	50.3	20.0	21.9	7.8
Not employed	41.3	12.0	15.2	31.5
Family income[c]				
Poor	60.0	13.8	6.2	20.0
Low-income	39.2	19.5	19.2	22.1
Middle-income	30.0	18.4	44.8	6.9[b]
High-income	12.9	13.2	72.1	1.7[b]
Place of residence				
Metropolitan service area	24.4	21.4	35.4	18.9
Nonmetro area				
At least 10 persons per square mile	48.7	13.0	21.3	17.0
Fewer than 10 persons per square mile	57.7	14.4	16.3	11.6
IHS facilities				
Hospital	54.0	15.6	16.4	14.1
Clinics only	32.3	18.1	29.7	20.0
No facilities	21.7[b]	15.7[b]	51.8	10.9[b]

[a]Employed full-time includes those working at least 35 hours per week. Employed all year includes those employed at least 45 weeks during 1987.

[b]Standard error greater than 30 percent of the estimate.

[c]Poor refers to individuals in families with incomes below the poverty line; low-income to those with incomes between the poverty line and 200 percent of the poverty line; middle-income to those with incomes over 200 to 400 percent of the poverty line; and high-income to those with incomes over 400 percent of the poverty line.

SOURCE: Agency for Health Care Policy and Research. National Medical Expenditure Survey—Survey of American Indians and Alaska Natives.

from urban areas, factors that combine to make private health insurance coverage difficult to obtain. Thus, IHS eligible persons residing in the most sparsely populated areas have the lowest rates of private health insurance coverage and are more likely to rely exclusively on IHS coverage.

Regular Source of Healthcare

The ability to identify a regular source of care—as well as the type of place—is strongly associated with the use of health services (Aday and Andersen, 1975; Aday et al., 1980). Since IHS facilities and services are targeted specifically to the IHS eligible population, it is perhaps not surprising that over 91 percent of the SAIAN population reported having a regular source of healthcare, compared with 81.6 percent of the general U.S. population (estimates not shown). For both populations, most persons who did not have a regular source of care said they did not need a doctor or had no need for healthcare (findings not shown). Only a very small percentage reported not having a regular source of care because of problems associated with the cost of care or the availability of providers.

Of greater interest is the extent to which IHS eligible persons identify a non-IHS facility as their regular source of care and whether particular demographic and socioeconomic characteristics are associated with this response. Table 13-3 shows that almost one-third of the SAIAN population identified a non-IHS provider as their regular source of healthcare, although this response was strongly associated with living in a metro area, having a higher income, having other healthcare coverage, and living in an area with relatively few IHS facilities.

In particular, the differences by urban/rural location are striking. While 63.2 percent of the SAIAN population in metro areas had a non-IHS regular source of care, this was the case for only 25.3 percent in nonmetro areas with relatively high population density and 6.3 percent in very low-density areas. While the percentage with a non-IHS regular source of care was generally higher for residents of metropolitan than nonmetro areas, regardless of healthcare coverage or income level, there were some important differences within metro and nonmetro areas. For example, the proportion of metropolitan residents with a non-IHS regular source of care was considerably smaller for persons with only IHS coverage all year (33.4 percent), persons with family incomes below the poverty line (34.4 percent), and persons living in areas with an IHS hospital (19.1 percent). By contrast, 87.5 percent of metro residents with private insurance, 74.5 percent of middle-income persons, 91.2 percent with high incomes, and 74.8 living in areas with no IHS hospital had a non-IHS regular source of care.

TABLE 13-3 Percentage of SAIAN Population with Regular Source of Healthcare Other Than IHS Facility

Characteristic	All Areas (%)	Metropolitan Service Area (%)	Nonmetro Area (at least 10 persons per square mile) (%)	Nonmetro Area (less than 10 persons per square mile) (%)
All persons	32.9	63.2	25.3	6.3
Healthcare coverage				
IHS only				
All year	12.2	33.4	11.8	2.9[a]
Part of year	32.1	49.7	25.0	10.0
Other coverage				
All year				
Any private	60.4	87.5	47.6	12.2
Public only	44.7	68.5	36.6	10.1[a]
Family income[b]				
Poor	17.6	34.4	21.2	3.8
Low-income	31.6	62.8	20.7	8.0[a]
Middle-income	47.8	74.5	33.3	7.7
High-income	63.9	91.2	55.9	12.9[a]
Perceived health				
Excellent/good	34.4	64.1	23.6	4.3[a]
Fair/poor	29.8	60.7	23.6	3.6
IHS facilities				
Hospital	11.1	19.1	17.1	4.8
Clinics only	52.1	74.8	35.4	15.5
No facilities	77.5	77.5	—[c]	—[c]

[a]Standard error greater than 30 percent of the estimate.

[b]Poor refers to individuals in families with incomes below the poverty line; low-income to those with incomes between the poverty line and 200 percent of the poverty line; middle-income to those with incomes over 200 to 400 percent of the poverty line; and high-income to those with incomes over 400 percent of the poverty line.

[c]No sample persons in this category.

SOURCE: Agency for Health Care Policy and Research. National Medical Expenditure Survey—Survey of American Indians and Alaska Natives.

In nonmetro areas with relatively high population density, the proportion with a non-IHS regular source of care exceeded 50 percent only for high-income persons. In very low-density nonmetro areas, the proportion with a non-IHS regular source of care did not exceed 20 percent, regardless of income or healthcare coverage. These findings suggest that persons in remote areas rely on IHS as their primary or sole source of healthcare, and that the role of IHS in these areas could not be replaced merely by providing increased financial coverage for other services.

Other research based on the SAIAN and the Household Survey has shown that IHS eligibles generally have longer travel times to their regular providers than the general U.S. population and longer average waiting times in their provider offices once they arrive (Beauregard et al., 1991). However, persons with a non-IHS regular provider have on average both shorter travel times and waiting times than persons with an IHS regular provider (Beauregard et al., 1991). In fact, on measures of waiting and travel time, persons with non-IHS regular providers are more comparable to the U.S. population as a whole than to persons having an IHS regular provider.

Use of Healthcare Services

About 82 percent of the SAIAN population used some kind of healthcare in 1987, including hospital care, ambulatory medical and home care, dental and vision services, and prescribed medicine and medical equipment purchases (findings not shown). This was slightly less than the 85.3 of the general U.S. population that used some kind of healthcare in 1987. Ambulatory care—including visits to emergency rooms, hospital outpatient departments, outpatient clinics, and physicians' offices—was by far the most commonly used type of healthcare for both the SAIAN and general U.S. populations.

Services received from non-IHS providers contributed significantly to the total healthcare use by the SAIAN population. For example, about 43 percent of the SAIAN population had made an ambulatory visit to a facility other than an IHS facility, including 15.6 percent who visited a contract care provider and 26.9 percent who visited other non-IHS providers (findings not shown). Visits to all non-IHS providers amounted to about 45 percent of all ambulatory visits in 1987.

In an effort to understand more clearly the factors associated with the use of healthcare, and in particular the factors associated with the use of non-IHS healthcare, multivariate regression analysis was used to examine the use of ambulatory care (the most common type of healthcare use). The analysis involved logistic regression analysis of the likelihood of using any ambulatory care in 1987, the likelihood of making a visit to an IHS or tribal facility, and the likelihood of making a visit to a non-IHS facility. For persons who used ambulatory care, weighted least-squares regression was used to examine the number of all ambulatory visits and, separately, visits to IHS and non-IHS providers. All individuals were included in the multivariate analysis, regardless of whether they had a usual source of care.

Andersen's (1968) behavioral model of healthcare utilization was the conceptual framework for selecting the independent variables. In this model, ambulatory care is conceptualized as a function of need and enabling and predisposing factors. Enabling factors include both individual and community resources that allow persons to satisfy a need for healthcare use. Measures of individual resources include family income and healthcare coverage. Community resources include metropolitan or non-metropolitan residence, whether there is an IHS hospital in the county of residence, the number of IHS clinics and health stations per 10,000 persons in the county of residence, and whether the county of residence is part of a federally designated health manpower shortage area (as an indicator of the availability of private providers). Need factors are the most immediate reason for using healthcare and are represented for this analysis by perceived health status (excellent, good, fair, or poor) and the number of chronic conditions.

Predisposing factors indicate the propensity of individuals to use health services. These factors include gender, age, educational attainment, family size, and cultural factors. While measures of culture are limited in the SAIAN results, they are important because they may indicate preferences for using IHS or non-IHS services. For example, IHS eligibles who are less acculturated in the mainstream American culture may have a preference for IHS facilities because medical staff at those facilities are more likely to be familiar with the local culture and language. Conversely, these same individuals may be less inclined to use non-IHS providers because of language barriers or past experiences with discrimination. To control for cultural preferences for IHS and non-IHS care, the present analysis includes whether the person's primary language (i.e., the language learned first) was English and whether he or she participated in the Native American Church or any other tribal activities, ceremonies, or rituals.

Table 13-4 shows the results of the logistic regression analysis for the likelihood of a visit. Since all eligibles can receive services at IHS facilities free of charge, one might not expect to see any differences in the likelihood of a visit between persons with other insurance and those with IHS coverage only, controlling for the availability of IHS facilities. However, persons with private or other public coverage all year were more likely than persons with IHS coverage only to have made an ambulatory visit to any site. The effects on use of having other insurance coverage were especially important for the likelihood of any non-IHS use.

The effects of family income on use were somewhat contradictory. While middle-income persons were more likely than the poor to use both IHS and non-IHS services, there were no statistically significant differences between high-income and poor persons in any ambulatory use or in visits to either IHS or non-IHS facilities. While there were no statistically significant differences between metro and nonmetro residents in the use of IHS services, nonmetro residents were still less likely than metro residents to use any healthcare, primarily as a result of their lower likelihood of using non-IHS services. While the likelihood of any ambulatory use increased along with the number of IHS clinics, the presence of IHS facilities had opposite effects on IHS and non-IHS use: persons living in counties with IHS hospitals were much more likely to have made an IHS facility visit but much less likely to have made a non-IHS visit compared with persons in counties with no IHS hospitals.

Other results in Table 13-4 show a strong association between use of both IHS and non-IHS services and health status and chronic conditions. Females had higher levels of use than males, while the negative coefficient for age and the positive coefficient for age squared indicate a U-shaped distribution, with both the very young and the elderly having the highest likelihood of use. Persons who had some college background were more likely to use any healthcare than persons with less than a high school education, mainly as a result of their higher likelihood of making a non-IHS ambulatory visit. Cultural factors appear to have had some effect on utilization in that persons whose primary language was not English were less likely to make a non-IHS visit. This suggests that IHS eligibles who are less acculturated in American society are more likely to experience language or cultural barriers to using non-IHS providers.

Similar results were found in analyzing the number of ambulatory visits (Table 13-5).[5] While there were no differences in the number of visits to IHS facilities across categories of healthcare coverage, the number of visits to non-IHS providers was sharply higher for persons with other healthcare coverage. The result was that the number of all ambulatory visits was higher for persons with other private and public healthcare coverage. Higher family incomes were associated with a higher number of ambulatory visits, primarily because of heavier use of non-IHS providers. As with the likelihood of ambulatory use, there were no differences between residents of metro and nonmetro areas in the number of ambulatory visits to IHS facilities. However, because residents of nonmetro areas made fewer visits to non-IHS providers than metro residents, they made fewer ambulatory visits overall. The existence of a greater number of IHS facilities tended to increase visits to these facilities and decrease visits to non-IHS providers.

While health status, insurance coverage, and the supply of IHS pro-

---

[5]The natural log of the number of visits was used to normalize the skewed distribution of the variable.

TABLE 13-4 Results of Logistic Regression Analysis for Probability of an Ambulatory Visit for SAIAN Population, 1987

Characteristic	Beta Coefficients		
	Likelihood of Any Ambulatory Use	Likelihood of a Visit at an IHS Facility[a]	Likelihood of a Visit to a non-IHS Provider[b]
Intercept	2.85**	1.64**	0.50**
Perceived health status (Poor health is omitted category)			
Excellent	−0.77**	−0.84**	−0.64**
Good	−0.48	−0.63**	−0.43*
Fair	−0.29	−0.36	−0.22
Missing	−0.70*	−0.66**	−0.57
One chronic condition	1.75**	1.14**	0.70**
Two or more chronic conditions	2.25**	1.71**	1.07**
Gender (1=male)	−0.47**	−0.37**	−0.17**
Age	−0.07**	−0.06**	−0.03**
Age squared × 10^{-2}	0.07**	0.06**	0.02*
Family size	−0.08**	−0.06**	−0.06**
Education (less than high school is omitted category)			
High school	0.06	−0.06	0.09
Some college	0.44**	0.11	0.51**
Missing	−0.09	−0.14	−0.28
Healthcare coverage (IHS only all year is omitted category)			
Other private coverage all year	0.55**	−0.36**	1.27**
Other public coverage all year	0.54	0.05	1.10
IHS only part of year	0.29	0.21**	0.70**
Income[c] (poor is omitted category)			
Low-income	0.18*	0.13	0.22**
Middle-income	0.34**	0.23**	0.32**
High-income	−0.08	−0.10	0.21
Primary language other than English	−0.19	0.05	−0.38**
Participates in tribal activities	0.10	−0.02	−0.13
Place of residence (metro area is omitted category)			
Nonmetro (10 persons per square mile or more)	−0.54**	−0.12	−0.47**
Nonmetro (fewer than 10 persons per square mile)	−0.54**	−0.01	−1.01**

TABLE 13-4 Continued

	Beta Coefficients		
	---	---	---
Characteristic	Likelihood of Any Ambulatory Use	Likelihood of a Visit at an IHS Facility[a]	Likelihood of a Visit to a non-IHS Provider[b]
IHS hospital in county of residence	0.15	1.05**	−1.14**
Log of number of IHS clinics in county per 10,000 persons	0.29**	0.42**	−0.09
Health professional shortage area designation (no shortage area is omitted category)			
All of county is shortage area	−0.34**	−0.53**	0.19
Part of county is shortage area	−0.43**	−0.83**	0.38
N	6,473	6,473	6,473

NOTE: * p < .05; ** p < .01

[a]Includes visits at IHS direct care facilities and IHS facilities under tribal management.

[b]Includes visits to IHS contract care providers and providers with no affiliation with IHS.

[c]Poor refers to individuals in families with incomes below the poverty line; low-income to those with incomes between the poverty line and 200 percent of the poverty line; middle-income to those with incomes over 200 to 400 percent of the poverty line; and high-income to those with incomes over 400 percent of the poverty line.

SOURCE: Agency for Health Care Policy and Research. National Medical Expenditure Survey—Survey of American Indians and Alaska Natives.

viders tended to be the major factors associated with use, cultural factors were also significant. Participants in tribal cultural activities made a higher number of visits to IHS facilities, while those whose primary language was other than English made fewer visits to non-IHS providers. As in the previous analyses, these findings suggest greater barriers to the use of non-IHS providers for individuals who are less acculturated in the mainstream American culture.

Out-Of-Pocket Expenditures

Since IHS services—both direct care and contract care services—involve no deductibles or copayments for IHS eligible persons, one would expect out-of-pocket healthcare expenditures for this population to be quite low relative to the general U.S. population. Table 13-6 shows that

TABLE 13-5 Results of Weighted Least Squares Regression Analysis for
Log of Number of Ambulatory Visits for SAIAN Population, 1987

| | Regression Coefficients | | |
Characteristic	Log of Number of All Ambulatory Visits	Log of Number of Visits at IHS Facilities[a]	Log of Number of Visits to non-IHS Providers[b]
Intercept	2.09	1.32	1.53
Perceived health status (Poor health is omitted category)			
Excellent	−0.65**	−0.33**	−0.62**
Good	−0.43*	−0.21	−0.31**
Fair	−0.28*	−0.12	−0.22
Missing	−0.49	−0.16	−0.59**
One chronic condition	0.42**	0.32**	0.31**
Two or more chronic conditions	0.86**	0.75**	0.33*
Gender (1=male)	−0.22**	−0.18**	−0.21
Age	−0.03**	−0.02**	−0.02**
Age squared × 10⁻³	0.03**	0.02**	0.02*
Family size	−0.02**	−0.03*	−0.02
Education (less than high school is omitted category)			
High school	0.06	0.06	0.03
Some college	0.12	0.16**	0.05
Missing	−0.19	−0.05	−0.18
Healthcare coverage (IHS only all year is omitted category)			
Other private coverage all year	0.17**	−0.06	0.38**
Other public coverage all year	0.19**	−0.01	0.47**
IHS only part of year	0.10*	−0.02	0.24*
Income[c] (poor is omitted category)			
Low-income	0.10*	0.10*	0.07
Middle-income	0.17*	0.07	0.19*
High-income	0.16*	−0.06	0.27*
Primary language other than English	−0.09	0.01	−0.19*
Participates in tribal activities	−0.06	0.11*	−0.19
Place of residence (metro area is omitted category)			
Nonmetro (10 persons per square mile or more)	−0.16**	−0.05E-1	−0.23**
Nonmetro (fewer than 10 persons per square mile)	−0.08*	0.07	−0.23**

TABLE 13-5 Continued

| | Regression Coefficients | | |
| | --- | --- | --- |
Characteristic	Log of Number of All Ambulatory Visits	Log of Number of Visits at IHS Facilities[a]	Log of Number of Visits to non-IHS Providers[b]
IHS hospital in county of residence	0.01	0.18**	−0.11*
Log of number of IHS clinics in county per 10,000 persons	0.02	0.09*	−0.05
Health professional shortage area designation (no shortage area is omitted category)			
All of county is shortage area	0.03	−0.05	0.13
Part of county is shortage area	0.03	−0.06	0.14*
N	4,446	3,687	1,598

NOTE: * $p < .05$; ** $p < .01$

[a]Includes visits at IHS direct care facilities and IHS facilities under tribal management.

[b]Includes visits to IHS contract care providers and providers with no affiliation with IHS.

[c]Poor refers to individuals in families with incomes below the poverty line; low-income to those with incomes between the poverty line and 200 percent of the poverty line; middle-income to those with incomes over 200 to 400 percent of the poverty line; and high-income to those with incomes over 400 percent of the poverty line.

while about three-fourths of the general U.S. population had some kind of out-of-pocket healthcare expenditure (premiums for health insurance are excluded), only one-third of the SAIAN population had such expenditures. The percentage with out-of-pocket expenditures increased with age and family income, and was also higher for persons with private insurance, those in metropolitan areas, and those living in areas with fewer IHS facilities. While one might also expect the percentage with out-of-pocket expenditures to be higher for persons in fair or poor health (since their use of healthcare is higher than for persons in good health), there were no statistically significant differences in the percentage with out-of-pocket expenditures between persons in excellent or good health and those in fair or poor health. There was also no difference in the percentage with out-of-pocket expenditures between persons with only IHS coverage all year and persons with other public coverage (about 22 percent).

For persons who had out-of-pocket expenditures, the average expense

TABLE 13-6 Out-of-pocket healthcare Expenditures for Personal Health Services for U.S. and SAIAN Populations, 1987

Characteristic	Percentage with Any Out-of Pocket Expense	Average Out-of-Pocket Expenses for Persons with an Expense ($)
Total U.S. population	75.7	476
SAIAN population	33.0	360
Age (SAIAN population)		
0-5	18.1	178
6-17	26.7	241
18-44	36.1	258
45-64	46.3	548
65 and over	48.0	884
Perceived health status		
Good or excellent	31.8	222
Fair or poor	34.7	365
Family income[a]		
Poor	19.3	415
Low-income	30.0	264
Middle-income	48.8	419
High-income	60.5	327
Healthcare coverage		
Not covered all year (other than IHS)	21.8	262
Covered part of year (other than IHS)	34.1	271
Covered all year		
Any private	58.6	374
Public only	21.9	704

in 1987 was more than $100 higher for the general U.S. population than for the SAIAN population. For the SAIAN population, average out-of-pocket expenditures increased considerably with age, and persons in fair or poor health had somewhat higher expenses than persons in good or excellent health. The relationship between family income and out-of-pocket expenditures was not linear: poor and middle-income persons had somewhat higher expenses than persons with low and high incomes, possibly because of the confounding effects of differential health status and healthcare coverage by family income. Of the different types of healthcare coverage, persons with other public coverage had much higher expenditures ($704) than those with other coverage types, mainly as a result of elderly persons with Medicare coverage and nonelderly persons in poor health with Medicaid coverage. Average expenditures were also highest in areas with no IHS facilities.

TABLE 13-6 Continued

Characteristic	Percentage with Any Out-of Pocket Expense	Average Out-of-Pocket Expenses for Persons with an Expense ($)
IHS facilities		
Hospital	20.7	231
Clinics only	44.0	387
No facilities	55.5	531
Place of residence		
Metropolitan statistical area	49.7	382
Nonmetro area		
At least 10 persons per square mile	26.3	411
Fewer than 10 persons per square mile	20.1	224

NOTE: Includes expenditures for inpatient hospital and physician services and ambulatory physician and nonphysician services, including vision care and telephone calls with a charge, prescribed medicines, home healthcare services, dental services, and medical equipment purchases and rentals.

[a]Poor refers to individuals in families with incomes below the poverty line; low-income to those with incomes between the poverty line and 200 percent of the poverty line; middle-income to those with incomes over 200 to 400 percent of the poverty line; and high-income to those with incomes over 400 percent of the poverty line.

SOURCE: Agency for Health Care Policy and Research. National Medical Expenditure Survey—Survey of American Indians and Alaska Natives and Household Survey.

Out-of-pocket expenditures are a concern to the extent that they impose a heavy financial burden on families and households with sick family members who require intensive healthcare use. A common way of assessing the burden of healthcare expenses is to compute the ratio of out-of-pocket expenditures to family income for households. Table 13-7 shows that SAIAN households generally had less of a financial burden due to healthcare expenses than did the general U.S. population. More than one-third of SAIAN households had no out-of-pocket healthcare expenditures in 1987, compared with only 11 percent of all U.S. households. Slightly fewer than half of SAIAN households had healthcare expenditures that comprised between 0 and 5 percent of family income (compared with about 68 percent of all U.S. households), while about 6 percent of SAIAN households had expenditures that amounted to 10 percent or more of family income (compared with about 11 percent of all U.S. households).

TABLE 13-7 Annual Family Out-of-Pocket Expenditures for Personal Health Services As a Percentage of Family Income, SAIAN and General U.S. Population, 1987

Percentage of Family Income	Percentage Distribution of Families	
	Total U.S. population	SAIAN population
No expenditure	11.0	35.1
0.01-0.99%	30.4	23.9
1.00-1.99%	17.3	10.8
2.00-4.99%	20.7	13.3
5.00-9.99%	10.2	6.8
10.00-19.99%	5.6	3.1
20.00% or more	4.4	3.3
No income	0.4	3.8

NOTE: Includes expenditure for inpatient hospital and physician services and ambulatory physician and nonphysician services, including vision care and telephone calls with a charge, prescribed medicines, home healthcare services, dental services, and medical equipment purchases and rentals.

SOURCE: Agency for Health Care Policy and Research. National Medical Expenditure Survey—Survey of American Indians and Alaska Natives and Household Survey.

Despite the overall lower level of financial burden experienced by the SAIAN population relative to the general U.S. population, it is noteworthy that there was no statistically significant difference in the percentage of "very high burden" families (about 3 percent for the SAIAN population and 4 percent for the general U.S. population), defined as having out-of-pocket expenditures that were 20 percent or more of family income. Also, differences between the SAIAN and general U.S. populations are not as large as one might expect, given that IHS eligibles by definition require no out-of-pocket healthcare expenditures. The smaller-than-expected differences are largely the result of the SAIAN population's having a considerably smaller denominator (i.e., family income) in the calculation of the ratios. Thus, even relatively modest out-of-pocket expenditures incurred by many IHS eligibles can be financially burdensome.

DISCUSSION

Characteristics of the population eligible for IHS services indicate that many would be seriously underserved with respect to healthcare if not for the availability of IHS-supported services. The IHS eligible population has lower rates of employment and much higher rates of poverty (37 percent) than the general U.S. population, most IHS eligibles lack other types of health insurance on a continuous basis, and a high proportion of the population lives in some of the most sparsely populated areas in the United States. IHS eligibles with these characteristics tend to rely quite heavily on IHS as their primary or sole source of healthcare.

On the other hand, there is considerable diversity among the IHS eligible population, not only culturally, but also in demographic and socioeconomic characteristics. Among the SAIAN population, almost one-third were middle- or high-income individuals, over 40 percent had some other healthcare coverage, and more than one-third lived in or near a metropolitan area. This diversity is also reflected in the healthcare utilization and expenditures of IHS eligibles, even though all can receive IHS services free of charge. Many IHS eligibles do have other sources of healthcare, and the effects of other health insurance on patterns of utilization are quite profound. IHS eligibles in metropolitan areas with high income and other health coverage—especially private insurance—tend to have a non-IHS regular source of care.

The findings also show that persons with other healthcare coverage are more likely to make use of any ambulatory care than persons with IHS coverage only, mainly as a result of higher use of non-IHS care. Moreover, the findings suggest that persons who use non-IHS services do not merely substitute non-IHS healthcare for services they would otherwise have received at IHS facilities. Because there are generally no differences in the use of IHS ambulatory care by type of healthcare coverage, it is possible that persons with other coverage supplement rather than substitute services received at IHS facilities.

Of course, the ability to procure other healthcare services has much to do with geographic location. Almost two-thirds of the SAIAN population lived in nonmetropolitan areas, and almost one-third lived in areas with very low population density. Persons in these areas were much less likely to have other healthcare coverage (in part because of high rates of unemployment, which makes private insurance less available), and there were few other alternatives to IHS facilities. Persons who had other private and public coverage in nonmetro areas (especially low-density areas) were much less likely than persons with other coverage in metro areas to have a non-IHS regular source of care. The targeting of IHS facilities in very remote areas appears to have considerably enhanced access to care for persons in these areas. Among SAIAN respondents, travel times to IHS providers in low-density nonmetropolitan areas were actually shorter than in other areas (i.e., other nonmetro and metro areas), and there were no statistically significant differences in the use of ambulatory care at IHS facilities between persons in metro and nonmetro areas. Nevertheless, persons in nonmetro areas still used less ambulatory care overall than persons in metro areas as a result of their more restricted access to non-IHS services.

The multivariate results also suggest that some IHS eligibles experience language or cultural barriers to the use of non-IHS providers. These findings are consistent with those of other studies that have found disparities in access and health service utilization for ethnic groups that are less acculturated in American society (Wells et al., 1989). This is a difficult issue to address from a policy perspective because it suggests that merely extending health insurance coverage or enhancing physical access to non-IHS providers could still leave disparities in access to care and health service utilization. Thus, having "culturally competent" providers available to serve the local population is an important consideration in reforming healthcare for IHS eligibles, especially for communities that are more culturally isolated from mainstream American society.

Even though the healthcare provided by IHS is comprehensive, and much of the IHS eligible population relies almost exclusively on IHS, the intent of IHS is not necessarily to be the sole or even primary provider of health services to the eligible population. As noted earlier, IHS was designed to be a residual provider of health services and is further restricted in providing all of the healthcare needed by its eligible population because it is not an entitlement program, and revenues are appropriated on an annual basis. Therefore, improvements in healthcare for the IHS eligible population will depend increasingly on utilizing other resources, particularly from the private sector. This is already occurring to a large extent through the IHS contract care system and IHS eligibles who rely on their own resources to use other healthcare. Portions of the service population already use the private-sector delivery system extensively, and this proportion could probably be expanded if there were greater subsidization for these services. IHS is also pursuing contracts with HMOs to provide all health services to eligible persons in a given area (e.g., the Pascua Yaqui tribe in Tucson), and tribal governments are increasingly taking over the management and operation of IHS facilities and services in their areas.

The availability of other healthcare resources in some IHS areas results in inequities in access to and use of health services among IHS eligibles by income level, healthcare coverage, and residential location. As IHS relies increasingly on the private sector and individual tribes to provide health services to its eligible population, the task will be to distinguish between areas and individuals that can be served effectively by other health systems and individuals who have no recourse other than publicly provided healthcare.

REFERENCES

Aday, L.A., and R. Andersen
  1975 *Development of Indices of Access to Medical Care.* Ann Arbor, MI: Health Administration Press.
Aday, L.A., R. Anderson, and G. Fleming
  1980 *Healthcare in the U.S.: Equitable for Whom?* Beverly Hills, CA: Sage Publications.
Anderson, R.
  1968 *A Behavioral Model of Families' Use of Health Services.* Chicago, IL: Center for Health Administration Studies.
Beauregard, K., P. Cunningham, and L. Cornelius
  1991 *Access to Healthcare: Findings from the Survey of American Indians and Alaska Natives.* (AHCPR Pub. No. 91-0028). National Medical Expenditure Survey Research Findings 9. Rockville, MD: Agency for Healthcare Policy and Research.
Berk, M.L., A.B. Bernstein, and A.K. Taylor
  1983 The use and availability of medical care in health manpower shortage areas. *Inquiry* 20(4):369-380.
Cunningham, P.J., and B.M. Altman
  1993 The use of ambulatory health care services by American Indians with disabilities. *Medical Care* 31(7):600-616.
Cunningham, P.J., and L.J. Cornelius
  1995 Access to ambulatory care for American Indians and Alaska Natives: The relative importance of personal and community resources. *Social Science and Medicine* 40(3):393-407.
Cunningham, P.J.
  1993 Access to care in the Indian Health Service. *Health Affairs* 12(3):224-233.
Davis, K., and D. Rowland
  1983 Uninsured and underserved: Inequities in healthcare in the United States. *Milbank Memorial Fund Quarterly* 61(2):149-176.
Edwards, W., and M. Berlin
  1989 *Questionnaires and Data Collection Methods for the Household Survey and Survey of American Indians and Alaska Natives.* DHHS Publication No. (PHS) 89-3450. Rockville, MD: Agency for Health Care Policy and Research.
Freeman, H.E., R.J. Blendon, L.H. Aiken, S. Sudman, C.F. Mullinix, and C.R. Corey
  1987 Americans report on their access to healthcare. *Health Affairs* 6(2):6-18.
Harper, T., R. Apodaca, D. Northrup, and R. DiGaetano
  1991 *National Medical Expenditure Survey. Survey of American Indians and Alaska Natives: Final Methodology Report.* Rockville, MD: Agency for Health Care Policy and Research.
Lee, R.C.
  1991 Current approaches to shortage area designation. *Journal of Rural Health* 7(4):437-450.
Office of Technology Assessment, U.S. Congress
  1986 *Indian Health Care* (OTA-H-290). Washington, D.C.: U.S. Government Printing Office.
Rowland, D., and B. Lyons
  1989 Triple jeopardy: Rural, poor, and uninsured. *Health Services Research* 23(6):975-1004.
Spillman, B.C.
  1992 The impact of being uninsured on utilization of basic health services. *Inquiry* 29(4):457-466.

Susser, M., W. Watson, and K. Hopper
   1985   Culture and health. Chapter 4 in *Sociology in Medicine*. New York: Oxford University Press.
Tourangeau, K., and E. Ward
   1992   *Questionnaires and Data Collection Methods for the Medical Provider Survey* (AHCPR Pub. No. 92-0042). National Medical Expenditure Survey Methods 4, Rockville, MD: Agency for Health Care Policy and Research.
U.S. General Accounting Office
   1991   *Indian Health Service: Funding Based on Historical Patterns, Not Need* (GAO/HRD-91/5). Washington, D.C.: U.S. Government Printing Office.
Wells, K.B., J.M. Golding, R.L. Hough, M.A. Burnam, and M. Karno
   1989   Acculturation and the probability of use of health services by Mexican Americans. *Health Services Research* 24(2):237-257.